HOW LONG WILL ISRAEL SURVIVE?

GREGG CARLSTROM

How Long Will Israel Survive?

The Threat From Within

OXFORD
UNIVERSITY PRESS

OXFORD
UNIVERSITY PRESS

Oxford University Press is a department of the
University of Oxford. It furthers the University's objective
of excellence in research, scholarship, and education
by publishing worldwide.

Oxford   New York

Auckland   Cape Town   Dar es Salaam   Hong Kong   Karachi
Kuala Lumpur   Madrid   Melbourne   Mexico City   Nairobi
New Delhi   Shanghai   Taipei   Toronto

With offices in

Argentina   Austria   Brazil   Chile   Czech Republic   France   Greece
Guatemala   Hungary   Italy   Japan   Poland   Portugal   Singapore
South Korea   Switzerland   Thailand   Turkey   Ukraine   Vietnam

Oxford is a registered trade mark of Oxford University Press
in the UK and certain other countries.

Published in the United States of America by
Oxford University Press
198 Madison Avenue, New York, NY 10016

Library of Congress Cataloging-in-Publication Data is available
Gregg Carlstrom.
How Long Will Israel Survive? The Threat From Within.
ISBN: 9780190843441

Printed and in Great Britain by Bell and Bain Ltd, Glasgow

To Lillian Goldston, who taught me to ask questions

CONTENTS

ACKNOWLEDGEMENTS

I've worked as a journalist for a decade. I still don't understand why anyone bothers to talk to me. This book is the product of thousands of interviews and informal conversations over the past few years. Dozens of Israeli officials—politicians, diplomats, religious leaders, army officers and others—shared their views. Countless other people, from Majdal Shams to Ashkelon, took the time to chat with a nosy reporter. I chose to build this narrative around events, rather than characters, so most of their names do not appear in the book. But their opinions and stories enlivened the manuscript and enlightened my thinking.

My publishers at Hurst, particularly Michael Dwyer and Jon de Peyer, shaped a very scattered idea into the rather more coherent book you are reading. They also put up with my very flexible definition of the phrase "I'll send it this weekend." No writer enjoys being edited, but Rachel Halliburton did a wonderful job tightening my prose, sharpening my arguments, and moderating my apparent obsession with the word "bizarre".

Parts of this book were adapted from articles that I wrote for other publications, and benefited from the efforts of numerous other editors. At *The Times* and *The Economist*, my primary employers, they include David Byers, Alastair Dawber, Suzy Jagger, Anton La Guardia, Christopher Lockwood, Jim McLean, Philippe Naughton, Jonathan Rosenthal and Roland Watson. Elsewhere I would thank Vanessa Gezari, Michael Hirsh, David Kenner, Siddhartha Mahanta, Elizabeth Ralph, Jebediah Reed and Max Strasser.

During three years of writing and rewriting, countless people were kind enough to discuss parts of the book, read draft chapters, or simply offer their thoughts and support. My thanks to the following: Luke Baker, Daria Carmon, Steven Cook, Lina Dakheel, Hafsa Halawa, Gemma Mangione, Yael Mizrahi, Anshel Pfeffer, Dimi Reider, Grant Rumley, Bel Trew, Amir Tibon, and Rania Zabaneh. A particular thank-you goes to H. A. Hellyer, who connected me with my publisher.

Dalia Hatuqa and Nour Samaha, two dear friends and talented colleagues, probably heard every anecdote in this book over three years of meals and phone calls and WhatsApp conversations. They stayed interested to the end, or at least did a flawless job of pretending.

My dog Mila, a two-year-old Saluki mix, was a much-needed distraction, a reason to drag myself away from the computer. She also tried to type a few paragraphs, though sadly her contributions did not survive the editing process.

This book is dedicated to my late maternal grandmother, Lillian Goldston, whose offhanded comment about a Jerusalem garbageman planted a seed decades ago. She embodied everything that this agnostic and assimilated journalist finds powerful about the Jewish tradition: a deep sense of humanism, a critical mind, and a willingness to ask questions and challenge settled ideas. I hope she would have been proud, though I suspect she would also have some detailed criticism.

Finally, I met Harriet Salem just before this project began, and for three years she gave me her intellect, her support, and her love. The book made it out the other end; we didn't. But I couldn't have finished it without her.

PREFACE

"The state of Israel will prove itself not by material wealth, not by military might or technical achievement, but by its moral character and human values."

David Ben-Gurion

The soldier, a young Israeli conscript, fired a single bullet into the head of the young Palestinian lying supine on the ground. The killing was hardly the worst thing to happen in greater Israel over the past few years—it was just one death among thousands. Yet that single bullet would shake an entire government and bring down the most powerful man in Israel's military. If you want to understand the seismic changes taking place in Israeli society, it is a good place to start.

It was Purim, March 2016, a Jewish holiday that commemorates the deliverance of the Jews from Haman, a cruel vizier of the Persian Empire. Some describe this holiday as the Jewish Mardi Gras, which many Israelis celebrate by wearing costumes and feasting. It is marked by public readings of the *Megillah*, or the book of Esther—the young Jewish woman and queen of Persia who saved the Jews by exposing Haman's plot to kill them.

It has a particularly dark history in Hebron because it was on Purim in 1994 that Baruch Goldstein, a US-born Israeli immigrant, went on a shooting rampage. A former physician for the Israeli army, he killed twenty-nine Palestinians and wounded 125 more inside the Cave of the Patriarchs (known to Muslims as the Ibrahimi Mosque). The alleys near the mosque are still lined with faded posters bearing the faces of the victims.

Hebron is the largest city in the occupied West Bank, and about 80 per cent—known as H1—is under full Palestinian control. The rest of it—H2—is controlled by the Israeli military, because it is home to about 800 Israeli settlers, who live under heavy guard among 35,000 Palestinians. It is the only place in the West Bank where the two populations live cheek-by-jowl, the place where Israel's half-century occupation appears in starkest relief. Around the time of the shooting, it had also become a focal point for the "lone wolf *intifada*", an outbreak of Palestinian attacks across the Holy Land that started in October 2015. During the first month alone there were 14 attacks (mostly stabbings) in Hebron, which accounted for more than a quarter of the nationwide total.

The events of 24 March followed a familiar pattern. Two Palestinians, Ramzi al-Kasrawi and Abdel Fattah al-Sharif, approached a group of Israeli soldiers and stabbed one of them. They were quickly shot, and the Israeli army issued the kind of statement that it had put out almost daily since the winter: "Forces responded to the attack and shot the assailants, which resulted in their deaths."

But then B'Tselem, a prominent Israeli human rights group, released a video shot by a Palestinian employee who lived nearby. The initial shooting only resulted in the death of one attacker, Kasrawi. The three-minute clip, posted on YouTube, showed the wounded Sharif lying supine on the street, surrounded by a group of soldiers. A voice, probably one of the soldiers, warned the others that "the terrorist is still alive, the dog." The soldiers conferred amongst themselves—then one of them shot Sharif in the head. The camera captured his blood trickling down the pavement while an ambulance slowly maneuvered into place to collect his body. The routine shooting was actually an execution.

A spokesman for the army quickly called it "very serious and atypical." Indeed, while there had been several other questionable shootings over the past few months, none had been so brazen, nor had they been caught on tape. The soldier responsible, a 19-year-old army medic named Elor Azaria, would soon be charged with manslaughter in military court.

In previous decades, this might have been uncontroversial. One of the closest parallels—a 1984 incident in which officers killed two Palestinian bus hijackers after they were already in handcuffs—ultimately led to prosecutions. (It also led to the resignation of a director of Israel's internal security agency, the Shin Bet, who tried to cover up the affair). But in 2016, the Azaria case polarized the nation. Members of the right-wing ruling coalition lined up to praise him. Avigdor Lieberman, who would soon be named defense minister, called him a hero. Benjamin Netanyahu, the prime minister, called the soldier's father to offer condolences, a move that stunned what little remained of Israel's liberal civil society. An overwhelming majority of the Israeli public said Azaria did not deserve to face criminal charges, and a petition to grant him a medal for heroism quickly garnered more than 63,000 signatures.

But perhaps the most telling response was the first one, from Azaria's fellow soldiers—at least one of them an officer, judging by the insignia on his uniform. The B'Tselem video captured their immediate reaction to the unprovoked shooting. Or, to put it more bluntly, their lack of reaction. As Azaria delivered the shot to the head, they didn't even flinch.

The Second Third Intifada

Israelis couldn't even agree on what to call it: the wave of terror, the knife intifada, the lone wolf intifada. Some simply called it the third intifada, though that was problematic, because a few commentators had already labeled the events of the previous winter the third intifada. (The "second third intifada", perhaps?)

However, one thing could not be disputed. It was the worst bout of sustained violence in Israel and the West Bank in more than a decade. Scores of young men and women, most of them armed with knives, struck nearly one hundred times in the first two months—not only in Jerusalem and other perennial hotbeds, but in sleepy suburbs like Petah Tikva and Ra'anana, far from Israel's contested borders. A middle-aged couple was shot dead on a West Bank highway with their four young children in the back seat. A rabbi was hacked to death with a meat cleaver in broad daylight on a busy Jerusalem street. Gunmen ordered dessert in a popular Tel Aviv restaurant, then pulled out their weapons and opened fire, killing four people.

One of the most puzzling aspects of the violence was that nobody seemed to be directing it. Security officials said there was little evidence that any of the attackers were linked to militant groups or political factions. Instead the violence was like a fire that fed itself. At first it had seemed to be a response to religious tensions on the Temple Mount, the site in Jerusalem sacred to both Jews and Muslims (who revere it as *Haram al-Sharif*, the "Noble Sanctuary"). As it continued, assailants told their Israeli interrogators that they had been provoked by the widely-circulated videos of their predecessors being shot dead. The violence subsided after the new year, from an average of three daily attacks to one, but it continued for months at that lower level. "This has become our new normal, even though it isn't normal," said Col Gilad Eisen, who was then the top intelligence officer in the West Bank.

A poll conducted in December 2015 found that 77 per cent of Jewish Israelis felt unsafe, and that nearly half were reluctant to attend public Hanukkah celebrations.[1] After an attack in a supermarket, one of Israel's largest grocery chains pulled the knives and scissors from its aisles—even the pizza cutters, just to be safe. Gun stores, on the other hand, did a brisk business. The number of new applications for firearms permits soared.

In most countries, wars and acts of terrorism bring a "rally-around-the-flag" effect—as in the United States after 9/11, or France after the *Charlie Hebdo* massacre. Historically, Israel was no different; indeed, it had pulled together as recently as 2014, when the army had gone to war against Hamas and other militant groups in Gaza. Months later, a prominent leader of the settler movement reminisced almost nostalgically about the "sense of togetherness" he felt during the war. He compared the atmosphere to that during the 1973 Yom Kippur War, a conflict that threatened the very existence of the state.

Yet months of daily attacks produced no such unity in 2015. Outside Jerusalem, where the worst violence occurred, religious settlers held a protest in November—not because of the stabbings, but because of the Supreme Court's order to demolish the synagogue they had built illegally on private Palestinian land. They stockpiled explosives and warned that, "There will be a struggle here, and there are gas cylinders, and everything is permissible." Other hardliners chose a football match around the twentieth anniversary of Prime Minister Yitzhak Rabin's death to chant the name of his assassin "Yigal" [Amir], as if they were celebrating him. In a further manifestation of the surging right, in October Amir's brother

Hagai was arrested for inciting violence against the sitting president, Reuven Rivlin, on Facebook. Though Rivlin is a conservative opponent of the two-state solution, he has nonetheless earned the enmity of the Israeli right for urging coexistence between Jews and Arabs.

The reaction of the political establishment was underwhelming. The Labor Party, that scion of Israel's old secular, Zionist majority, briefly took notice of all this, then went back to haggling over a nominee to head the Jewish National Fund, a quasi-governmental body that develops land and plants trees. The country's Arab minority was beset by infighting, with the head of its parliamentary bloc and the mayor of its largest city bickering on live television about the economic danger that daily knifings posed to hummus restaurants and pastry shops in Nazareth.

Then there was the tragic absurdity of the letter to Palestinians published in broken Arabic in *Mishpacha*, a popular weekly newspaper for ultra-Orthodox Jews. Many had been targeted in the Old City, probably because of their conspicuous garb. Yet, the authors explained, they did not pray on the Temple Mount because their rabbis deemed it sacrilegious. Since the intifada had been kicked off by disputes about praying there, they felt they should be exempted, imploring, "please stop murdering us."

A changing climate

Netanyahu's surprise victory in the March 2015 election had put him on course to surpass David Ben-Gurion, the founder of the state, as Israel's longest-serving prime minister. But he didn't seem to particularly enjoy the start of his fourth term. The government he pieced together after weeks of negotiations was Israel's most conservative in decades; Netanyahu was actually one of its most liberal members, and he struggled to contain the hawkish impulses of his coalition partners. He had to endure a volley of criticism from the right, particularly from Lieberman, the head of a hawkish nationalist party that had initially elected to stay in the opposition. And his coalition had just 61 members, a one-seat majority in the Israeli parliament, the Knesset. This narrow margin exposed him to endless blackmail from backbenchers. Two Likud members, David Amsalem and Avraham Nagosa, hinted that they might vote against the budget unless Netanyahu agreed to bring

1,300 Falashmura—Ethiopians with a tenuous connection to Judaism—to Israel. If the budget vote failed, the Knesset would dissolve, and Netanyahu's rule would be in danger.

So the violence compounded an already precarious situation, threatening his image as the level-headed guardian of Israel's security, his main (arguably, his only) selling point to voters. It also opened a rift between Netanyahu and the army leadership. In February the chief of staff, General Gadi Eizenkot, urged his soldiers to exercise restraint. "When there's a 13-year-old girl holding scissors or a knife, and there's some distance between her and the soldiers, I don't want to see a soldier open fire and empty his magazine," he said at a meeting with high school students in Bat Yam.

The Israeli army, like all modern armies, has rules that govern the escalation of force. Eizenkot was merely restating those rules. Yet he was immediately attacked by politicians on the right, who accused him of handcuffing the army and endangering the public. Yitzhak Yosef, one of Israel's two chief rabbis, repeated the Talmudic injunction, "If someone comes to kill you, rise up and kill him first." Soldiers shouldn't worry about the courts, "or if some chief of staff says something else," he said in a sermon, a clear rebuke to Eizenkot.[2]

Netanyahu kept quiet for four days after Eizenkot's speech, then finally dismissed the furor as "pointless". It was a half-hearted defense of his top general, but it was enough to silence the controversy—until it roared back after the Hebron shooting. The prime minister's initial statement, issued hours after the incident, declared that Azaria "does not represent the values of the IDF [Israel Defense Forces]." The backlash was immediate: social media—including the WhatsApp groups favored by Likud members—was filled with angry invective that accused Netanyahu of abandoning Azaria to "the Arabs" and "the left". Right-wing activists circulated a photo of Israeli Defense Minister Moshe Ya'alon, in the crosshairs of a gun, with the words "politically eliminated" written in red below.

The prime minister read the political winds, and on 31 March he made an unusual phone call to Azaria's father, Charlie. "As the father of a soldier, I understand your distress," Netanyahu told him. "The soldiers are forced to make decisions in the field, in real time, under stress and conditions of uncertainty. This is not a simple reality."[3]

Yet this was a charitable interpretation. The shooting didn't happen in real time; the B'Tselem video showed Azaria standing around for several minutes before he pulled the trigger. He had told other soldiers that Sharif "deserved to die", according to army investigators. His Facebook page revealed a history of racist posts, including his support for Meir Kahane, the right-wing rabbi whose political party (Kach) was banned as a terrorist organization in Israel in 1994.

Some Israeli commentators were incredulous. Since when do heads of government pay condolence calls to the relatives of manslaughter suspects? It particularly infuriated Ya'alon and the army brass, because it seemed to throw the military prosecution under the bus. They delivered their response on 4 May, Holocaust Remembrance Day. General Yair Golan, the deputy chief of staff, warned that the "disgusting trends" in Israeli society—racism, "hatred of the other"—were reminiscent of events in Europe, "particularly Germany", on the eve of World War II.

The speech came as a bombshell. The prime minister condemned it at the next weekly cabinet meeting, and asked Ya'alon to demand an apology from Golan, thought to be a future contender for army chief. Ya'alon refused, and then went one step further, encouraging other officers to follow Golan's lead. "I call on you, the commanders of the IDF, to say what is in your heart," he said the following week at an Independence Day celebration. He urged them to follow their "moral compass", not to act "according to which way the winds are blowing."

It would be his farewell address. Netanyahu summoned him for a dressing-down on Sunday. On Wednesday he offered the defense ministry to Lieberman, an ultra-nationalist who had spent the previous year attacking him from the opposition. At 9 am on Friday, Ya'alon announced his resignation in a tweet, saying he had "lost confidence" in the prime minister.

A former commando and army chief, Ya'alon is a soft-spoken and uncharismatic politician, often visibly uncomfortable with the trappings of his new profession. With his bald pate and penchant for short-sleeved Oxfords, he looks more like a retiree at a Sizzler in Florida than a hardened veteran. But the press conference he gave at the defense ministry on 20 May, hours after he announced his departure, was positively scathing. "Unfortunately, Israel and the Likud party were taken over by extremist and dangerous elements," he said. "This is not the Likud party I joined."

It was a dramatic change, not only for Ya'alon, but for Israel. Lieberman is a hawkish politician who has suggested toppling the Palestinian Authority, beheading "disloyal" citizens with axes, and bombing the Aswan High Dam in Egypt. Benny Begin, a Likud lawmaker and the son of the party's first prime minister, called the appointment "delusional". Moshe Arens, a three-time defense minister and Likud stalwart, called it a "turning point" in Israel's political history.[4]

Palestinians and Israelis, like people trapped in an unhappy marriage, can be incisive observers of each other's flaws. A few weeks after the shooting, I met in Gaza with Bassem Naim, a Hamas official and an adviser to former prime minister Ismail Haniyeh. He reminisced about the defense minister's past as an elite army commando: Ya'alon had taken part in the 1988 raid that killed Khalil al-Wazir, a leading Palestinian militant. Wazir, who went by the *nom de guerre* Abu Jihad, was shot dead in front of his wife and children at his home in Tunis.

Yet Naim was still surprised at his treatment by right-wing activists. He asked if I had seen the photos of Ya'alon in the crosshairs. "They put a target on his face," he said, incredulously. "We don't even do that, and he's the one who shot Abu Jihad."

INTRODUCTION

This book is based primarily on thousands of interviews and conversations conducted over three years with people from Acre to Be'er Sheva. Unless otherwise specified, all quotes and anecdotes are from my own reporting. Some of it is based on articles I wrote for other publications during that time. It also relies on a vast range of Hebrew, Arabic and English secondary sources, which are listed at the end of the book.

I have chosen to use the most commonly accepted transliterations of Hebrew and Arabic names, except in the cases of well-known public figures who use alternative spellings. Hence the opposition leader is Isaac Herzog, not Yitzhak. I also use the common English renderings of place names, which tend to be the Hebrew ones: Negev instead of Naqab, Hebron instead of Al-Khalil (but also Nablus instead of Shekhem). This is not a political statement, merely an attempt to make the book more accessible. In a country where even highway signs become heated political disputes, you can't please everyone.

Similarly, I adopt some Israeli euphemisms, like the phrase "illegal outpost" in reference to West Bank settlements that were built without government approval. This is not an endorsement of the Israeli position that the other settlements are legitimate, only an effort to improve readability. "Arab Israelis" and "Palestinian citizens of Israel" are used interchangeably—both to improve the prose and to reflect the community's own internal disagreements over identity.

Finally, a word about myself. I am a correspondent for *The Economist* and for *The Times* of London, and my longer-form work has been published in a number of other newspapers and magazines. I have lived in

Israel for the past three-plus years, and I have made reporting trips here throughout the past decade, criss-crossing the country to cover two Gaza wars, two "third intifadas", an election campaign, and countless other stories, interviewing everyone from religious settlers to cannabis entrepreneurs (who occasionally have proved to be one and the same). I've also spent considerable time in the Palestinian-controlled parts of the West Bank, and I make regular visits to Gaza.

I do not claim to know everything about this place, with its endless complexity and deep divides; no one does. Nor do I claim to be an unbiased observer; no one is. But this book is, I hope, a good-faith effort to document the events of three tumultuous years, viewed from all sides, and to use that as a prism through which to consider the future.

My own politics are very much on the left side of the spectrum. I do not believe in the two-state solution, either on practical grounds or ideological ones. And yet some of the most enlightening conversations I've had about the "peace process" have been with right-wing settlers, those who also believe that partitioning the land is impossible. We disagree on the details, of course, but I find their overall views to be more realistic and clear-eyed than those of the graying Labor "peace camp" or the lifelong negotiators in Jerusalem, Ramallah and Washington.

The conclusions and insights presented here, if I may call them that, are drawn from a wide range of sources. Any mistakes, of course, are mine alone.

1

THE BATTLE FOR ISRAEL'S SOUL

"If all or any of the French Jews protest against this scheme on account of their own 'assimilation', my answer is simple: The whole thing does not concern them at all. They are Jewish Frenchmen, well and good! This is a private affair for the Jews alone."

Theodor Herzl

How long will Israel survive? In years past, the answer to this question would have dwelt on its physical survival as a small Jewish state surrounded by hostile Arab neighbors. But the Israel of 2017 faces no existential threats. This assessment comes not from dovish leftists but from hard-nosed, security-minded realists like former defense minister Moshe Ya'alon. It would also have asked about the shortages and scarcity that plagued Israel's economy for decades. Again, these are a thing of the past.

Modern Israel presents a paradox. While the country has never been safer, more prosperous, and more accepted than it is today, these improved material circumstances have coincided with a deterioration not just in its politics, but in the very fabric of its society.

There are three important questions to consider about Israel's future. The first concerns its security situation. This book was never meant to be about "the conflict" or "the peace process", subjects about which there is almost nothing original left to say. It was meant to be strictly about Israeli society: the people inside the 1948 borders, in East Jerusalem and the

Golan Heights, and in Area C, the two-thirds of the occupied West Bank that remains under complete Israeli control. But, as the prologue suggests, *haMatzav*—"the situation"—kept finding a way to intrude. Israeli politicians, except those on the far left, have become resigned to a seemingly endless state of conflict and occupation. So has a broad swathe of the public. Whether or not you agree with their logic, this dynamic is troubling. It is slowly poisoning the relationship between the nation and the army, long seen as a melting pot and a guardian of values, and between Jews and Arabs. It is also having a coarsening effect on society, empowering harsh strains of nationalism.

The second question is about its socioeconomic survival. The Israel that is marketed to the world is a land of startups and entrepreneurs, an emerging energy powerhouse, and a world-class destination for tourists. But it is also a country of profound inequality—the worst in the Organization for Economic Cooperation and Development (OECD). Israel's fastest-growing demographic, the ultra-Orthodox, often finish school without learning even the basic precepts of math and science. Beyond this, its various groups, Jewish and Arab, religious and secular, hawks and doves, have fundamentally incompatible visions of what it means to be Israeli. The country is so divided that one former Mossad chief mused openly about the possibility of civil war.

The final question, perhaps the most troubling in the short term, addresses its survival as a democracy. Israel, its leaders never tire of saying, is the only democracy in the Middle East, a country that affords its citizens vastly more political and personal freedoms than the autocratic republics and stifling monarchies that surround it. Yet the past eight years of Netanyahu's rule have been marked by a growing climate of illiberalism. Civil society is threatened, with a raft of initiatives meant to curtail the activities of left-leaning groups. The media is under pressure too. Israel has a panoply of news outlets, but a strikingly limited range of opinions, and the prime minister has used his perch to threaten and cajole critical voices. The political system is increasingly fragmented, unable to deal with profound issues of Israel's identity and its future. Two former heads of the Shin Bet, the internal security agency, have dubbed all of this a process of "incremental tyranny."

Despite the occasional diatribes in Beirut and Tehran—and the often overheated rhetoric in Jerusalem—no one seriously doubts that Israel will survive. But it is much harder to say what sort of Israel will survive, and this question has profound implications both for the country itself and for the half of world Jewry that lives outside of it.

The crisis of Zionism

The question of Israel's future has been a fixation for Western commentators in recent years, particularly Jewish ones. The American journalist Peter Beinart brought the subject into the mainstream in 2012 with his book *The Crisis of Zionism*, which argued that the ongoing occupation, now past its fiftieth anniversary, threatens Israeli democracy and alienates American Jews from Israel.

The events of the subsequent few years, particularly the outcomes of two elections and the devastating Gaza war in the summer of 2014, brought a sense of urgency to this discussion. Jonathan Freedland, a leading columnist for Britain's liberal newspaper *The Guardian*, wrote that there was still hope, with liberal Zionists "better placed than most to move Zionist, including Israeli, opinion."[1] Antony Lerman, another British writer, thought the liberal Zionist movement was already past its sell-by date. He instead urged well-meaning leftists to push for "a movement to achieve equal rights and self-determination for all in Israel-Palestine", beyond the tired and failed efforts for a two-state solution.[2] There was also Roger Cohen, the *New York Times* columnist, who visited Israel before the 2015 election and concluded that the Zionist Camp (the main center-left party) represented the last chance to stave off a looming binational catastrophe:

> A battle has been engaged for Israel's soul... the two-state idea is alive but ever more tenuous. It is compatible with an Israel true to its founding principles. It is incompatible with an Israel bent on Jewish supremacy and annexation of all or most of the land between the Mediterranean Sea and the Jordan River. It can be resurrected, because there is no plausible alternative, despite the fact that almost a half-century of dominion over another people has produced ever greater damage, distrust and division. It can be buried only at the expense of Israel as a Jewish and democratic state, for no democracy can indefinitely control the lives of millions of disenfranchised people—and that is what many Palestinians are.[3]

Days before the election, Beinart also warned Israeli voters that reinstalling Netanyahu would irreparably damage their relationship with the US. The message obviously fell on deaf ears:

Bibi is putting Israel on an ideological collision course with the people who will likely dominate American politics in the years to come. He's alienating the young and non-white voters who backed Obama not merely because he's treated Obama with disrespect but, more fundamentally, because he flouts the values that led them to support Obama in the first place.[4]

The main source of their angst is the Israeli occupation of the West Bank, East Jerusalem and the Gaza Strip. The average diaspora Jew is a liberal. "There are more than twice as many self-identified Jewish liberals as conservatives, while among the general public, this balance is nearly reversed," the Pew Research Center wrote in a wide-ranging 2013 survey of American Jewry.[5] These numbers have stayed remarkably consistent across the generations: 72 per cent of American Jews aged 65 and up identified as Democrats, as did 75 per cent of those aged 18 to 29. Apart from the Orthodox, not a single Jewish demographic group votes Republican.

The occupation was once thought to be a temporary phenomenon, particularly during the heady days of the 1990s, the era of the Oslo Accords, which allowed many in the diaspora to believe that it would end after a few years of negotiations. But the Oslo process went nowhere, and eventually led to the second intifada—four years of gruesome suicide bombings that silenced any talk of a negotiated agreement.

The years that followed 2005 cannot be classified so easily, but can perhaps best be described as a sort of lost decade. On the one hand, they embodied a time of relative peace and prosperity for Israel. Despite four wars against militant groups in Gaza and Lebanon, and a sustained wave of stabbings and hit-and-run attacks, overall violence went down. The Israeli economy thrived, at least on a macro level. The Palestinian Authority had recently been taken over by Mahmoud Abbas, a man who, for his many flaws, is firmly committed to nonviolence. Israel forged relationships with new allies in Asia and Africa—and even in the Middle East, where a mutual fear of Iran brought the Gulf monarchies into a quiet cooperation with their onetime foe.

Yet the decade also marked a time of diplomatic drift and inaction. Although the contours of a two-state solution are widely understood, countless attempts at diplomacy ended in failure. The last round of peace talks collapsed in 2014. At the time of writing, between Netanyahu's right-wing government and the Palestinians' intractable internal divisions, progress seems highly unlikely—despite Donald Trump's efforts. Hence the angst. How can one be both a liberal and a Zionist, when the latter seems to mean supporting a permanent occupation?

A fluttering flag

Israel had to do its own soul-searching about Zionism during the 2015 campaign. Zionism is the animating ideology of Israel, quite literally the state's *raison d'être*. It originated in Europe in the late nineteenth century as a predominantly secular movement which believed that the long-persecuted Jews could only be safe in a country of their own. The religious establishment was broadly hostile to Zionism; rabbis saw it as a sacrilegious attempt to hasten the return of the Messiah. So it was led by secular men, products of the *haskalah*, the European Jewish enlightenment of the eighteenth and nineteenth centuries.

The early Zionist movement took various forms. There was the "political Zionism" of Chaim Weizmann, the leader of the World Zionist Organization, who focused on lobbying the international community to create a Jewish state. Labor Zionists, who would shape Israel in its first decades, emphasized the need for a progressive society with liberal economic policies, and gave birth to the *kibbutzim*. The Revisionist movement, the forerunner of today's Likud, believed that Jews should control all of *Eretz Yisrael*, literally "the land of Israel", the territory between the Mediterranean and the Jordan River (and perhaps more: some Revisionists lumped in the stretch of desert that is modern-day Jordan).

More than a century later, these ideologies feel somewhat anachronistic. The Jewish state is an established fact; the land is settled, and Israel is now an advanced neoliberal economy, where many *kibbutzim* are better known for luxury holiday cabins and steakhouses than for dairy farms. Jews have *de facto* control, if not official sovereignty, over all of the land from the river to the sea. Asking the average Israeli if she is a Zionist is a bit like asking an American how she feels about manifest destiny. The word tends only to enter political discourse in its negative form—an anti-Zionist is a liberal Israeli Jew, unpatriotic, perhaps even pro-Palestinian.

Enter the Zionist Camp. The party was the offspring of a shotgun wedding between Isaac Herzog's Labor Party, the antecedent of the Labor Zionist movement, and *HaTnuah* ("The Movement"), a centrist party led by former justice minister and lifelong political carpetbagger Tzipi Livni. They spent much of their campaign trying to reclaim the word "Zionist" from the right. (A co-founder of the far-right activist group Im Tirtzu actually filed a lawsuit to block them from using the name. He claimed it was misleading to voters because Herzog and Livni were not true Zionists.)

Two months before the election, the party released a campaign spot entitled "What is Zionism?" It looked a bit like an educational video shot in the 1980s, the sort of thing that might have aired on state television. One by one, candidates appeared in front of a fluttering Israeli flag and outlined views of Zionism that seemed simple to the point of banality. "For me Zionism is a house, allowing security for all the citizens of the state," Herzog explained. "Zionism is to maintain that no one can transfer our money under the table," added Stav Shaffir, a young Labor MK who rose to prominence as a social activist and fought in the Knesset against funneling money to illegal West Bank settlements. "Zionism is responsibility. Responsibility of the state for education, for livelihood, for health care—for all of us," said Shelly Yachimovich, who served as Labor chairwoman before Herzog.

If the video was meant to challenge anyone, that person was Naftali Bennett, one of the most charismatic politicians in Israel—a source of either inspiration or terror, depending on your political leanings. Bennett is the leader of the Jewish Home, a right-wing party that draws its support largely from the "national-religious" sector (*dati leumi*, in Hebrew). The term conjures up images of bearded settlers, but in reality the community is heterogeneous and hard to define. Pollsters from the Israel Democracy Institute (IDI), a respected middle-of-the-road think tank, tried to do so in a comprehensive 2014 survey, but admitted they weren't even sure how to choose a sample population.[6] Some 3 per cent of Israelis who identified as national-religious also paradoxically described themselves as secular. Bennett himself is not a settler, but a high-tech entrepreneur who lives in Ra'anana, a stony suburb north of liberal Tel Aviv. He is a Modern Orthodox Jew, but his wife was not religious before they met. His party's popular second-in-command, Ayelet Shaked, is also secular.

Still, as the name suggests, the national-religious camp trends towards a more religious, nationalistic worldview. Among the respondents to the survey, 78 per cent told IDI they identified as right-wing on foreign policy and security issues. A plurality opposed both civil marriage and allowing same-sex couples to join their synagogues, while a majority believed that rabbis should have authority over the votes of religious Knesset members. Three-quarters of them agreed that students should be segregated by gender. In the 2013 election, center-left parties received 37 per cent of the overall vote, but just 9 per cent from the national-religious electorate.

Most significantly, the survey found that nearly a quarter of Israeli Jews identify as *dati leumi*. Previously the group was thought to comprise no more than 10 per cent of the Jewish population. And the growth of this sector seems to be accelerating. One-third of the Israeli Jewish population is aged 18 to 34; another third is 55 and up. But the younger group comprises 42 per cent of the national-religious camp, while their elders represent just 26 per cent. They have a particular foothold in the army, where national-religious soldiers make up a growing share of the officer corps. "The community is gradually taking root in formal and informal positions of power, and entrenching itself at the very heart of public discourse in Israel," the survey noted.

This is a profound shift in the definition of "Zionism". It is no longer a secular movement, nor one concerned solely with safety and self-determination for Jews. Indeed, in a combative debate with former US ambassador Martin Indyk at the Saban Forum in Washington in late 2014, Bennett pronounced the era of secular Zionism over. "Modern Zionism was all about creating a shelter for the Jews… it was a secular approach that had the audacity to change history", Bennett said. "But one hundred years on… the reason we're in Israel is not because it's a shelter. It's our homeland. I want every Israeli child to know our history."[7]

In Israel, as among the diaspora, there is a debate over the future of Zionism. But it is not one that cares much about the occupation. One side adopts a religious, messianic worldview—the territorial maximalism of the Revisionist movement, without the secularism of its founder, Ze'ev Jabotinsky. The other, it seems, defines Zionism as a belief in transparent accounting.

The garbageman

My late maternal grandmother, Lillian Goldston, was the archetype of a twentieth-century first-generation Ashkenazi immigrant to America.

Her parents made the prescient decision to leave Poland in the early 1900s, eager to escape both worsening anti-Semitism and the strictures of *shtetl* life. They arrived in Queens and opened a fruit-and-vegetable shop. Their daughter, my grandmother, went to college, worked in sales, married an accountant; the family, like so many others, became more comfortable and less observant.

In the early 1990s, she made her first trip to Israel. I asked her about it when she came back, and remember her telling me, "It was very strange. I stepped out of my hotel in Jerusalem on the first morning, and there was a garbageman emptying the bins. I noticed that he was wearing a yarmulke. A garbageman! With a yarmulke! And I just stopped and stared, because I couldn't believe it. We don't do that kind of work!"

Of course the garbageman was Jewish, in a country where 80 per cent of the population is Jewish. But she came from a world where Jews were overwhelmingly educated middle-class professionals, like her own family. The garbageman didn't fit her lived experience.

The same disconnect exists in much of the discussion taking place today in New York and London. Diaspora Jews, particularly younger ones, increasingly view the occupation as a moral outrage and worry about its corroding influence—not only on Israel's democracy, but on its society and culture. You see this in the outpouring of "liberal Zionist" commentary, in the rise of lobby groups like J Street fighting the status quo, and in the discussions that take place at *shul* and around Shabbat tables.

Their initial premise, however, is an idealized Israel, the egalitarian society of hardy, secular pioneers striving for peace with their neighbors, the outmatched David who won miraculous battles against the Arab Goliath. This rosy impression isn't confined to American Jews. President Obama, in a Shabbat address at a Washington synagogue in 2015, described his own first impressions of the country. "I came to know Israel as a young man through these incredible images of *kibbutzim*, and Moshe Dayan, and Golda Meir, and Israel overcoming incredible odds in the '67 war," he said. "The notion of pioneers who set out not only to safeguard a nation, but to remake the world. Not only to make the desert bloom, but to allow their values to flourish; to ensure that the best of Judaism would thrive."[8]

As the Jewish community has become more assimilated, support for Israel has become a central marker of Jewish identity. In a separate poll, conducted in 2016, Pew asked both American and Israeli Jews what it meant to be Jewish. A majority of the American Jews chose "leading an ethical and moral life" and "working for justice and equality". Among their number, 43 per cent also said that caring about Israel was an essential part of Jewishness. Just 19 per cent chose "observing Jewish law", which ranked well below "having a good sense of humor". The Israelis, on the other hand, couldn't seem to agree on an answer: the only choice that elicited majority support was "remembering the Holocaust".[9]

The diaspora, in other words, is engaged in self-projection. It views Israel as a reflection of itself: liberal, moral, committed to social justice. And thus the occupation of 1967 is viewed as a singularly corrupting force, a misstep that pulled Israel away from its true path. "Liberal", then, has acquired a particular meaning in the Israeli-Palestinian context, a way to mark oneself out as a critic of the occupation, a supporter of both Palestinian self-determination and a return to this idyllic *status quo ante*. For the liberal Zionists, this is Israel's most pressing concern. It needs to end "the conflict" in order to save its identity—its very soul, as Roger Cohen wrote—and arrest the rightward shift.

A compelling argument, simple and elegant. But it is also based on three major misconceptions.

First, the idealized past was hardly ideal, at least for Israelis outside of the secular Ashkenazi elite. Mizrahi and Sephardic Jews were subject to widespread discrimination. The founder of the state, David Ben-Gurion, once described them as having "[not] a trace of Jewish or human education." The ultra-Orthodox, too, were seen as backwards, in need of "secularizing". The early Zionists granted them a number of concessions, like an exemption from army service, because they believed the *haredim* to be a vestige of exile, one that would quickly disappear. The Palestinian minority lived under martial law for nearly two decades. Israel was ruled by left-wing Labor governments that were hardly less militaristic than today's Likud-led coalition. It was a Labor government that blessed the first Israeli settlements.

The other two misconceptions are deeply intertwined. One is the belief that the alarming trends in Israeli society are blips, aberrations that can be easily undone. The other is the assumption that they are a pressing concern for many Israelis, like they are for many American Jews. Yet the problems that alarm the "liberal Zionist" intelligentsia— the settler movement, growing nationalism and religiosity, racism, efforts to undermine democracy—are features, not bugs. They are either the results of conscious government decisions, some of which were taken by "good" Labor leaders, or they are inevitable outgrowths of Zionism itself. Nor do they provoke the same level of concern inside Israel, where the public is increasingly right-wing, hawkish, and focused on socioeconomic problems.

Israel is not an outpost of the Jewish diaspora on the Mediterranean. The belief that it is says more about the state of Western Jewry than it does about Israel. Nor is it a Western-style democracy that made a single bad choice in 1967. It is something else entirely, and to believe otherwise is unhelpful: for Israelis, who must wake up to the very real battle over their nation's identity; for the diaspora, who ground their relationship with Israel in fantasy; and for the rest of the world, where governments fail to take a clear-eyed approach to the country and its problems.

2

CONFLICT

"War is a bad and contemptible thing, but people at war are sometimes better than in everyday life."

Ze'ev Jabotinsky

In the summer the hills around Nablus are parched and barren, almost a moonscape; in the winter they are cold, damp, windswept. The homes built atop them enjoy stunning views, but they are modest properties, without the swimming pools or stone patios found in some of the larger and wealthier Israeli settlements. Infrastructure is modest—narrow streets lined with beat-up minivans. There are no nearby Israeli cities for shopping or entertainment. Jerusalem is 50 kilometers down a winding two-lane highway that is often clogged with traffic. Even if you set aside the political and ideological problems with living there, Israel boasts far nicer places to raise a family.

But of course ideology is precisely the point. Austere settlements have taken root on the hilltops in almost every direction around Nablus: Eli to the south; Kedumim to the west; Elon Moreh to the east. The families who live here are mostly religious, drawn by the area's prominent role in the Old Testament. Shiloh, for example, was the focal point of Jewish worship before the First Temple was built in Jerusalem.

In recent years these settlements have gained notoriety for something else: the regular acts of violence and arson their inhabitants com-

13

mit against the nearby Palestinian villages. They are known (in both English and Hebrew) as "price tag" attacks, because they are meant to extract a "price" for Israeli or Palestinian actions against the settler movement. Such causal logic seems irrelevant in an era of right-wing rule. Benjamin Netanyahu is hardly an enemy of the settlers, even if his role as a supporter is often exaggerated. Still, the attacks continue. The settlers often dismiss them as pranks—harmless graffiti on mosques, an occasional tree set ablaze by mischievous teenagers. Official statistics from the United Nations paint a somewhat more serious picture. Some 50 people were injured and more than 2,500 trees damaged in 2011 alone. (About half of Palestine's farmland is planted with olive trees, and the industry supports some 80,000 families.)

Yitzhar has perhaps the most outsized reputation. In that particular year, it earned the distinction of carrying out more attacks than any other settlement: seventy in all, one-sixth of the year's total, despite having fewer than 2,000 residents.[1] Most of the violence is directed at Palestinians; their homes, churches and mosques; and their olive groves.

In an indication of the changing times, however, the settlers are also turning their ire on the Israeli army that protects them. This happened in Yitzhar in April 2014, after the border police (a paramilitary force which operates mostly in the occupied territories) demolished five houses that had been built without the proper permits. They were confronted by hundreds of angry residents, throwing stones and burning tires to block the streets. Six officers were injured. The settlers later trashed the army post inside the settlement, even slashing the tires on a colonel's jeep. It was the second time his vehicle had been vandalized there in three months.

The authorities responded by shuttering one of Israel's most notorious *yeshivot*, or Jewish religious schools, called *Od Yosef Chai* ("Joseph Still Lives"). It had originally been located inside Joseph's Tomb, a religious site in the Palestinian-controlled outskirts of Nablus, but it was relocated to Yitzhar after the outbreak of the second intifada. Yitzhak Shapira, formerly one of its top rabbis, penned an infamous tract in 2009 called *Torat HaMelech* ("The King's Torah"), which argued that Jews were permitted to kill non-Jews who threatened them, even children. "It is reasonable to harm children if it is clear that they will grow up to harm us," he wrote.

The Israeli army said the yeshiva had become a "hub" for launching attacks on the surrounding communities. "The reason [for the closure] is twofold, first because of the rising violence that is originating from the area of the yeshiva", said Lt Col Peter Lerner, an army spokesman. "And secondly, because of the recent violence there directed at the army. This vandalism is a major concern for us."

Within Yitzhar, all of this became the subject of an unexpected debate. Residents decided to hold an unofficial referendum on whether stone-throwing and other actions against the army were a valid response to future home demolitions. Municipal officials said they would resign if the town voted in favor. "The army may come and do things that upset us, but there have to be limits," said Ezri Tubi, a resident who serves as a spokesman for the settlement. "This vote is an internal vote, to decide what boundaries need to be set in harsh situations like this."

The blue-eyed paratrooper

The settlements are perhaps the clearest example of a modern problem created by Israel's oft-romanticized early governments. They did not simply appear out of thin air. Nor were they solely the work of a few determined individuals, as the more hagiographical works written about the settler movement can suggest. Instead they were the result of a specific policy decision by the Israeli government—a decision that was taken in the face of objections from the government's own legal adviser.

The first settlement was established in September 1967, just months after the Six-Day War that gave Israel control of the West Bank. Shortly after the ceasefire, Israeli activists started to petition the government to authorize Jewish communities in the newly-occupied territories. One of them was Hanan Porat, a young man who grew up in Kfar Etzion, a pre-state community southwest of Bethlehem. His village had particular emotional resonance for Israelis: it had been destroyed by Arab armies in a fierce two-day battle during the war of independence. More than 120 people (a mix of combatants and civilians) had been killed. In some accounts of the battle, they had been shot after the village surrendered. Porat, a former paratrooper, wanted to rebuild it.

The government asked Theodor Meron, the legal adviser at the foreign ministry, to draft an opinion on the relevant points of international law. His classified memo—which was not released until forty years later—was fairly unequivocal, outlining the Fourth Geneva Convention's ban on settling civilians in occupied territory. "The prohibition therefore is categorical and not conditional upon the motives for the transfer or its objectives," he wrote. "If it is decided to go ahead with Jewish settlement in the administered territories, it seems to me vital, therefore, that settlement is carried out by military and not civilian entities. It is also important, in my view, that such settlement is in the framework of camps and is, on the face of it, of a temporary rather than permanent nature."

He did offer a suggestion for how Israel could circumvent the law, by arguing that the West Bank was in essence still part of Mandatory Palestine, which had never been officially divided into two political entities. But "in truth," he added, "even certain actions by Israel are inconsistent with the claim that the [West] Bank is not occupied territory." Around the same time, four officials from the Mossad, the foreign intelligence service, went out to survey Palestinian public opinion. They too returned with a clear recommendation: Israel should hasten to establish a Palestinian state, they wrote, because "the vast majority of West Bank leaders, including the most extreme among them, are prepared at this time to reach a permanent peace agreement."

The Labor government, led by Levi Eshkol, ignored their advice and allowed Porat to establish Kfar Etzion anyway. "The secular Labor leaders, themselves former pioneers, could not resist," Akiva Eldar and Idith Zertal wrote in *Lords of the Land*, their detailed history of the settler movement. "They perceived the blue-eyed fighter, paratrooper, and religious settler of the land [Porat] as a new incarnation and avatar of the soldier-tiller of the land, the cherished icon of national movements that fight for territory."[2]

The following year, a group of Israeli Jews moved into a hotel in Hebron. They pretended to be Swiss tourists celebrating Passover, and then refused to leave. Eshkol decided not to force them out, and thus Kiryat Arba was born, the first of five Israeli settlements in and around Hebron. It remains the only Palestinian city with a settler presence inside its borders, and its residents are among the West Bank's most ideological, a major source of friction to this day.

From there, the settlements grew in fits and starts—slowly at first, during the next decade of Labor rule, and then rapidly once Menachem

Begin brought Likud to power in 1977. Netanyahu, despite his right-wing rhetoric, has taken a middle road. The settler population has grown rapidly during his term in office: up by 37 per cent over eight years, to a total of 385,000 people, compared to 14 per cent growth for Israel as a whole. (A roughly equal number of Israelis live in occupied East Jerusalem, but they are a very different group, ideologically and legally; we will return to them later.) Much of this, however, is "natural growth"—settlers having children. New construction is relatively slow. Except for 2013, developers broke ground on fewer than 2,000 new homes per year or "construction starts", as they're known. This annual average is lower than it was under both of Netanyahu's predecessors, the right-wing Ariel Sharon and the center-left Ehud Olmert.

The reluctance to approve major new construction has been a constant source of tension between the settlers and the Netanyahu government, which depends heavily on their support. The prime minister frequently blamed the slow pace of housing starts on Barack Obama. For all their personal animosity, the American president was an invaluable asset to Netanyahu, who invoked his name in cabinet meetings like a stern father warning unruly children about the boogeyman. A building spree in the West Bank, he advised, could bring consequences from Washington: an unfavorable military aid package, perhaps, or reduced support at the United Nations. His ministers usually fell in line. Yet the rank-and-file of the settler movement wasn't convinced. This is what gave rise to the "price tag" phenomenon.

Jews on Jews

The residents of Yitzhar and neighboring settlements largely belong to the national-religious movement. In the 2015 election, nearly three-quarters of Yitzhar's votes went to Yachad, an extremist party that ultimately failed to clear the threshold to enter the Knesset. (One of the candidates on Yachad's list believes homosexuality is a disease; another was charged with assaulting a Palestinian shortly before the election.) About 20 per cent of the vote went to the Jewish Home, the mainstream political vehicle for the settlers. Likud received exactly eight votes. It narrowly edged out the pro-marijuana legalization party, which got four.

One of the many divisions within the national-religious camp revolves around the concept of *mamlachtiyut*, a word that is roughly translated as "statism". The vast majority of national-religious Israelis belong to the *mamlachti* trend: they often disagree with Israeli policy, but they accept it, because it is the consensus decision of a Jewish government. A minority, however, subscribe to an anti-*mamlachti* worldview, which holds that certain actions—dividing the land of Israel, for example—are beyond the pale. An Israeli government that pursues them is also illegitimate and should be opposed, often passively, but occasionally with violence. The assassination of Prime Minister Yitzhak Rabin in 1995 was the most extreme manifestation of this ideology. (Readers familiar with the Arab world will see a parallel in Sunni Islamist discourse, in the argument over participation in democratic governments between groups like the Muslim Brotherhood and more rigid *salafis*.)

So the attacks on the army in Yitzhar were not unprecedented. Settlers broke into the regional army command near Beit El in 2012 to protest demolitions in the Migron outpost and elsewhere. A similar riot in 2011 targeted an army base in the Jordan Valley. "There's a long history of this kind of behavior," said Yehuda Shaul, a member of Breaking the Silence, a group of former Israeli soldiers who document the army's activities in the West Bank. "The discrimination in law enforcement is embedded in the system. The fact is that police are not given orders to crack down on settler violence."

The residents of Yitzhar, like their neighbors in other settlements, often accuse the army of doing the exact opposite—turning a blind eye to acts of Palestinian violence against them. Four times in the winter of 2014, they said, buses carrying girls back from school were attacked with Molotov cocktails, and they complained that the army did nothing to stop it. "Sometimes we feel that the army is more like the United Nations, in between [us], to separate [us], and there are complaints about it," Tubi said. (Lerner dismissed the criticism, calling it "outright wrong.")

But the bulk of the violence goes in the other direction, as the UN statistics indicate. The Israeli army and police are often ill-prepared, or simply unwilling, to respond. In January of 2014, for example, masked settlers from Yitzhar raided a water reservoir being built in the nearly Palestinian village of Urif. They threw stones at schools and family homes. A video released by the human rights group B'Tselem showed Israeli soldiers standing nearby, watching idly. They made no effort to stop the violence or arrest the perpetrators. The army is required (under the Geneva Conventions) to protect Palestinians living under its control, but it rarely does. The Shin Bet has a "Jewish division", meant to crack down on extremists, but it was long seen as a backwater, the sort of "promotion" that might derail a career.

Yitzhar and the other ideological communities near Nablus are often described as a blight on the settler movement—not least by the settler leaders themselves. Dani Dayan, who was then a senior member of the Yesha Council, an umbrella organisation of settler groups, said he would support jailing violent settlers in Yitzhar under "administrative detention". This is a policy that Israel routinely employs to hold Palestinians without charge, but almost never uses against Jews. "Of course I would prefer the main tool to be indictments, but if that's not possible... then I don't mind the use of other means that the law allows," he said.

Elazar Stern, a Knesset member from the centrist HaTnuah party, called for similar steps. "The settlement of Yitzhar should be marked as a place which sends out terrorists," he said, calling for checkpoints at the entrance and army raids at night. The Labor Party's Omer Bar-Lev went even further, arguing that the "continuous violence" left no choice but to close Yitzhar and evict its residents. "This is a decisive step, but if we don't act today with determination, this will end with more than tires punctured and policemen lightly injured," he said.

Any decisions ultimately fell to the cabinet, however, and in particular to the defense minister, Moshe Ya'alon. He was sharply critical of the Yitzhar attack, calling it "terrorism, to all intents and purposes." But he was also a man of the right, an opponent of Palestinian statehood thought to enjoy good relations with the settler movement (though not for long). Days after closing Od Yosef Chai, Ya'alon allowed settlers to move into a building on the outskirts of Hebron, the first expansion there in decades. "They're trying to divert attention from the real issue," Shaul said of the closure in Yitzhar. "It's a show. The next day they announce a new settlement in Hebron. To close a *yeshiva*, it's just a stunt."

About 200 of Yitzhar's 350 registered voters ultimately turned out for the "referendum" at the end of April, and 97 per cent of them rejected further attacks on soldiers. Yitzhak Ginsburgh, the head of Od Yosef Chai, urged residents to halt the violence. "I am distressed by any clash of Jews on Jews," he wrote in an article. His decree, and the vote, were respected. The army spent a year in Od Yosef Chai, but would eventually withdraw and allow it to reopen.

Still, it was clear that not everyone was satisfied. A week after the vote, *Yediot Aharonot* published emails from the settlement's internal mailing list. Several residents defended the attacks on soldiers in remarkably blunt language. "I'm in favor of throwing stones (at the Jews; of course there's no question about the Arabs) in certain situations," wrote one 22-year-old woman, "even if the stone brings the death of a soldier." She would soon be arrested for incitement. "There is no *halachic* problem with killing a soldier in a nighttime evacuation [of a settlement building]," wrote another resident, a 17-year-old boy.[3]

The problems in Yitzhar would return to the headlines the following summer, in the nearby village of Douma, where a group of young settlers carried out another "price tag" attack. Even the most outspoken settler activist couldn't dismiss it as a prank: an 18-month-old baby and his parents were burned to death. Dayan would get his wish, as the Shin Bet employed "administrative detention" against Jewish extremists for the first time in decades. And Ya'alon and the army would continue to clash with the national-religious movement, until Elor Azaria's bullet ended his storied career.

"We helped you"

An hour to the north, Israelis were having a very different debate about the army. Shortly after the Yitzhar controversy started, I drove up to Jish, a picturesque hilltop village in northern Galilee. The Lebanese border sits barely five kilometers to the north. On a clear day you can see across the frontier to Maroun al-Ras, the site of one of the first major battles during the 2006 Lebanon war.

The 3,000 inhabitants of Jish are mostly Maronites, followers of a Christian sect founded by Saint Maroun in the fourth century in the mountains of modern-day Lebanon. Some arrived centuries ago: others have come over the course of the past three decades, during and immediately after Israel's 18-year occupation of south Lebanon. (Israel's proxy force, the South Lebanon Army, included thousands of Maronites, many of whom fled south as Israeli troops withdrew.) The village would be unremarkable, though, just one of dozens that dot the Galilee, were it not for the efforts of its best-known resident. Shadi Khalloul has emerged as a prominent activist for two issues: Christian enlistment in the Israeli army, and the creation of an "Aramaic" identity for Maronites.

On this particular Friday, a group of elderly Jewish visitors from a nearby *kibbutz* was touring the town and learning about the Maronite community. "The big change here, the big problem, was the Arab occupation, the Islamic occupation," Khalloul told them, as he guided them through history dating from the early caliph Mu'awiyah up to the Ottoman empire. The Maronites, he complained, were unhappily forced to Arabize, so they were optimistic when the first waves of European Jews began immigrating to Palestine. "We helped you," he said, brandishing a copy of a letter from a man named Yossi Nachman, a resident of the Galilee in the *yishuv*, the pre-state Jewish community, who thanked the Maronites for their help. "And we continue to help you," he added, explaining that many Maronites serve in the army. Khalloul himself is a reserve captain in the paratroopers.

"We live better than in all the surrounding countries," Khalloul told me later, over a chicken lunch; he pointedly refused to speak in Arabic, offering to do the interview in Hebrew, Aramaic, or English. "Where I'm standing now, it's only two hours from Damascus, from Syria. Can you imagine if these guys could enter this land? What would happen to us? So today I evaluate the situation, and I value being under Israeli Jewish control."

In the earliest days of the Israeli state, Arabs were viewed as a potential fifth column. They were allowed to vote and run for office, and Arab lawmakers have served in every Knesset. But they lived for decades under martial law, subject to nightly curfews and periodic expulsion from their homes and villages. The military regulations were not fully lifted until 1966.

Israel's first conscription law, drafted in 1949, was neutral on gender, religion and ethnicity. It required everyone to serve in the army, except for mothers and pregnant women. But it allowed the defense minister to make exemptions, a prerogative that David Ben-Gurion used to excuse the Arab minority from military service.

His successor, Pinhas Lavon, canceled that exemption in 1954 and ordered the army to begin drafting Arabs. Lavon's career would be short-lived, though. He resigned in February 1955 after it was revealed that he had recruited Egyptian Jews to bomb British- and American-owned targets in Cairo and Alexandria. The disastrous plot, dubbed the "Lavon Affair", was rooted in the fear that Egypt would nationalize the Suez Canal. Lavon hoped that the bombings would damage Britain's relationship with the Egyptian government and convince London to maintain troops in the canal zone.

Ben-Gurion returned to the defense ministry after Lavon's departure, and quickly halted the draft program. Instead he struck a deal in 1956 with the leaders of the small Druze community, a secretive sect that practices a syncretic offshoot of Islam, who agreed to send their young men to the army. The decision was deeply controversial. Indeed, a 1956 report from the Israeli army found that a majority of the Druze opposed the decision. Opponents formed a group, the "Free Druze Youth Organization", which encouraged young men to ignore the draft notices; those who did were sentenced to stiff prison terms. But the leadership saw loyalty to the state as their best guarantee of safety, a pattern the Druze have followed in neighboring countries as well: in Syria, they have remained largely loyal to the Assad regime; the leader of the Lebanese Druze, Walid Jumblatt, is known as the weathervane of his country's politics.

The small Circassian minority made their own deal two years later, in 1958. (While they are not ethnic Arabs, some of them speak Arabic, owing to the century they spent scattered across the Ottoman Empire after their expulsion from the Caucasus.) Now, Khalloul argued, it was time for the Christians—or at least the Maronites—to do the same. "This is our country. If we don't defend our country, we will have Syria," he said.

Enemies and friends

It was a complicated moment for Israel's Christian community. They were eagerly awaiting a high-profile guest: Pope Francis, the newly-installed and very popular head of the Catholic Church. The Maronite patriarch, Bishara al-Rai, planned to fly from Lebanon to accompany him on his trip, the first such visit by a Maronite leader in half a century. Khalloul and his co-religionists were hoping for an audience.

Francis took office in 2013 after his predecessor's unexpected resignation and quickly built a reputation as a liberal reformer, at least for a pope: washing the feet of women and Muslims in a ceremony typically reserved for Catholic men, for example. A longtime friend of the Jewish community in his native Buenos Aires, Francis spoke out strongly against anti-Semitism, working to mend the church's historic schism with the Jews.

Even before he had descended from a Jordanian helicopter at Ben-Gurion International Airport, however, he was already courting controversy in Israel. He started his Middle East tour in Jordan, then flew to the West Bank, where he was due to preside over mass at the Church of the Nativity, the site where Jesus was born. En route to the church, however, his convoy passed by the separation wall, the eight-meter-high concrete barrier that separates Bethlehem from Jerusalem. Francis unexpectedly asked the cars to stop and descended to pray at the barrier. This image—the pope hunched in prayer, next to the words "Free Palestine" scrawled in red paint—would define his trip. Prime Minister Netanyahu responded quickly by asking the pontiff to amend his itinerary and include a stop at the national memorial for victims of terrorism on Mount Herzl.

Politics aside, many Christians in Israel saw the visit as a welcome show of solidarity with their embattled coreligionists across the region. It ended amicably, with an invitation for the Israeli and Palestinian presidents, Shimon Peres and Mahmoud Abbas, to join him at the Vatican on 8 June and pray for peace. (The prayer summit would be Peres' last major act on the world stage; it would be an unfortunate coda, given his reputation as a peacemaker, since war would begin again a few weeks later.)

Yet there was more controversy when, around the same time, the Israeli army sent a batch of "voluntary draft notices" to Christians. They were under no obligation to respond, but the army thought that sending the letters, rather than simply waiting for Christians to show up at the induction center, might boost enlistment. Khalloul, needless to say, supported the move. So did Father Gabriel Naddaf, a Greek Orthodox priest who had become a controversial figure for his own outspoken pro-Israel views. He was a frequent guest at the Knesset (until mid-2016, when he was accused of soliciting sexual favors from children). But it caused a major upset in other parts of the Christian community, with protests in Nazareth and other cities.

"[It's] a good opportunity to try the old Zionist policy of divide-and-rule," said Basel Ghattas, a Palestinian member of the Knesset, a Christian himself, and a critic of the plan. "They've created an argument within the Christian community. There is a huge debate, a huge crisis." (Ghattas would be arrested two years later on suspicion of smuggling mobile phones to Palestinian prisoners in Israeli jails. He lost his seat after pleading guilty, and was sentenced to jail time.)

About 21 per cent of Israel's 8.2 million citizens are members of the Arab minority. Jewish politicians and the Israeli media often describe them, simply, as the "Arab sector" (*mizgar aravi*), a term that elides the vast religious, political and cultural differences within the community. Their numbers include 180,000 Christians—roughly 2 per cent of the national population, making them the third-largest religious group, behind Jews and Muslims. Israeli officials occasionally describe their country as the only one in the Middle East with a growing Christian population, which is untrue. The Copts in Egypt, and the various Christian sects in Lebanon, are growing as well. But it is undeniably one of the safest, most tolerant places for Christians in the region, free from the communal violence and sectarian rhetoric that is prevalent in Egypt, to say nothing of the carnage in Iraq and Syria.

Despite this, Christians (like Muslims) have not exactly been eager to enlist in the Israeli army. Recruitment numbers were historically quite low, just a few dozen young men annually, from a pool (in recent years) of perhaps 1,400 potential recruits. The plight of the Palestinians—the desire not to serve in an occupying force—is of course a major reason. Abd el-Aziz el-Zoubi, an Arab Knesset member in the 1960s and 1970s, described his people as one "whose country is at war with its nation."

"If you accept yourself as a Palestinian, you don't go into an army which maintains occupation or kills Palestinians," Michel Sabbah, the former Latin Patriarch of Jerusalem, said before the pope's visit.

Yet there are signs of a change. If enlistment numbers are any guide, a growing number of Christians disagree with Sabbah. Since 2012, the number of annual Christian recruits has climbed above 100—small in absolute terms, but a notable increase in relative terms. Officials expect it will keep rising. It is hard to ignore the link with the worsening violence across the Levant. Several teenagers in Jish who were mulling whether or not to enlist mentioned the battle of Ma'loula, an ancient Aramaic-speaking village in Syria that was occupied by the jihadi group Jabhat al-Nusra in late 2013. The group, which is the Syrian branch of Al-Qaeda (now known as Jabhat Fatah al-Sham), kidnapped a dozen Greek Orthodox nuns and held them hostage for months.

There are also less idealistic reasons for enlisting. Veterans are accorded a range of benefits in Israeli society. In the weeks before the pope's visit, Yair Lapid, then the finance minister, was pushing a bill to exempt first-time homebuyers from tax. He wanted to limit the benefit to Israelis who had served in the army, or the officially sanctioned "national service" program, which offers a civilian alternative to military service. Some employers use army service as a criterion for hiring, which effectively discriminates against Christian and Muslim applicants. And the army can provide useful skills: many of Israel's high-tech entrepreneurs, for example, are veterans of Unit 8200, an elite branch of the intelligence services. (It cocreated the Stuxnet virus that wreaked havoc on Iran's nuclear facilities, causing centrifuges to spin out of control.)

Yet these benefits have not accrued to the Arab communities that send their sons into the army. The Druze have a higher unemployment rate than Jews or Christians, and their villages have historically been underfunded. The same is true of the tiny Circassian community, which numbers about 4,000. Israel's Central Bureau of Statistics generally does not offer a detailed breakdown of socioeconomic data by sect, instead lumping together all of the Arabic-speaking minorities as one population group. A drive around the rutted streets of a crowded Druze village is enough to underscore the lack of investment, however.

At one point the Netanyahu government did make an effort to improve the status of Arab communities, drawing up a 15-billion-shekel plan to improve health care, education, and infrastructure. The cabinet approved the plan, only to freeze it days later after a shooting in Tel Aviv carried out by a single Arab Israeli.

"It's hard to talk about discrimination against Christians, because they are regarded as part of the Arab population," said Sawsan Zaher, a lawyer from Adalah, a legal center for Palestinian rights in Israel. "In education, in housing, in employment, it's overall discrimination against Arabs, Christian or Muslim or Druze. You cannot come and divide between [them]."

Indeed, Khalloul's approach was emblematic of the country's bigger problems. He has carved out another separate identity—not just Arabs, or Christian Arabs, but Aramaic Christians of Arab descent. Jish now has a school, founded in 2008, that teaches in Aramaic, the language used during the time of Christ. A few months after I visited, the interior ministry agreed to recognize "Aramean" as an identity. In October, his 2-year-old son Ya'akov was the first to have it listed on his identity card. "You don't have this in Lebanon, the source of the Maronites," Khalloul said. "And we here in Israel, as they say, the enemy state, they gave us the right to teach our heritage and language. So you see who is the enemy and who is your friend."

The race for the presidency

Ten people have served as the president of Israel, a ceremonial post with a seven-year term. Some use the job to conduct diplomacy and steer the nation. Yitzhak Navon, a Sephardic Jew who spoke eloquent Arabic, helped to cement the peace treaty with Egypt on his historic 1980 visit to Cairo. Others were less distinguished: Moshe Katsav, who held the post from 2000 to 2007, is best known for resigning amidst rape allegations and then being sentenced to prison.

None had the stature of the nonagenarian Shimon Peres, a leading figure on the Israeli political scene for nearly half a century and a darling of the international community. President Obama awarded him the Medal of Freedom in 2012, calling him "the essence of Israel itself, an indomitable spirit that will not be denied." His ninetieth birthday celebration the following year drew an A-list crowd, from Bill Clinton and Mikhail Gorbachev to Barbra Streisand and Robert DeNiro. "Shimon, you are the world's social Einstein. You have tried to put together a unified theory of meaning," Clinton told him.

In some ways, the reputation was undeserved. As the defense minister in 1975, Peres helped to authorize one of the earliest Israeli settlements, Ofra. He was an advocate for the settler movement, describing it in 1976 as the "roots and eyes of Israel."[4] He genuinely moved to the left in his later years, but his main goal was always political survival. Even during his time as president—which would clearly be his final job, his last chance to leave a mark—he spent five-plus years offering political cover to Netanyahu.

In a December 2012 interview with *Der Spiegel*, he insisted that the hawkish prime minister would surprise his critics. "Netanyahu agreed to a two-state solution," Peres said, when asked about the four-year period after Netanyahu took office, during which he broke off talks with the Palestinians. "Those four years will not be repeated... I am sure Netanyahu doesn't want a binational state."[5] It was only in late 2015, more than a year after his retirement, that Peres finally spoke the truth. Netanyahu's overtures, he admitted to the Associated Press, had never "escaped the domain of talking."[6] An obvious conclusion for anyone familiar with Netanyahu's history—but Peres denied it until his voice no longer carried any official weight.

Nobody harbored any such illusions about Reuven Rivlin, one of the two candidates who led the spring 2014 race to replace Peres. He was, and is, a staunch opponent of the two-state solution, and a supporter of continued settlement in the occupied territories. His candidacy also provoked unease within the Reform community, the dominant Jewish sect in the United States: an observant (though not Orthodox) Jew, Rivlin once said he was "stunned" after attending his first Reform service in New Jersey, which he described with a Hebrew phrase often translated as "idol worship."[7]

The president is selected by the Knesset, not the Israeli public, so it has historically been a vote between two candidates backed by the major left- and right-wing parties. Rivlin, a longtime Knesset speaker who enjoyed warm relations with many of his colleagues, was a logical choice for Likud. But he had one prominent enemy: Netanyahu. The prime minister has harbored a grudge against him for years, partly because Rivlin blocked bills introduced by right-wing lawmakers that he viewed as anti-democratic or racist. (Rivlin also occasionally made jokes about Netanyahu's wife, Sara, a controversial figure who plays a major behind-the-scenes role in her husband's administration.) In a bid to block Rivlin's candidacy, Netanyahu first tried the nuclear option. He proposed eliminating the presidency altogether. When that failed, he pushed Holocaust survivor and Nobel laureate Elie Wiesel as an alternative to Rivlin. That effort failed too. Wiesel refused the job. He wasn't eligible anyway: he wasn't an Israeli citizen. Rivlin eventually got the nomination.

Labor threw its backing behind one of its own long-serving parliamentarians, Binyamin Ben-Eliezer, a thirty-year veteran of the Knesset (and longtime friend of Hosni Mubarak). But Ben-Eliezer, popularly known as "Fouad", was indicted on corruption charges days before the vote and quickly withdrew. His replacement, Meir Sheetrit, had enjoyed a long but unremarkable career in the Knesset, which opened a space for three other candidates to join the race, including a former high court justice and a chemistry professor. Rivlin defeated Sheetrit on the second ballot with 54 per cent of the vote.

After he won, the *New York Times* dryly observed, "Rivlin's politics are far from mainstream."[8] So it would prove—sometimes in surprising ways.

A man of contradictions

Like his predecessor, Rivlin is a career politician. He was elected to the Knesset in 1988, and it would be his home for the next twenty-five years, save for a short period in the 1990s. But the similarities do not go much further. Peres craved the spotlight, the visits to foreign capitals, the celebrity friends he accumulated over the years. Rivlin, with his bulbous nose and bemused grin, often seems uncomfortable with the trappings of state—as if he would much rather be eating falafel and holding court in a streetside cafe.

The Rivlin family traces its roots to Lithuania, but his ancestors moved to Jerusalem more than two centuries ago, when it was still an Ottoman territory. His biography, somewhat unique among Israeli politicians, has done much to shape his worldview. Many of his colleagues speak of Jerusalem as a symbol, a collection of holy places and old stones. Rivlin is one of the few who imbues it with life, reminiscing about his time in the Scouts, or his competition with childhood friends to collect autographs at the Knesset. "You could trade six Menachem Begins for a David Ben-Gurion," he joked. His father Yosef, a scholar of Semitic languages, translated the Qur'an and the *One Thousand and One*

Nights into Hebrew. Rivlin himself speaks fluent Arabic (though he occasionally makes self-effacing jokes about his Hebrew accent). He hails from the political right, yet his closest friend in the Knesset was Ahmad Tibi, an Arab nationalist who served as an adviser to Yasser Arafat.

Rivlin has a reputation in the Knesset for niceness and decency—adjectives not often deployed in Israel's raucous parliament. In many ways, his politics could be described as classical liberalism: he believes in civil liberties and individual freedoms, and as the Knesset speaker, he often blocked legislation that infringed upon those rights. In 2011 he publicly opposed the "Boycott Law", which imposed civil penalties on Israelis who supported boycotts against their country. "Woe betide the Jewish democratic state that turns freedom of expression into a civil offense," he wrote in a *Ha'aretz* op-ed. "[The law] threatens to catapult us into an era in which gagging people becomes accepted legal practice."[9] He denounced efforts to remove Arab MK Hanin Zoabi from the parliament after she joined a Turkish aid flotilla to Gaza, as well as a law that allowed Israel to detain refugees indefinitely. When the Knesset debated a bill designed to push the small Arab parties out of the Knesset, Rivlin was the sole dissenting vote from Likud. He loudly condemned a ruling from a group of municipal rabbis that urged landlords not to rent apartments to Arabs, saying it "shamed the Jewish people."

"I blocked the passage of several laws that the prime minister would have had much difficulty explaining to the world," he said in a 2013 interview with Channel 10.[10]

Rivlin made a particular effort to combat the endemic anti-Arab racism in Israel. Like Netanyahu, he is a longtime supporter of Beitar Jerusalem, one of Israel's top football clubs. In early 2013, after the club signed two Muslim players from Chechnya, fans hoisted a banner that read "Beitar, forever pure". They chanted "no entry to Arabs", and called the club's owner a "whore". The Beitar coach, Eli Cohen, condemned the fans, but offered a bit of his own racism in response: the Chechens, he explained, were good European Muslims, and not the more sinister sort found "in the Middle East." Rivlin's response, delivered on International Holocaust Remembrance Day, was unequivocal. "Imagine the outcry if groups in England or Germany said that Jews could not play for them," he said.

"He really believes it. He's not just the 'tolerant' sort who goes to the Arab village occasionally for hummus," Tibi said. "He genuinely respects the Arab community." At a 2012 *iftar*, the meal that breaks the Ramadan fast, Rivlin described an effort to draft Israeli Arabs as "hypocrisy", even malice: "You don't have to be a genius to realize that it's impossible to draft the Arab public." A few months after his election, Rivlin became the first Israeli president to attend the annual memorial for the victims of the 1956 Kafr Qassem massacre, in which dozens of Israeli Arab civilians were gunned down by border police officers. "The Arab population in Israel is not a marginal group," he said. "We are destined to live side by side and we share the same fate."

Early in the 2014 school year, George Amire made a video about the bullying he received in school. The 11-year-old boy, a Christian from Jaffa, had been called "homo", "faggot", and other epithets by his classmates. He didn't speak in the video; instead he held up sheets of paper, first with the names he was called, then with a message to his bullies. "Don't judge people by how they look," said one. "Look at me, and then look at yourselves. We are the same." The video soon went viral, with hundreds of thousands of views on Facebook.

Rivlin quickly invited Amire to his office in Jerusalem, and they agreed to make a new video, sitting side-by-side on a couch, each holding up cards. Amire's bullying was not racist, but Rivlin connected it to the broader trends in society. "Violence, hostility, thuggery, racism, [these] are only a part of the bad things people encounter every day here in Israel, [and] that must not be in our state," their papers read. Perhaps the most powerful piece of the video was the simple imagery: a small Arab boy and the Ashkenazi head of state, wordlessly delivering the same message.

All of this made Rivlin, a man of the right, into a prime target for vitriol from his own political camp. One photo circulated on social media showed him in an SS uniform offering a Nazi salute. Another portrayed him in a keffiyeh, with the logo of the Palestine Liberation Organization over his right shoulder. "Reuven Rivlin is a kike·traitor, may his name and memory be obliterated," read the caption.[11] The Shin Bet was called in on various occasions to investigate threats against the president's life.

It was another sign that the "peace process" is no longer an operative issue in Israeli politics. Peres, after all, was a universally beloved elder statesman during his presidency; he was never subjected to such criticism, even though his political views were anathema to the Israeli right. In the final year of his presidency, according to IDI, 67 per cent of right-wing Israeli Jews trusted him. Rivlin only won 55 per cent of their support in 2016. But 90 per cent of liberal Israelis had confidence in the conservative president who opposed the two-state solution that had long been the left's defining cause.

One state, two states

Perhaps his views were irrelevant in any case: there was no peace process to speak of. The last round of US-brokered peace talks had collapsed in April 2014. It started amidst great fanfare the previous summer. Over the next nine months, Secretary of State John Kerry would hold more than 100 meetings with Netanyahu, Abbas, and their envoys. None of this work yielded much progress, however, and the talks ran aground at the end of March, when Israel refused to free a group of twenty-six Palestinian prisoners—the last tranche of four amnesties meant as "confidence-building measures", gestures to bring the Palestinians to the table. Abbas retaliated by acceding the "State of Palestine" to fifteen international treaties—including, with no sense of irony, the UN Convention against Corruption—while Israel announced hundreds of new settler homes in the occupied territories. Kerry frantically tried to extend the late-April deadline for ending the negotiations, but his efforts failed.

It was no big surprise to the diplomats and journalists who follow the conflict. Indeed, the whole process would later be revealed as a tragic farce. At one point Yitzhak Molcho, the prime minister's personal envoy, was holding secret back-channel talks with a Palestinian negotiator who wasn't actually authorized to negotiate.[12]

This was the backdrop to the Herzliya Conference, a high-profile annual powwow for security and diplomatic types. It was unusually subdued in 2014: there was the usual chatter about Iran's nuclear program and the worsening civil war in Syria, but it had little of the urgency of past years, when a possible Israeli strike on Iran's nuclear facilities seemed to be imminent.

So the organizers invited the heads of major Israeli political parties to discuss their vision for the future. The result was a bizarre back-and-forth between Naftali Bennett, the head of the national-religious Jewish Home party, and Yair Lapid, from the centrist Yesh Atid. The latter ran for the first time in the 2013 election, and won a surprising nineteen seats, becoming the second-largest party after Netanyahu's Likud. It was a stunning victory. Lapid achieved it by talking almost exclusively about the economy, a hot topic after the major socioeconomic protests of 2011. He promised to lower housing prices, and to compel the ultra-Orthodox to "share the burden" in Israeli society by slashing their welfare benefits and drafting them into the army.

He found time, though, to make a rare foray back into foreign affairs at the conference, warning against the talk of unilateral annexation in the West Bank that had been gaining traction since the latest round of negotiations stalled in April. "If there is an attempt to annex even a single settlement unilaterally, Yesh Atid will not only withdraw from the government, it will bring it down," he said. (Israel has not formally annexed the West Bank, which would foreclose any possibility of a Palestinian state, though it has applied parts of Israeli law to the settlements, a sort of *de facto* annexation.)

Lapid was followed by Bennett, whose supporters were busy working the conference hall, handing out glossy brochures touting his "sovereignty plan". The Oslo process had reached a "dead end", he said, and it was time to move forward unilaterally and seize permanent control of "Area C", a designation created by Oslo for the two-thirds of the West Bank which remained under Israeli security control. It includes the Jordan Valley, the breadbasket of the West Bank, and most of the land around Jerusalem, along with all of the settlements dotted across the territory.

It is hard to capture the absurdity of the moment. Two prominent ministers offering their views on the most important issue for Israel's long-term survival as a Jewish state—one threatening to blow up the government, and the other happily offering him the dynamite. Clearly Lapid and Bennett could only coexist in the same cabinet if peace was low on the agenda—if Netanyahu, and the public at large, were content to preserve the status quo.

A senior member of his party made that point explicitly. "The conflict will not be solved in the near future," said Gideon Sa'ar, then the number-two man in Likud, speaking shortly after Lapid and Bennett. "The status quo is a better alternative, under these circumstances."

CONFLICT

The teenagers

The status quo survived for another four nights.

On 12 June, three Jewish teenagers—Eyal Yifrach, 19, Gilad Shaer, 16, and Naftali Fraenkel, 16—were heading home from their *yeshiva*, or religious seminary, in the occupied West Bank. They were hitchhiking, a common practice in a region where buses run infrequently. A Hyundai pulled up around 10.25pm and offered them a ride. The boys got in, and quickly realized their mistake—the drivers were two Palestinian men looking to abduct Israeli settlers. Shaer made a rushed phone call to police, whispering that he had been kidnapped. Moments later, the trio were dead.

Rumors of the abduction began to spread the next morning, and within twenty-four hours the boys were the subject of a major manhunt and nationwide concern. Their faces adorned the front pages of newspapers for days. Television news became an around-the-clock vigil, with correspondents obsessing over the latest tidbits of gossip. There were endless press conferences and statements, even a worldwide "Bring Back Our Boys" campaign on social media, appropriating a similar effort for the hundreds of Nigerian schoolgirls kidnapped by Boko Haram. Posters appeared across the country praying for their safe return.

Netanyahu quickly blamed Hamas for the abduction, and authorized a major crackdown on the group. Hundreds of its members were arrested across the West Bank, thousands of homes were raided, and at least six Palestinians were killed in confrontations with Israeli soldiers.

The search concentrated on Hebron, just down the road from the hitching post where the boys were abducted. Military correspondents embedded with the troops carrying out night raids there, and produced sensational stories with headlines like "a night in the city of terror".[13] But the arrests were not confined to the southern West Bank. Soldiers raided homes as far north as Nablus and Jenin, and even downtown Ramallah, where an overnight operation set off some of the worst clashes there since the Second Intifada. Some Israeli politicians thought Netanyahu didn't go far enough, however. Danny Danon, the deputy defense minister, proposed shutting off the electricity across the West Bank (which relies mostly on Israeli power plants).

All of this might have been justified, had it been possible that the teenagers were still alive. Yet the assumption was false. The security services had understood from the very beginning that they were probably dead. In a recording of Shaer's last phone call, he could be heard whispering "they kidnapped me," followed by what sounded like silenced gunshots—and then total silence.[14] Police had initially dismissed the call as a prank, and did not start investigating until hours later, when the boys' parents reported them missing. Soldiers searching the area had quickly located the torched remains of the Hyundai; inside they found blood, shell casings, and eight bullet holes.

Local journalists were barred from reporting these details, however, because of a gag order issued by the prime minister's office, a common practice on security-related stories in Israel. A few tried to push the envelope: Amos Harel, for example, made it clear in a 13 June piece for *Ha'aretz* that the teens were unlikely to be rescued.[15]

> One thing should be stated with care: As the hours go by, the chances of this affair ending well are diminishing... [in the West Bank], in most cases, they murder their hostages a short time after kidnapping them; they assume a live hostage leaves behind a greater "intelligence footprint" than a discarded body. A hostage needs to be guarded, fed, held and hidden— all actions that leave traces behind and can send security forces running to the rescue.

But much of the Israeli press swallowed the official spin. They were egged on by the army spokesman, Gen Moti Almoz, who held regular briefings on the search, and promoted the incorrect belief that the teenagers were alive. Politicians were in on the act, too: Lapid said in an interview that the emergency call was "impossible to decipher", a claim that was quickly proved false once the recording was made public.

After eighteen days of searching, the trio's bodies were found dumped in a field outside of Hebron, not far from the kidnapping site. They were buried on 1 July. Their funeral, in their hometown of Modi'in, attracted tens of thousands of people, the crowd spilling beyond the cemetery onto the surrounding hills. The mood was somber, if not angry. Mourners wanted revenge, but were unsure about what form it should take. "We need to send a message, and we need to be sure that [these three] did not die for nothing," said one man, voicing a fairly representative opinion.

Vengeance

Some thirty-six hours later, three Jewish Israelis were cruising the night-time streets of East Jerusalem in their own white Hyundai, hopped up on cigarettes and energy drinks. "We were hot-headed and angry," the driver later said. They had five large soda bottles filled with gasoline in the car; they doffed their kippahs and donned less conspicuous secular clothing. They were looking for a target—looking to send their own message.

They found one shortly before dawn in Shuafat, a middle-class neigh-borhood north of the old city: Mohammed Abu Khdair, a slight 16-year-old boy who spoke broken Hebrew. He was outside the local mosque, just steps away from the family home, waiting for his father to finish prayers before *suhoor*, the morning meal before the Ramadan fast begins. "We can overpower him, get out of the car quickly," Yosef Haim Ben-David told his two passengers, both minors. One of them slapped Abu Khdair; the other covered his mouth to stop him from screaming. They forced him into the car and choked him until he lost consciousness.

From Shuafat it was a short drive to the Jerusalem Forest, west of the city, where Ben-David dragged his captive outside and beat him with a crowbar. "This is for the Fogel family; this is for Shalhevet Pass," he shouted, referring to murders carried out by Palestinians in the West Bank in 2011 and 2001, respectively. The three doused him with gasoline. "I took a lighter and I set the boy ablaze," Ben-David con-cluded. An autopsy would later find that Abu Khdair was still alive when he was set on fire.

Three Jewish teenagers were dead, and now so was a Palestinian teenager, in an act of revenge. Ben-David would later recount the inci-dent for police in chillingly clinical detail. The plot was hatched on 30 June, the night the teens were found dead, when he met with one of his accomplices. "We decided that we had to take revenge for what they did. Both of us were saying, 'let's get revenge.' I said my blood was boiling, and he said his blood was boiling, and the whole country was silent, and we were wondering, 'why did they do this to them, and what were they guilty of?'"

They spent two nights searching for the right victim. On the first, they assaulted a Palestinian woman pushing her young child in a stroller, who quickly fled. "We said she shouldn't bring any more children into the world," Ben-David recalled. They found Abu Khdair the following night, after the second minor joined their group. (The names of both accomplices were sealed by the court because of their ages.)

Abu Khdair's slaying appalled the vast majority of Israelis, and was roundly condemned by the entire political class. "The murder of your son is abhorrent and cannot be countenanced by any human being," Netanyahu told the boy's father, Hussein, several days later. Elyakim Levanon, a hardline rabbi affiliated with the settler movement (who once threatened to "cut off" Netanyahu's hand if he tried to dismantle an illegal outpost), called for Abu Khdair's killers to face the death penalty, which has not been applied in Israel since the Nazi leader Adolf Eichmann was executed in 1962. The police moved swiftly, and within four days the suspects were apprehended. The case was over—an outlier, everyone swiftly agreed. There was unequivocal condemnation in the pages of *Israel HaYom*, the country's most widely-read newspaper:

> We are commanded to throw up from within us, and also to condemn, the tiny minority that, as was published yesterday, is suspected of murdering and burning to death the Arab boy. We are compelled to ask and cry aloud the words of the prophet Ezekiel, "You shed blood; shall you then possess the land?"[16]

So too in *Arutz Sheva*, a website popular with the settler movement: "No one in the state of Israel believed in committing murder in such horrific circumstances… the value of human dignity and the sanctity of life, they are the basis of Jewish ethics."[17]

The killers were similar to Yigal Amir, pundits argued, the extremist who assassinated Prime Minister Yitzhak Rabin in 1995. They acted alone, and their actions were unconnected to the prevailing political climate in the country. "There is this pernicious belief that half the country assassinated Rabin," one acquaintance complained. "And now it's going to rear its head again."

Collective responsibility

It had to be such—because the alternative would imply a degree of collective responsibility, and would implicate people like Ayelet Shaked, a prominent member of the Jewish Home party. She strongly condemned Abu Khdair's murder, denouncing his killers as "heinous". "Murderers who murder children in cold blood, youth, women and innocent men, should spend the rest of their lives in prison," she said. Less than twenty-four hours earlier, though, Shaked had told her supporters that the "entire Palestinian population is the enemy." An incendiary statement on her Facebook page—described as an "unpublished speech" written more than a decade earlier by Uri Elitzur, a onetime adviser to Netanyahu—argued "that the Palestinian population has declared war on us, and we must reply with war." (The post has since been deleted, but the text was preserved on various Israeli websites.)

> Behind every terrorist stand tens of men and women, without whom he could not engage in terrorism… they are all enemy fighters, and their blood shall be on their heads. Now this also includes the mothers of the martyrs, who send them to hell with flowers and kisses. They need to follow their sons; nothing would be more just than that. They need to go, and also the physical homes in which they raised their sons. Otherwise, they will raise more little snakes there.[18]

It is hard to interpret this as anything but a call for mass murder, though Shaked later accused critics of misinterpreting this "sober, legally-minded discussion" and dismissed them as "militant leftists".[19]

Both sets of murders plumbed unspeakable depths. No circumstances can justify plucking teenagers off the street and killing them. Even so, it bears noting that the Israeli teenagers—two of them minors—were studying in what is still effectively a conflict zone, a territory that the Israeli supreme court has described as being under "belligerent occupation". Their parents sent them to the West Bank, and their government supported their presence there.

Some argued that Netanyahu himself had played a role in stoking tensions. That summer Israeli journalists found themselves briefly tied up in an incongruous debate about the overlap between literary allusion and politics. At the centre of the discussion was a series of tweets sent by the prime minister himself. Had he been calling for revenge? Hours after the bodies of the Israeli teenagers were found, he began his tweet with a quote from the work of Chaim Bialik, a Ukrainian-born Jew who eventually became known as Israel's national poet. "'Vengeance for the blood of a small child, Satan has not yet created.' Neither has vengeance for the blood of three pure youths who were on their way home to their parents who will not see them anymore. Hamas is responsible and Hamas will pay. May the memories of the three boys be blessed," he wrote.

Netanyahu's supporters argued that his words were misinterpreted, and they have a point. The Bialik quote (the first sentence quoted above) comes from the final stanza of "On the Slaughter", a lamentation the poet wrote shortly after dozens of Jews were killed in a 1903 pogrom in Kishinev. The poem is about Bialik's own crisis of faith—his anger that divine justice did not "show itself immediately". Netanyahu had omitted the first three words, *v'arur haomer "nkom"*, "cursed be he who says, 'avenge!'"

But it is worth considering the larger body of Bialik's work, which is familiar to many Israeli schoolchildren. He wrote a much longer poem in 1904, after interviewing survivors of the massacre, called "In the City of Slaughter". Here he laments not just the inaction of heaven, but also of men, "Crushed in their shame, they saw it all/they did not stir or move/they did not pluck their eyes out/they beat not their brains against the wall"; "they crawled forth from their holes/they fled to the house of the Lord/they offered thanks to Him/the sweet bene-dictory word."

A century separates the massacre in Kishinev from the murders in Kfar Etzion. The Jews who once "cowered... in their holes" now have a modern state, an army, a legal system. Bialik's words conjure a feeling of Jewish powerlessness and victimhood, from an era when justice was the subject of desperate prayers to an indifferent God. They have little relevance in modern-day Israel. Yet Netanyahu still chose to invoke them.

It was Yossi Melman, a veteran journalist who writes on security and intelligence issues, who raised the comparison with Rabin's assassination in a column for the Jerusalem Post. It was true, he noted, that Abu Khdair's murderers, like Amir, acted alone. But they didn't exist in a vacuum: they emerged from a society in which, as President Rivlin would soon argue, anti-Arab racism was widespread, and in which its ideologues were often coddled by the authorities.

In recent years, the religious dimension has manifested itself in young right-wing terrorists and thugs from Jewish settlements in the West Bank, wrongly known as the Hillside Youth. They have burned and desecrated Arab mosques and cemeteries. Unfortunately the Shin Bet, police and other law enforcement agencies, including the courts, have responded by either turning a blind eye or not acting harshly enough. This is at least partially caused by the refusal of the government to declare their cells a terrorist organization and to impose on them the same anti-terrorist laws and regulations that are used against Palestinian terrorists.

Now, with the murder of the Palestinian boy, we may embark on the most dangerous stage, which is the nightmarish scenario of the Shin Bet. This may be the era in which local gangs, incited by politicians or poisoned by anti-Arab sentiments and atmosphere, turn into vigilantes and take the law into their own hands.[20]

Indeed, the incitement and racism would soon grow worse, becoming a regular fixture of political discourse. The following summer, the "vigilantes" would commit a crime that rivaled the Abu Khdair murder in its brutality.

The "martyr of the dawn"

Mourners tucked into plates of rice and lamb as the sun set over their colorful funeral tent, adorned with photos of the young-looking Abu Khdair—who they called "the martyr of the dawn". The tent was watched from both ends of the street by black-clad members of the *magav*, the paramilitary border police, clutching tear gas launchers and automatic rifles. Broken glass and chunks of concrete littered the street; charred dumpsters rendered it impassible, forcing the few cars passing through to use the railroad tracks.

Not that it mattered, since the light rail had been out of service for days. "Price tag: Death to Israel, death to Jews," someone had spray-painted in Hebrew on the trashed station nearby.

"Don't cause too much trouble. This week has been difficult," an elderly woman warned a group of young men as she shuffled home. Several of them ignored her advice: They climbed to the roof of a nearby building, shooting fireworks over the heads of the officers and sending everyone running for cover.

In quieter times the Shuafat neighborhood is a middle-class redoubt, full of villas populated by East Jerusalem's professional class. Many of the mourners at Abu Khdair's funeral tent were doctors, nurses, lawyers; some were Palestinians from the US and Europe, visiting family for the summer.

Yet that July was not a quiet time. The riots started on the morning of 2 July, shortly after police found Abu Khdair's body in the forest. It was so badly charred that it would take more than twenty-four hours to make an official identification, but the neighborhood knew Abu Khdair had been abducted, and quickly connected the two events. The crowds that day were not huge, only a few dozen local youth fighting with police. At times there seemed to be more journalists than protesters (not an unusual phenomenon here).

But they were the largest clashes that had been seen in East Jerusalem for decades—the biggest since the first intifada, residents said. They dragged on for twelve hours; at one point the imam of the local mosque came down and urged protesters to break their Ramadan fasts. "He said anyone who is fighting has permission to eat and drink," one protester, Yazid, told me. The staccato pop of sound bombs echoed down empty streets, and clouds of thick black smoke lingered in the air where protesters had burned tires. The pavement was a carpet of rocks. It fizzled out after sunset, only to resume the next day, and the day after that. Hundreds of people were injured, hundreds more arrested.

The Israeli press dismissed it as pointless rioting. Though the cause justified the anger, what ensued seemed to compound the hopelessness. Veolia, the company that operated the light rail, said it would take weeks to repair the damage to tracks and stations. Streets and sidewalks were broken apart for ammunition. A poorly-aimed Molotov cocktail even went through an upper window of the Abu Khdair family home, though the fire was quickly extinguished.

However, there was also a half-century's worth of frustration to account for. When Israel occupied East Jerusalem in 1967, most residents had elected not to become Israeli citizens. Instead they were treated as a special category, allowed to move and work freely, but not to vote in national elections. They were also subject to losing their legal status if they moved out of Jerusalem. More than 14,300 Palestinians have had their residency revoked since 1967 (though Israel has scaled back this practice in recent years).

Half a century after the occupation, there remains a vast disparity between east and west on virtually every indicator. Among East Jerusalem residents, 75 per cent live below the poverty line, and one-third of children do not complete a full twelve years of school. Building permits in the east are expensive and difficult to obtain, and the resultant housing crisis has pushed population density to nearly twice the level of the west. Basic services are scarce, from health care to sewage to post offices. Shuafat refugee camp, which borders the "ordinary" Shuafat neighborhood but is separated by a high concrete wall and a checkpoint, had no running water for three months before Abu Khdair's murder.

"We're treated like fifth-class citizens in this country," said Abed Basit, a nurse from neighboring Beit Hanina who visited the mourning tent one night.

So there was a siege mentality in this part of town, even before Abu Khdair's murder. On 15 May, Israel's Independence Day on the Gregorian calendar, several Palestinians were arrested at Damascus Gate for trying to commemorate the *Nakba* ("catastrophe"), the Arabic name for the mass expulsion and displacement of Palestinians that accompanied the creation of the state. "We live here but the state does not see us as equals, it sees us as a threat," said one of them, Abed Hassoura. He held a portrait of his son Louay, who had been jailed three years before on vague security-related charges.

Two weeks later, tens of thousands of religious Jews descended on the city for Jerusalem Day, the annual state-sponsored outpouring of racism that commemorates the 1967 occupation. They marched through the Old City, singing nationalist songs and harassing the Palestinians who live and work there. Naftali Bennett led a midnight march through Sheikh Jarrah while the neighborhood's residents shut their doors and windows.

Outside Damascus Gate, a mother explained to her two sons in New York-accented English that "this is an Arab neighborhood, so we don't normally come here, but we can today because God chose us to have this city, not them." They stopped to take in the view, and her younger son, who couldn't have been more than five years old, unfurled an Israeli flag. In its center, next to the star of David, was a large sticker. It declared, "Kahane was right," in reference to the ultranationalist Rabbi Meir Kahane, the leader of Kach, which was banned in 1994 and declared a terrorist organization.

A handful of people, most of them women, tried to stage a small counter-protest at the gate, peaceably unfurling a Palestinian flag. They were hauled away by police, who barricaded the residents of Sheikh Jarrah and other areas inside their neighborhoods. An elderly resident of

Silwan asked me to check on his son, who had been arrested for demonstrating. Then he scurried away, fearing he would also be detained.

One wonders whether the Ashkenazi Jews of a century ago would find these scenes disquietingly familiar: a fearful minority huddled inside its homes; a raucous mob marching through the streets outside, asserting its ethnoreligious supremacy.

This was the incendiary climate in East Jerusalem, even before Abu Khdair was murdered. Netanyahu tried to calm the situation after his death, urging "all sides not to take the law into their own hands... Israel is a nation of laws for all, and all are compelled to follow the law." But the riots dragged on for days, steps away from the funeral tent where friends and relatives were holding a vigil. Ahmad Tibi made several appearances, demanding that Israel move quickly to find the killers. "Palestinian blood is no less valuable than the blood of settlers," he said.

The body was returned to the family on Friday, 4 July, shortly after midday prayers, unceremoniously dropped off in the middle of the street by an ambulance. The funeral march wound down Shuafat's main street, along the trashed light rail tracks, until it reached a turnoff: the crowd could continue down the main road, toward central Jerusalem, or hang a right towards the cemetery. Most people did the latter. But dozens of local youth tried to continue their march to the Old City, chanting "to Al-Aqsa!" They were blocked by a line of the now-ubiquitous riot police, sparking hours of clashes in which more than forty people were hurt.

It was an absurd and tragic end: mourners banged on the windows of a nearby restaurant, where a group of waiters was setting tables for *iftar*, the meal that breaks the Ramadan fast. They eventually came out with a bucket of sliced onions, an effective remedy for the clouds of tear gas swirling everywhere. A group of pallbearers holding a simple coffin, draped in the Palestinian flag, scurried down the hill, covering their faces against the fumes.

"Gaza is a graveyard"

A crowd gathered after sunset, perhaps 2,000 people chanting about peace, asking the people of Gaza for forgiveness. A line of police separated them from a smaller counter-protest, a uniform sea of blue and white, where right-wing Israelis sang approving slogans like "Gaza is a graveyard". Both demonstrations had to stop earlier than expected, under police orders, but the ultra-nationalists did not go home. They roamed the streets, searching for "leftists", pepper-spraying them and beating them with chairs from a nearby cafe.

A plane rumbled overhead, its cargo of leaflets fluttering down like snowflakes. "Hamas has created a disaster for the residents of the Gaza Strip by opening an unequal war against the state of Israel," the fliers announced in Arabic. A middle-aged man retrieved one from the branches of a tree and stared uncomprehending at the sloping, curved letters. "I hope that's not all we're dropping on them," he muttered.

A woman leaned on a metal barricade at the military cemetery, watching from a distance as a mother sobbed over her son's coffin. Next to it was another freshly-dug grave. The man's father, his black T-shirt torn in keeping with Jewish custom, stood to the side and wept quietly. The woman, a casual acquaintance, was there to show her support. "We should kill a hundred of theirs for every one of ours," she said.

Just like its political history, Israel's military history can be cleaved roughly into two halves. There have been thirteen wars since the country was founded in 1948, according to the defense ministry. For the first few decades, these were mostly conventional battles against states: the counterproductive invasion of Sinai in 1956, alongside France and the United Kingdom; the stunning victory in 1967; the near-catastrophe in 1973. The following years brought a change in politics, as the Likud party took power, ending thirty years of Labor dominance, and in war, as Israel invaded Lebanon in 1982 to strike at the Palestine Liberation Organization, which had carried out repeated attacks across the border. The invasion and the main fighting lasted only a few months, but the subsequent occupation would drag on for nearly two decades. It offered a preview of future conflicts in the Middle East: insurgents, proxy militias and suicide bombings, a technique perfected in Lebanon by Hezbollah and other anti-Israeli factions.

That war enjoyed near-unanimous support from Israel's political class, at least in its earliest days. On 8 June 1982, two days after the invasion, the joint Jewish-Arab Communist party Hadash introduced a no-confidence motion in the Knesset, warning that the government was "leading Israel to the abyss". The measure was defeated by 94 votes to 3; only the Hadash MKs voted in favor.[21] Herzl Rosenblum, the editor of *Yediot Aharonot*, suggested prosecuting them for treason.

One of his journalists, Amiram Nir, soon coined the phrase *sheket, yorim*: "quiet, we're shooting". It was a plea for national unity in the midst of a controversial military campaign: public criticism, he argued, would damage the war effort.[22]

"Now there is no opposition, there is no Likud and Alignment [a now-defunct center-left bloc]. There is no religious and secular, rich and poor... now all of us are one, in uniforms. Now we are shooting. Quiet."

In fact, there was opposition. Anti-war protests started almost immediately. On 5 July, less than a month into the fighting, a relatively new group called Peace Now organized an anti-war rally in Tel Aviv. About 100,000 people turned up—then equal to one-third of the city's population. "They called for the removal of Defense Minister Ariel Sharon and an end of the war," the Jewish Telegraphic Agency reported. "Speakers urged the government not to order an attack on PLO forces holding out in west Beirut."[23] The protests would continue for months, and grew in intensity after the Sabra and Shatila massacre in September 1982, in which the Israeli army stood idle while its Lebanese Christian allies murdered hundreds of Palestinians in and around a Beirut refugee camp. Peace Now called for another demonstration in Tel Aviv on 25 September. It drew 400,000 protesters, which at the time represented a tenth of Israel's population.

Critics denounced the conflict in Lebanon as *milkhamat breirah*, a "war of choice", contrasting it with the wars of necessity in 1967 and 1973. Another new group, Yesh Gvul ("there is a limit"—*gvul* also means "border"), urged combat soldiers to sign a pledge not to serve in occupied Lebanon. About 3,000 of them ultimately did, and dozens were court-martialed for refusing to obey orders.

Peace Now and its allies did not bring peace, then or now. But the anti-war efforts of the 1980s created a "peace camp", one that questioned not just Israel's tactics but the entire foundation of its security policies. They would use their newfound clout a decade later to help Yitzhak Rabin implement the Oslo Accords, despite fierce political opposition. They made peace the defining issue in Israeli politics over the coming decade.

For fifty-one days in the summer of 2014, Israel was again at war. It was the second-longest war in the country's history, only behind the

1948 battle for independence, which pitted a nascent state against the combined forces of more than a half-dozen Arab nations. By 2014 the balance of power had been reversed: the most powerful army in the Middle East fought a motley collection of militants armed with rudimentary rockets and mortars, a network of underground attack tunnels, and at least one suicide donkey. Israeli jets and artillery dropped thousands of tons of ordnance on Gaza, reducing entire neighborhoods to rubble. And still, for more than seven weeks, the war refused to end.

Nir died in a plane crash in 1988. Had he lived to see 2014, though, he might have been satisfied. The summer-long war was, in many ways, also an unnecessary conflict, born of lies and miscalculations by Israel's political establishment, and a conflict without a clear objective. Yet it produced no real dissent. Quite the opposite: the fractiousness that had come to define Israeli society had all but disappeared. The largest anti-war rally, in Tel Aviv on the night of 26 July, drew perhaps 5,000 people. There were no representatives from the Labor Party, the Zionist center-left's main political vehicle. Even Peace Now, ironically, avoided this pro-peace demonstration. It was also the high-water mark. Rallies in Jerusalem, Haifa and other cities over the following weeks attracted at best a few hundred people. Netanyahu's approval ratings soared, and most of the Knesset rallied behind him. The media became a nationalist choir. Squabbles over politics and religion and identity were replaced by near-unanimous support for "the operation", which was backed by more than 90 per cent of Jewish Israelis, according to polls.[24]

Israelis, of course, are hardly the only people to rally around the flag during wartime. But the mood in 2014, with its intolerance for dissent and its occasional violence, was particularly striking. In hindsight, it was a watershed moment. Six months after the ceasefire, I had coffee in the lobby of Jerusalem's Crowne Plaza with Dani Dayan, the settler leader, who was making a brief and unsuccessful turn as a politician. (Dayan is now Israel's consul-general in New York.) He reminisced—almost nostalgically—about the atmosphere during the war. "It reminded me of 1973," he said, reaching back to the war that had threatened Israel's very survival. "I hadn't felt the country come together like that for a long time."

Shadows and lions

After decades of conflict in the Holy Land, it seems almost futile to talk about what started the 2014 war. Israeli officials point to the kidnapping of the three teenagers in June. Perhaps the point of departure came earlier, when Palestinian groups vowed to take revenge after Israeli soldiers killed two unarmed teenagers at a Nakba Day protest on 15 May. Or maybe the chain of cause and effect went back even further: to 1948, and or even earlier.

The proximate cause, though, was indisputably the kidnappings and the Israeli crackdown that followed, dubbed "Operation Brother's Keeper". Virtually the entire Hamas leadership in the West Bank were among the hundreds of Palestinians arrested during nightly raids. So were fifty-eight prisoners released in the 2011 agreement to free Gilad Shalit, the Israeli soldier captured by Hamas in 2006. The campaign sent the Hamas leadership in Gaza into a panic. The officials I spoke with in mid-June figured they were next. It wasn't an unreasonable fear. Israel had assassinated the group's leaders in Gaza before; one such airstrike in 2012 touched off the second Israel-Hamas war.

Despite its ideology, Hamas can be a very pragmatic actor when it wants to be. The group has tight control over its own cadres, and usually works aggressively to stop other militant groups from firing rockets at Israel; perpetrators are quickly arrested and jailed. But as the Israeli operation dragged on—six Palestinians were killed during clashes and raids—the Hamas leadership went into hiding, and their security forces stopped enforcing the ban on launches. Sixty-five rockets and mortars were fired in June, up from just seven in May.

Israel responded with ever-larger rounds of airstrikes. On the evening of 29 June, one of them killed a Hamas militant. The group fired back with a barrage of rockets, its first since the ceasefire that ended the previous war, in 2012. A week later, as the back-and-forth continued, Israel bombed the house of a Hamas official in the southern city of Khan Younis, killing seven people. The group dubbed it a "massacre". From there, things escalated quickly to a full-blown war. On 8 July Israel launched what it called (in English) "Operation Protective Edge", a conflict that would eventually kill more than 2,000 Palestinians, the majority of them civilians. (In Hebrew it was *Tzuk Eitan*, "Firm Cliff".)

At the time, it all seemed bewildering and abrupt. (I was eating dinner with mourners at Abu Khdair's wake in Shuafat when it started—still reporting the last story.) In hindsight, though, it was inevitable. Lies and miscalculations: the former, Israel's insistence on pretending that the kidnapped teenagers were still alive; the latter, the misguided belief that a massive clampdown on Hamas would pass without further consequences. As J. J. Goldberg wrote a few days later in *The Forward*, "the [kidnapping and murder] set off a chain of events in which Israel gradually lost control of the situation, finally ending up on the brink of a war that nobody wanted."[25]

The first week and a half was a confusing blur. Hamas launched an average of 143 rockets per day, but they were almost entirely ineffective; only one Israeli was killed, an ultra-Orthodox man who had volunteered to distribute food to soldiers on the border. Israel carried out more than 200 daily airstrikes, which killed 241 Palestinians, a figure that would soon seem modest. The army-backed government in Cairo, which has a warm security relationship with Israel and an abiding hatred for Hamas—it rightly accuses the group of working with militants on the Sinai Peninsula—tried to broker a ceasefire with the quiet assistance of former British Prime Minister Tony Blair. It was hard to tell whether the war would be a rerun of 2012, a relatively restrained eight-day battle, or 2008–9, a fierce ground campaign.

From the Israeli side, in those early days, it was still largely a conflict happening "over there", a bombing campaign beyond the wall that occasionally intruded on daily life. On 12 July, Hamas announced that it would fire a new kind of rocket at Tel Aviv at exactly 9 pm, a PR stunt timed for maximum exposure on the evening news. A few minutes before the barrage, I sat on my balcony overlooking Jaffa's trendy flea market and watched a group of young Israelis—drinks in hand—totter into my parking garage, which was doubling as a bomb shelter. The sirens went off (a few minutes late, because it was the Middle East); the rockets were intercepted by the Iron Dome defense system, or missed their marks; and the partygoers wandered back to the bar to top off their drinks.

In an ironic twist, the Hamas-run TV channel took a live feed from Channel 2, Israel's largest broadcaster, hoping to show its viewers images of panic and destruction in Tel Aviv. The hoped-for images never came, so Hamas accused the network of using recorded video. When Al Jazeera, the Qatari-funded pan-Arabic broadcaster, described Tel Aviv as a "ghost town", the Israeli army's Arabic spokesman quipped back, "I'm sure life in Tel Aviv is more vibrant than Doha at the moment."

There was one scene of panic that evening, but it wasn't caused by rockets. A few kilometers from Jaffa, next to the national theater on Tel Aviv's central HaBima Square, a few hundred Israelis were holding an anti-war demonstration. They faced off with a smaller group of counter-demonstrators, who had come at the behest of Yoav Eliasi, a failed Israeli rapper who calls himself "The Shadow", and one of the summer's stranger characters. Eliasi released a hit album with another rapper in 2002, but his career quickly soured, and his solo debut in 2008 was a flop. After living off his residual fame for a while—"if I didn't screw four women a night in the club bathroom, I couldn't go home," he told an interviewer in 2011—he reinvented himself as a far-right activist, and built a following with his incendiary, nationalist posts on Facebook. On the afternoon of 12 July, hours before the rally, he urged them to hit the streets. "The leftist demonstration will be at HaBima at 20:00… and we'll come like lions," he wrote. "I'll bring a crowbar to spill their blood, and the blood of their families," one person responded. Another urged everyone to "take your 9mm [pistols]."

They shouted back and forth for a while—"Jews and Arabs refuse to be enemies" on one side, "death to Arabs" on the other. But the protest quickly dispersed after Hamas fired its barrage of rockets. The "lions" followed the liberals through the streets, throwing punches and insults. Some of the left-wingers sought refuge inside a nearby café. The right-wing group stormed the place, overturning tables, breaking glasses, even cracking someone over the head with a chair. At least one person was hospitalized. Nobody was arrested, and a police spokesman would later blame the anti-war protesters for the melee, saying, "the organizers didn't inform the police about the gathering, and didn't ask for a permit."

The protest, needless to say, had no impact on the war. The Egyptian ceasefire initiative quickly failed, and the rocket fire continued. On the night of 17 July, Netanyahu ordered a ground invasion of Gaza, and the first tanks rolled across the border.

CONFLICT

"The worst to the air force"

The images that came out of Gaza during the next few weeks shocked the world. In the space of one morning on 20 July, the neighborhood of Shuja'iya was largely reduced to rubble; the first journalists to arrive shot footage of dead and dying Palestinians crumpled in the streets. Two weeks later, Hamas briefly captured an Israeli soldier in the southern city of Rafah. The army employed the "Hannibal doctrine", which instructs commanders to do everything in their power to prevent a capture, regardless of the consequences. Dozens of civilians were killed in the ensuing fusillade of artillery. (The doctrine took its name from a Carthaginian general who poisoned himself rather than be captured by the Romans.)

Very little of this filtered through into the Israeli media, however. Israel bars its own journalists from entering Gaza—a sensible enough policy, considering who runs the strip. Some of the older Palestinian affairs correspondents have contacts in Gaza from the days before 2006, when it was under Israeli control. The others rely on wire reports, foreign journalists, and the Arabic-language media. My landlord phoned me once to ask what was happening across the border, because the Israeli media devoted so little time to the subject.

It's not only truth, but also empathy that is among the first casualties of war: people will focus more on their own suffering than the enemy's, and journalists will accommodate them. But the lopsided nature of Israel's war in Gaza, and the entry ban, meant that editors often struggled to fill their newspapers and bulletins. The results could be blackly comic. Channel 10 aired a segment on a kitten rescued by a tank commander from the rubble of eastern Gaza. The confused animal wandered around the broadcast desk for a few minutes, poking its head into the hosts' coffee cups. On Channel 2, there was a tender report about an all-female artillery unit on the border. Young soldiers showed off a collection of donated hair-care products, stenciled their names on mortars, and munched on sushi delivered by one of their brothers, all of this punctuated by the frequent thump of outgoing projectiles.

One morning in late July, I sat down with Gideon Levy, the liberal *Ha'aretz* columnist. We had met during the previous war in a somewhat surreal cafe at Yad Mordechai, the last junction before the Erez crossing into Gaza. It attracts a motley wartime crowd of journalists and soldiers, smoking and filing copy while warplanes roar overhead. Ordinary civilians pull into the adjacent gas station to fill up, and occasionally have to scramble for cover at the sound of artillery fire. (The defense ministry had a spokesman posted there one day to brief reporters over iced coffee.)

Levy has long been among the country's most polarizing media figures—heroic truth-teller to the far left, traitor and propagandist to everyone else—but he spent much of that previous war reporting from the south, without any problems. In 2014, though, we met in his home in a quiet section of north Tel Aviv. A couple of weeks earlier, he had been accosted in Ashkelon while doing a live television interview. Since then, the newspaper had hired a bodyguard to accompany him on reporting trips.

The cause of this was a column he had published a week earlier, entitled *hara'im l'tayyis*—literally, "the worst to the air force", a subversion of the well-known phrase *hatovim l'tayyis*, "the best to the air force", a slogan adopted by the service decades ago to boost enlistment. He lamented that none of the pilots refused to serve in the war: "Are they really like robots?":

> They are the best of all, brother—they are the best to the air force, the best pilots, and now they do the worst deeds, the most cruel and vile. They have never seen an enemy plane in front of them—the service's last aerial battle took place before most of them were even born... they are heroes over the weak, the weakest, the powerless who do not even have an air force or air defense, barely even a kite.[26]

A controversial column, even for *Ha'aretz*, which published a rejoinder to itself two days later. But not a new one. Levy himself pointed out that he had published "almost word-for-word the same article" in 2008, during Operation Cast Lead.[27] "And then it passed, you know? There were many people furious at me, but nothing like the atmosphere now." Hours after the interview was published, Levy appeared on Channel 2 for an interview, and was quickly shouted down by an angry local resident. "You're a traitor," the man yelled. "You say that our pilots are murderers. Tell me, are you not ashamed? Do you have to live with Hamas? Our pilots are the most moral."[28]

It was not an isolated incident. Levy said he was constantly heckled for his politics throughout the war, even by his own bodyguards. Yariv Levin, a Knesset member from Likud and the chairman of the ruling coalition, suggested that Levy should be prosecuted for treason, calling him an "enemy mouthpiece" and the "lowest kind of provocateur".[29]

"I've never had it so harsh, so violent and so tense," Levy told me. "I'm quite experienced with public criticism, even with threats, attacks, but the recent days have really been the worst of all."

Levy often appears on international media, and his articles are widely shared by pro-Palestinian activists in the West. In Israel his following is far more limited; he is more of a canary in the coal mine, or—as his colleague Chemi Shalev called him—a "journalistic Iron Dome", a "lightning rod for angry outbursts, ever-multiplying, as the Israeli public's temper heats and its tolerance expires."

Sure enough, he wasn't the only target. Firas Khatib, a reporter for the BBC's Arabic service, was attacked during a live shot outside Sderot by an assailant who called him a "son of a whore" and knocked him out of the frame. Yonit Levi, one of the lead anchors for Channel 2, received countless death threats for her perceived "left-wing" views. Never mind that Levi did nothing to earn that ugliest of Israeli epithets—she never criticized the war, and even co-wrote a column afterwards that sympathetically explained why the Israeli media devoted so little attention to the suffering in Gaza. "When your child is spending their summer vacation running to find shelter… one has limited emotional capacity to see what is happening to the children on the other side," she wrote.[30]

Amnon Abramovich, another well-known figure on Channel 2, was attacked at the network's makeshift wartime studio outside the defense ministry on 29 July by a mob chanting "traitor" and "terrorist". Abramovich, unlike Levi, really is a left-wing commentator. But he is also a decorated combat veteran who suffered severe burns during the Yom Kippur War. The scars are visible to this day. No matter—the Tel Aviv police chief had to whisk Abramovich away from the angry crowds in his official car.

It was easier for foreigners, though the mood was hardly welcoming. Interviewees routinely asked me if I was Jewish, a kind of overt tribalism I rarely encountered in years of reporting from around the region.

"Jewish or Arab? Because I won't talk to Arabs," one elderly woman warned on a leafy residential street in Ashkelon.

Nor were journalists the only ones targeted for their views. Orna Banai, an actress and comedian, was fired from her job as the spokeswoman for a cruise company after she expressed sympathy for Palestinians. Hanoch Sheinman, a law professor at Bar-Ilan University, decided to revise his exam schedule because of the security situation. He emailed his students about the changes, and opened his letter by wishing that "that you, your families and those dear to you are not among the hundreds of people that were killed, the thousands wounded, or the tens of thousands whose homes were destroyed."

It was a clear, if understated, expression of sympathy for both sides in the conflict—no homes were destroyed in Israel, and the casualties numbered in the dozens. The dean of the law school quickly pronounced himself shocked at Sheinman's email, and wrote to students that Sheinman's "hurtful letter... contravene[s] the values of the university."

"Even this trivial expression of concern stirred such a backlash, and that's not trivial at all," Sheinman told me. "It actually tells you something important... to be shocked or angered, or allow yourself to be offended by a trivial expression of sympathy to everyone, is to betray a lack of such sympathy."

The peace camp

The "peace camp" had been withdrawing from the public sphere for years before the 2014 war. The violence of the Second Intifada led many Israelis to view the peaceniks as naive, and the years of quiet that followed took away any sense of urgency for reaching a deal with the Palestinians. Instead Netanyahu promoted "economic peace", the idea that Israel should marginally improve conditions for Palestinians in the West Bank without seriously trying to end the occupation. Gaza was an afterthought, an intractable problem that nobody wanted to deal with (including, to be fair, much of the Palestinian leadership).

The Israeli center-left shifted focus to economic issues. The summer of 2011 saw the largest demonstrations in Tel Aviv in two decades, which were focused not on peace but on prices. (They are somewhat jokingly known as the "cottage cheese protests", because the movement started with an angry Facebook post about the rising price of the popular dairy staple.) The protests started with a small tent city in HaBima Square in July. By September they had swelled to a mass movement, one that brought nearly half a million people into the streets. They were inspired, in part, by the pro-democracy protests sweeping the Arab world: their rallying cry, "the people demand social justice", had unmistakable echoes of the Arab Spring's most popular chant, "the people demand the downfall of the regime."

The anti-war protests in 2014 didn't even come close. The Israel Democracy Institute, a non-partisan think tank, carried out several surveys during the Gaza war. It found that, on average, 95 per cent of Israeli Jews thought the war was justified. By the end of the conflict, the air force alone had bombed Gaza some 5,000 times; fewer than 4 per cent of Israeli Jews thought this constituted excessive force, while more than a third thought the level of bombing was insufficient. "People were thrilled to feel this sense of togetherness, this feeling of 'us against them.' There's a good sense of nationalism, the likes of which this country has not seen in decades," said Dr Tamar Hermann, the chief pollster at IDI.

The organizers of the first rally tried again on 26 July, this time in Rabin Square, named after the prime minister who was slain there in 1995. The plaza, which sits below City Hall, is a focal point for Israeli civil society: it was the site of Peace Now's massive protest against the Lebanon war in 1982, and a popular location for election rallies.

Hours before the rally was meant to begin, though, the police canceled the permit, arguing that the threat of rocket attacks made such a large gathering unsafe. It was due to coincide with the end of a brief "humanitarian ceasefire". The permit was only reinstated an hour before the rally, too late for buses to bring in demonstrators from outside Tel Aviv. Just 5,000 people turned up. They spelled out the words "forgive us" in Hebrew using 1,043 candles—the number of Israelis and Palestinians who had been killed up to that point. A lawmaker from Hadash, the Communist party, gave a speech, as did Israeli and Palestinian members of Combatants for Peace, an organization that brings together former soldiers and militants. But there were no representatives of the larger political parties, nor leaders of activist groups like Peace Now. "We feel very isolated, it's true," one protester said at the Tel Aviv rally. "Nobody to the right of Zehava Gal-On [a prominent member of Meretz] has spoken out against the situation."

"It's still not the mainstream Israeli peace movement that was protesting," Hagit Ofran, the director of the settlement project at Peace Now, told me after the rally. "It's very hard to call for stopping the war when the emotions are so strong, when the feelings are that Hamas is not willing to stop either."

Officers had learned their lessons from the previous protest, and spent much of the evening trying to separate the crowd from a smaller group of pro-war demonstrators. They dispersed the rally at 10 pm, again citing the threat of rockets. As the anti-war protesters trickled away, they were chased down and attacked by their nationalist counterparts, beaten with metal rods and doused with pepper spray. This time at least eight people were hospitalized.

There were a few more scattered protests in the weeks to come, but nothing that attracted a sizable crowd, owing to a combination of fatigue and fear. The last one happened on 9 August, days before the ceasefire, where several right-wing protesters were photographed holding signs that read, in Hebrew, "one people, one state, one leader"—a translation of the famous Nazi propaganda slogan "*ein Volk, ein Reich, ein Fuhrer*". Standing in the background of one of the photos, surrounded by his lions, was The Shadow.

Death

During the brief 2012 conflict, I interviewed David Bouskila, the mayor of Sderot, a frontline town on the Gaza border. He raved about the success of the Iron Dome system: since it went online in mid-2011, he said, "just two or three" rockets had hit his town, compared to thousands in the preceding years. Ten minutes later, just a hundred meters down the road from where we spoke, a rocket crashed into a house. It was a small, unsophisticated projectile that caused only minor damage and no injuries, though it terrified the inhabitants. I ran into Bouskila again outside the home. "I need to update those figures I gave you," he said with a wry grin.

The Home Front Command, the branch of the Israeli army that handles civilian preparedness, issues a color-coded map that shows people how much time they have to find shelter once the air-raid siren sounds. The towns in the "Gaza envelope", marked in bright red, have less than fifteen seconds, if they get any warning at all. Mortars rarely show up on radar, so the first indication of incoming fire is the sound of a nearby explosion and the disorienting crash of a blast wave. The roads in Sderot are lined with bomb shelters, which look like bus stops made of concrete. Life there was intolerable for years.

By 2014, though, the threat of rockets was significantly diminished, thanks to Iron Dome, an extensive network of sirens and shelters, and the general shoddiness of Hamas' arsenal. In the first month of the war, they caused three deaths, all of them essentially preventable: the Jewish man killed on the border while delivering food to soldiers; an Israeli Bedouin, from a village with no sirens or bomb shelters; and a migrant worker from Thailand, fatally wounded by shrapnel while working in an open field. More Israeli civilians were killed by traffic accidents that summer than by rockets. But the threat was not completely neutralized.

Nahal Oz is an idyllic kibbutz on the Gaza border, a friendly village surrounded by rolling fields where the anemones bloom in spring. During the war, though, it was a ghost town: it was evacuated early on, like others in the area, and was almost empty when I visited in late July, save for a detachment of soldiers camped on the outskirts. In mid-August, however, with the fighting seemingly on the wane, community leaders urged residents to come back. The Israeli army encouraged it too. Dozens of families returned, including the Tragermans, but their happiness at being home was short-lived: the rocket fire continued.

They were packing their bags to leave again on the afternoon of 22 August when the siren went off. The Tragermans grabbed their two youngest children and ran for the shelter. But their eldest son, Daniel, didn't make it. A mortar hit a parked car nearby, and the shrapnel killed him. He was four years old.

He became the face of Israel's grief on social media and the front pages of newspapers: a photo of a young boy with tousled hair and a mischievous grin, wearing an oversized Messi jersey. He was "a boy too small to cross the road, because it is dangerous, but big enough to know what rocket sirens are," Rivlin said at his funeral. His death left a deep scar on Nahal Oz. Roughly one-fifth of the population—more than a dozen families, including the Tragermans—decided not to return after the ceasefire. (Two more civilians were killed by mortar fire in Nirim, a nearby kibbutz, hours before the ceasefire went into effect.)

A war, to what end?

It was hard to explain why Daniel Tragerman died—or indeed any of the other 2,200 people who lost their lives that summer. At the outset of the war, Israel's motto was "quiet for quiet": if Hamas stops firing rockets, we'll stop firing back. Netanyahu wanted a rerun of 2012. Hamas didn't. It had demands. Reasonable ones, many Palestinians agreed, like lifting the years-old blockade of the strip—a demand the Israeli government was unwilling to meet. So it kept shooting. "Hamas is willing to be practical in its behavior," said David Hacham, the defense ministry's top adviser for Arab affairs. "But we also need to speak about what's happening on the ground. It's not willing to give in on strategic demands."

From that point on, the conflict in Gaza was a war in search of an objective. Or perhaps more accurately, it was an open-ended conflict tied to the ever-more difficult political objective of sustaining an unsustainable status quo.

In a brief statement announcing the start of the ground invasion, Netanyahu said the troops had been ordered "to strike at the terrorist tunnels from the Gaza Strip into Israeli territory." Officials said the fighting would continue until the passages were destroyed, a process that should take "two or three days." The tunnels were not, strictly speaking, a new weapon: Hamas had used them before, as far back as 2006, when the militants who captured Gilad Shalit used an underground passage to sneak across the border and then spirit him back into Gaza. In the summer of 2014 they were upgraded to an "existential threat", as the head of the southern command told reporters; *Yediot Aharonot* warned that Hamas planned to sneak a force of 200 gunmen into Israel and seize control of a kibbutz on Rosh Hashanah, the Jewish new year.

Hyperbole aside, they were a real threat, a point that was underscored on 29 July, when Hamas killed five Israeli soldiers in a tunnel raid. The gunmen filmed it on a head-mounted camera; the eerie footage, posted on YouTube, shows them emerging from the passage and hiking through the desert before they open fire on an army post.

The Israeli government had known about this threat for years, though, and did nothing about it. The proposed Egyptian ceasefire, which Netanyahu eagerly accepted, would have left the tunnels intact—an existential threat with which, apparently, the prime minister was content to live. "They were a threat even before, but it's not always the case that if we have some threats we decide to go immediately to a big ground operation in order to neutralize it," Yuval Steinitz, the intelligence minister, tried unconvincingly to explain.

The military played its assigned role, targeting the rockets, then the tunnels. But rockets can be rebuilt, and tunnels re-dug. So in late July, with the Palestinian death toll already above 1,000, the rationale for war shifted again. Steinitz briefed foreign reporters, telling them that the war would only end once the international community agreed to "disarm" Hamas. "If we want a real comprehensive solution, that will bring not just an end to the current round of violence, but real relief for people on both sides of the fence: …you have to demilitarize Gaza, as it was supposed to be," he said. There was some aspirational chatter about putting the Palestinian Authority in charge of Gaza, though no one could articulate how this was meant to happen, short of strapping Abbas onto a Merkava tank and driving him across the border. "Like asking a priest to convert to Judaism," quipped Amos Yadlin, a former head of military intelligence.

While most Israelis supported the war, only a small minority—between 8 and 30 per cent across three polls in July—thought it would actually bring long-term quiet (like the 2006 Lebanon war, which ended with more than a decade of calm on the northern border). Yet there was no criticism from the left. Isaac Herzog, the Labor leader and the ostensible head of the opposition, acted as Netanyahu's unofficial spokesman. He convened dozens of foreign diplomats on 1 August—including the ambassadors from France, Germany and other European countries—to defend Israel's conduct in Gaza. A senior Brazilian diplomat asked him about a pair of Norwegian doctors who had traveled to Gaza to treat casualties; Israel had barred one of them from entering. "The world has remained silent about the massacres in Syria," Herzog replied, "and with all due respect to the important work of the Norwegian doctors, are these doctors aware of the missiles stored under the hospital?" Tal Schneider, an Israeli journalist who attended the briefing, said his remarks were "straight from Netanyahu's talking points."[31]

Instead the criticism came from the right. Before the war even started, Danny Danon, the deputy defense minister, urged the government to "shut off the electricity" in the West Bank and Gaza, to punish Palestinians for the kidnappings and the steadily increasing rocket fire. A few weeks later he called the Egyptian ceasefire proposal "humiliating". Netanyahu eventually fired him for insubordination.

Danon had long been a thorn in Netanyahu's side. He also served as the chairman of Likud's central committee, and helped to steer the party further to the right, effectively turning Netanyahu into the most liberal member of his own faction. This was an ironic turnabout, as Netanyahu had used the same tactics against Ariel Sharon a decade earlier. "My position is to make sure we're not becoming a construct of the left," Danon told me that summer. "As long as [Netanyahu] stays loyal, he'll have the backing of the party."

He didn't enjoy much backing from other parties, either. Naftali Bennett, the head of the right-wing Jewish Home, said Israel should "strike at Hamas mercilessly" until the group was disarmed or destroyed. Foreign Minister Avigdor Lieberman, meant to be Israel's top diplomat, veered even further off-message: a ceasefire would be "mere preparation" for the next war, he argued, so Israel should "go all the way" and reoccupy Gaza. (Even Tzipi Livni, the centrist former foreign minister, negotiator with the Palestinians, and Netanyahu critic, suggested helping the PA topple Hamas.) None of them were sacked, though the prime minister probably would have liked to have taken action. "They're the heads of parties, so the prime minister cannot fire them," Danon said. "The consequences would be new elections. That's the only issue, because if you compare my remarks to theirs, they were very similar."

Shamed and confused

Across the border, they claimed victory. Moments after the ceasefire was announced on 26 August, a clutch of Hamas officials gathered outside Shifa, the main hospital in Gaza City, yelling defiant slogans and praising the "steadfastness" of the resistance. "We scored victory when we destroyed the myth of the army that can't be defeated, and when we closed the Zionist airspace, shelled cities, and forced the

Zionists to go into hiding," said Sami Abu Zuhri, one of the group's Gaza-based spokesmen.

The next day it was Ismail Haniyeh's turn: The head of the Hamas politburo in Gaza drove through a victory rally in a white SUV, emerging from the sunroof to bust a few awkward dance moves before thousands of supporters. And on 28 August Khaled Mesha'al, the group's overall leader, seemed positively jubilant at a press conference in the Qatari capital. "Our resistance will continue until all our demands are met, and we are getting closer to victory," he said.

As victories go, this was a dubious one. More than 2,100 Palestinians had been killed during seven weeks of fighting, and even Israeli officials admitted that a majority of them were civilians. Tens of thousands of homes were destroyed, 25 per cent of the strip's population was displaced, and basic infrastructure was shattered. Aid agencies estimated that it would take decades to repair the damage, a prediction that was still accurate as this book went to press. The carnage finally ended with a warmed-over version of the ceasefire that had stopped the 2012 war—full of vague promises to ease the blockade, but little of substance. Most of them would go unfulfilled over the coming years.

Weeks after the truce, I interviewed desperate families living in the rubble of their homes, or in squalid tents by the roadside; when I returned to the same neighborhoods two years later, some of those same families were still there. A friend had moved to Nahal Oz not long after the war. On a visit to the kibbutz one evening, he pointed out the eerie darkness across the border. Even electricity remains in short supply in Gaza.

So Hamas' main accomplishment was simply to survive, to briefly interrupt flights out of Tel Aviv and to continue firing rockets on Tel Aviv until the final moments of the war. But they claimed victory nonetheless, and enjoyed a major short-term bump in popularity as a result. A post-war poll by the Palestine Center for Policy and Survey Research found Haniyeh to be vastly more popular than Mahmoud Abbas.[32] It was an "unprecedented" boost for the group, the largest since 2006, according to Dr Khalil Shikaki, the director of the center.

Not so on the other side. There was no Israeli counterpart to the jubilant press conference outside the hospital; in fact there was no press conference at all, not until more than 24 hours later. Netanyahu did not put the ceasefire to a cabinet vote, because he wanted to avoid the embarrassing spectacle of half his cabinet voting "no". Instead he accepted the truce unilaterally, notifying ministers in a series of rushed phone calls. When he addressed the public on 27 August, he looked exhausted and sounded defensive. Asked if the war would bring lasting quiet to southern Israel, he ducked the question, saying only that the "blows that Hamas has suffered and our ability to prevent their resurgence in the future... increase the chances of achieving that goal."

A poll broadcast on Channel 2 found that 54 per cent of Israelis opposed the truce, and only 29 per cent felt they had defeated Hamas during the conflict. Criticism came in from across the political spectrum, even from within his own Likud party: Danon accused him of ending the fight with Israel "shamed and confused." It was an ignominious end to Netanyahu's first major war as prime minister—and to a remarkable period of unity within the country.

The disappearing war

There is an old story, probably apocryphal, about a foreign diplomat who met an Israeli official in the early years after independence. The minister abruptly stopped talking at the top of the hour, turned up his radio, listened to the news bulletin, and then resumed the conversation. "I just wanted to know if we were at war," he told his slightly bewildered guest.

War remains a constant. The 2014 conflict, though it seemed to start abruptly, was also inevitable. As this book goes to press, there is renewed talk of a fourth round in Gaza, or a third on the northern border with Lebanon. The question is not "if", only "when", and what will spark it.

One can debate whether or not this inevitability is a permanent fixture of life in Israel—whether a different government could forge a lasting peace agreement with the Palestinians and the Arab world. It is fair to say that Hamas, which is plagued by deep internal divisions (and countenances violence against Israeli civilians), is not a viable partner for a long-term peace. But it could be a partner to interim agreements, which would provide an opportunity to change the political and economic realities in Gaza. As far back as the late 1990s, the group's leadership offered Israel a long-term *hudna*, or truce. The Israeli right insists that it will not negotiate with a terrorist organization. Yet even before the 2014 truce, the leader of the Israeli right, Benjamin Netanyahu, had already negotiated two separate deals with Hamas: the 2011 prisoner swap that freed Gilad Shalit, and the cease-fire that ended the brief 2012 war.

Many Israelis, however, don't bother with that debate. They accept the inevitability. The proof for this would be seen a few months after the 2014 war, when Netanyahu dissolved his government and called early elections: lawmakers barely mentioned the war. They can accept it because, for much of the country, the 2014 war was a nuisance. Life did not grind to a halt in Tel Aviv or Jerusalem. It was far more serious for the residents in the "Gaza envelope", some of whom never returned home, and of course for the soldiers who fought it. Hamas surprised even itself with its performance—fighting for more than seven weeks, deploying new offensive tactics like attack tunnels. But, to no one's surprise, it ultimately suffered a strategic defeat.

Israelis are fond of the phrase "status quo". Hebrew even borrows it as a loan expression from Latin. One lesson from reporting on Israel and Palestine, however, is that the status quo is never truly static. This is certainly true on the Palestinian side, where the ever-worsening misery in Gaza has fueled the birth of radical *salafi* groups. Their numbers are small—the largest has perhaps 300–400 members, according to both Israeli and Palestinian security officials. Alarmingly, though, many of those are disaffected militants from Hamas and Islamic Jihad. They have fired rockets at Israel more than a dozen times since the 2014 ceasefire, suggesting that they have at least some access to weapons. "They're angry that the factions didn't continue the war. They have this idea that we should have no agreements with Israel," a member of Islamic Jihad's military wing told me the following summer.

On the Israeli side, too, the constant wars are having an impact. Obviously there are tangible, physical effects. Seventy-two Israelis were killed during the 2014 war. In a small, close-knit society, their deaths touched thousands of families. The mobilization of tens of thousands of reservists damaged the Israeli economy, as did the abrupt cancellation of the summer tourist season, particularly the suspended flights, which also had a psychological impact—a country briefly losing its only real exit to the outside world. But the sharpest impact is political and social. The never-ending conflict continues to poison the relationship between the Jewish majority and the Arab minority. Perhaps more significantly, it continues to empower an aggressive strain of Jewish nationalism. You could hear it on the streets, in the intolerance for dissent and the lack of empathy for suffering on the Palestinian side. And you see it in the polls, which reflect a steady erosion in support for talks (or any sort of settlement) with the Palestinians.

Just as striking, though, was the speed with which the war disappeared from public discourse. When Israelis went to the ballot box, nine months later, it was barely mentioned. Instead the country turned back to arguing over its own equally intractable internal problems.

3

INEQUALITY

"What do we need all this Vatican for?"
Moshe Dayan

The attackers struck just after dawn on 18 November 2014, while the faithful were gathered inside the synagogue for morning prayers. They opened fire outside, then quickly moved inside the building, hacking at the worshippers with knives and axes. A shootout with police ended the assault seven minutes later. Four rabbis died inside, while a fifth person—a Druze policeman who was among the first responders—died in the hospital hours later. (Nearly a year later, a sixth and final individual, another rabbi, would also succumb to his wounds.)

The synagogue, Kehilat Bnei Torah, sits at the base of a steep hill in Har Nof, a largely ultra-Orthodox neighborhood in West Jerusalem. Many of the residents are English- or Spanish-speaking immigrants from the Americas. It is miles away from the Green Line, the disputed boundary between the two halves of the troubled holy city.

The bodies of the dead were still inside an hour after the attack, wrapped in their prayer shawls. A small crowd stood outside the building, chanting "death to terrorists" and "revenge". The synagogue's white facade, gleaming in the late November sunlight, was pockmarked with bullet holes. Workers from ZAKA, a religious organization that retrieves the bodies of the dead, were filtering in and out, collecting bits of flesh. "It was a very hard scene, a very complicated scene," said Matti Goldstein, one of the group's volunteers, later that morning. "The fact that the bodies are still in there after three hours... should tell you what we're dealing with."

It was the deadliest attack in Jerusalem in more than six years, but it came as little surprise. Four weeks earlier, on 22 October, Abdel Rahman al-Shalloudi had got behind the wheel of his father's gray Volkswagen sedan. Shalloudi, a Palestinian from East Jerusalem, had driven to Ammunition Hill, where a crowd of evening commuters was waiting to catch a tram, and had plowed the car into them. A three-month-old baby was killed; so was a 22-year-old woman from Ecuador, who had come to Israel to convert to Judaism after discovering she was descended from a *converso* (a Spanish Jew forced to become Catholic during the Inquisition). Shalloudi was shot dead by police.

A second vehicular attack, on 5 November, had killed three people and wounded thirteen at another light rail station on the seam line between east and west. In between the two attacks, a Palestinian man had tried to assassinate Yehuda Glick, an American-born activist who campaigns for Jewish access to the Temple Mount. He had previously been the executive director of the Temple Institute, a group that aims to build a new Jewish temple on the plateau. (In recent years it had started using *in vitro* fertilization to breed a red heifer, a cow required for sacrifices.) The violence had also included deadly stabbings at a train station in Tel Aviv and a bus stop in the West Bank.

Until the early-morning assault in Har Nof, though, Prime Minister Benjamin Netanyahu had opted for a fairly measured response. Police had installed concrete barriers around light rail stations, to shield passengers from vehicular attacks, and established checkpoints around a few restive neighborhoods in East Jerusalem. But the images of religious men murdered at prayer struck a nerve amongst the Israeli public, conjuring up collective memories of some of the darkest periods in Jewish history. (The Israeli government enthusiastically encouraged this. It shared graphic images on social media within hours of the attack, among them a photograph of a bloodied hand wrapped in *tefillin*—the cubic black leather box that observant Jewish men wear during weekday morning prayer.) Naftali Bennett, then the hawkish economy minister, told the government to "declare war" on the

Palestinian Authority. Aryeh Deri, the head of the ultra-Orthodox Shas party, wanted the army deployed in the streets of Jerusalem. "There are thousands of terrorists in East Jerusalem, and we need to arrest them all," said Baruch Marzel, a prominent settler activist who joined the mourners outside the synagogue.

The cabinet convened a spate of emergency meetings and deployed 1,000 extra policemen to the streets of Jerusalem. Ministers approved longer jail terms, up to twenty years, for Palestinians who threw stones. The army authorized soldiers to use live ammunition against rioters who shot fireworks. Ultimately, the synagogue attack even helped to bring down the Israeli government.

Yet in hindsight it was the peak of what the Israeli press dubbed the "silent intifada", or Palestinian uprising. The violence did not stop completely: two policemen were stabbed in the Old City and a young girl was seriously injured by a firebomb. But there was no further escalation. The media eagerly turned to coverage of the upcoming election, and talk of an intifada all but disappeared. The eleven fatalities of the violence, and the countless Palestinians swept up in the ensuing crackdown, barely elicited a mention during the three-month campaign. It was, if anything, the forgotten intifada—until it happened again.

The winter of 2014 would turn out to be a preview of a bloodier and more sustained wave of violence the following year, a glimpse of how a conflict thought to be manageable could still erupt. More importantly, it offered a glimpse at the fault lines running under Israel's supposedly undivided capital.

Jerusalem

The early Zionists did not care much for the holy city. "When I remember thee in days to come, O Jerusalem, it will not be with pleasure," Theodor Herzl wrote in his diary in 1898, after his only known visit to Palestine. He lamented the "musty deposits of 2,000 years of inhumanity, intolerance and foulness" found in the city's "reeking alleys". When he stood before the Western Wall, he felt no emotion—save for disgust at the "hideous, miserable, scrambling beggary" all around. Shai Agnon, the Austrian-born writer who would win a Nobel Prize for his work in Hebrew, was repulsed by the city's Jewish residents. "When you approach one of them he flees from you as if he has seen a ghost," he wrote. (Many of them were Orthodox Jews with little interest in political Zionism.)

Instead they lavished their attentions on Jaffa (and Tel Aviv, founded in 1909 on the dunes north of the ancient port), and on rural parts of Palestine. It was there, away from the stifling religious atmosphere of Jerusalem, that the pioneers believed they could craft a new Hebrew identity: secular, cultured, agrarian, with Jewish nationalism taking the place of Jewish dogma. They also viewed Jerusalem as a political problem. Herzl feared that Jewish sovereignty over the holy sites would make Zionism unpalatable to Christians, so he proposed making it an extra-territorial entity.

Attitudes began to change around 1918, under the leadership of Chaim Weizmann, the chairman of the Zionist Commission for Palestine. He felt that Jewish control of the Western Wall would be a powerful symbol. "We feel that at the present time, when the Jewry are looking forward to a revival of its national life, would be all times the most fitting for the carrying out of this project," Weizmann wrote in 1918. The city gained further importance after the riots of 1929, which were centered in Jerusalem. Yet even after the young state of Israel declared Jerusalem its capital in 1949, there was still little popular demand for a campaign to unite the city, as Bernard Wasserstein wrote in his 2001 history. "Few political voices in Israel and none in the government before June 1967 called for an irredentist policy towards east Jerusalem. The country thus found itself politically, diplomatically and psychologically unprepared when, quite unexpectedly, after nineteen years of division, Jerusalem was, almost overnight, reunited under Israeli rule."[1]

The reunification came in 1967, during the Six-Day War. The fighting was costly: three dozen Israeli soldiers were killed just to seize Ammunition Hill, a fortified Jordanian position near the border. By 7 June, though, two days into the war, the Israeli army had largely surrounded the walled Old City. A small detachment of soldiers fought their way through the winding alleys until they reached the Western Wall, the sole remaining edifice of the Biblical temple. Atop it sits the Temple Mount, the onetime site of the Holy of Holies, the inner sanctuary where Jews believe God dwelt. Their victory was recorded in the driest of military prose: the daily after-action log blandly notes *"har habayt b'yadeinu"*— "The Temple Mount is in our hands." Shlomo Goren, the army's chief rabbi, quickly made his way to the site, where he blew a *shofar* (ram's horn) and held the first Jewish prayers in nearly two decades.

But atop the plateau is also Al-Aqsa mosque, Islam's third-holiest, and the Dome of the Rock, where Muslims believe Mohammed made his "night journey", ascending to heaven on a winged horse. Elsewhere in the Old City, and radiating outward in neighborhoods like Silwan and Sheikh Jarrah, there were Palestinians. All of this was in Israel's hands, too.

Around this time Moshe Dayan, the storied Israeli general, made his way to Mount Scopus, which offers a commanding view of the city. He leaned over to Col Uzi Narkis, the head of the army's central command, and whispered a single question: "What do we need all this Vatican for?"

The city of peace

The holy city, the city of God, the city—all too ironically—of peace. Of the many names for Jerusalem, though, none is repeated so often as "our undivided, eternal capital". It's not only a right-wing slogan: Yair Lapid, the great centrist hope of Israel's Ashkenazi middle class, vows in one breath to solve the conflict with the Palestinians, and in the next to keep Jerusalem united forever. Isaac Herzog promised the same before the 2015 election.

The United Nations, the United States, the European Union, and much of the rest of the world consider East Jerusalem to be occupied territory. Israel insists that it is not. A casual visitor might be inclined to agree. Crossing Route 60, the four-lane boulevard that roughly follows the armistice line, hardly feels like traversing a border. In Sheikh Jarrah, a neighborhood adjacent to the Old City, the east side of the highway is lined with luxury hotels. Many of the tourists who stay there are unaware that their rooms are meant to be part of a future Palestinian state.

If you drive a bit further into East Jerusalem, though, the difference quickly becomes apparent. Silwan is built in a ravine. At the top, the neighborhood abuts the Zion Gate into the Old City, where tour buses queue up throughout the day. At the bottom, the roads are barely paved, and rubbish piles up in vacant lots; municipal services are spotty, to say the least.

Only a handful of the 300,000 Palestinians in East Jerusalem are Israeli citizens. They, or their ancestors, chose to keep their Jordanian nationality after 1967. So Israel treats them as "permanent residents": they hold the same blue ID cards as Israeli citizens, which allow them to work and travel freely throughout the country; but they cannot vote in national elections, nor can they apply for Israeli passports. Their status is tenuous, and can be revoked if they move abroad or otherwise lose their "center of life" in the city.

They can also apply for citizenship, though the annual number of requests used to be in the dozens. Lately it has grown more than tenfold: in 2012–13, there were 1,434 applications.[2] East Jerusalemites have not suddenly grown fond of the Israeli government, but citizenship feels permanent in a way that residency does not. The Israeli passport carries benefits, such as visa-free travel to the European Union, and a full franchise. There is also is a growing sense that the conflict will not end anytime soon.

Israel insists that it looks after Jerusalemites in all parts of the city, regardless of ethnicity or nationality. "Compare the quality of life of the Arab residents in Jerusalem to the quality of life in the region, in Gaza, in Lebanon, in Syria, in Iraq, and people understand, here in our city we care about them," said the mayor, Nir Barkat.

And indeed, compared to Raqqa, the capital of the Islamic State's self-proclaimed "caliphate," the residents of East Jerusalem are well off. But compared to Rehavia in the west, they are not. Schools in East Jerusalem have a shortage of 1,000 classrooms. One-third of households are not connected to the municipal water grid. Basic services, from hospitals to post offices, are woefully scarce, and most residents live below the poverty line. A 2013 United Nations study found that 40 per cent of the men were unemployed, and nearly twice as many women. Those with jobs mostly toil in construction, agriculture and the service industry.[3]

Around the time of Shalloudi's attack the city did try to fix one disparity: it started enforcing the finer points of municipal law. The protests that followed Abu Khdair's murder in July had never fully stopped, so the Palestinian districts in East Jerusalem were being targeted for punishment. A resident of the Old City was ordered to remove his home's water heater, because it was installed without permission; another man, from Beit Hanina, had his car towed because he was two payments behind on his *arnona*, a bi-monthly municipal tax. "I don't think they do this in Talpiot," he said, referring to a Jewish neighborhood in the west. In Shuafat, police handed out dozens of $130 fines for parking on the curb, a virtual necessity in a neighborhood with narrow streets and few parking lots.

Barkat denied that the crackdown was targeted at Palestinians, insisting that the law is applied equally. "The mayor has a clear policy of enforcing the law in all parts of Jerusalem," said his spokeswoman, Brachie Sprung. "People who live in West Jerusalem pay for things they do illegally, and the same applies in the east."

But some of the punishments were extreme, and in many cases, the city had never levied penalties before. It was hard to see the crackdown as anything but a punitive measure. "It seems that the municipality is basically using collective punishment against some of the most disenfranchised members of Jerusalem's population," said Sarit Michaeli, a spokeswoman for B'Tselem, the Israeli rights group.

Bombs and buyers

Not much survived the explosion in the Shalloudi apartment: an empty tub of hummus, a single slipper, a few decorative tiles in the kitchen. Shalloudi lived with his parents and five siblings at the base of the hill in Silwan. Their living room, which enjoys a scenic view of the Dome of the Rock, was a rubble-strewn expanse with no walls when I visited in late November.

Nearly a month after his hit-and-run attack, dozens of paramilitary border policemen arrived at the family home in the dead of night. They emptied the five-story apartment block, set charges, and blew up the flat. The whole affair was over in a matter of hours; the Shalloudi home was completely destroyed, and the blast caused minor damage to other apartments. A slab of concrete crushed a car parked on the street below. "The explosion was loud enough to wake all of Silwan," said his uncle, Talaat, the next morning. "They didn't even let the children take their belongings."

There were two stories that winter, both in Silwan, both related to housing, that undercut the notion of a united capital. On one side were the punitive home demolitions, which the Israeli government argues are a useful deterrent to Palestinian attackers. "When you're dealing with people who have no qualms whatsoever about killing themselves in order to kill others, deterrence is a problem," said Mark Regev, a spokesman for the prime minister (and later the Israeli ambassador in London). "How do you deter someone who's willing to kill themselves in order to get others?"

An Israeli army commission had studied that question more than a decade ago, though, and had concluded that home demolitions were not the answer: it had found they had little deterrent value. The panel, headed by Gen Udi Shani and convened as the second intifada died down in late 2004, was the first serious study on the subject, and its findings were stark. "There is no proof of the deterrent effect of house demolitions," it reported, after speaking with everyone from military officers to philosophers. As a result, the policy was largely suspended, only to be revived with little public debate in 2014. "If anything, the study found that the demolitions inflame the public and probably generate more attacks," said Jeff Halper, the founder of the International Committee Against Home Demolitions, a local activist group. "And there hasn't been another committee convened that said conditions have changed."

The practice dates back to 1945, before the state of Israel was founded. The British Mandate passed an emergency resolution that gave military commanders latitude to destroy any house from which they suspected a weapon was fired, or whose inhabitants attempted to violate military law. When Israel occupied the West Bank, it applied a bewildering mix of Jordanian, Ottoman, British and Israeli law, including the 1945 regulation. Over the next twenty years, it demolished or sealed some 1,300 homes; in more than half of those cases, the inhabitants had not committed "actions that involve injury or loss of life."[4] Hundreds of additional homes were destroyed during both the First and Second Intifadas. (The same regulation is used to justify demolitions in East Jerusalem, even though it has been formally annexed to Israel.)

The policy has regularly been condemned by human rights organizations and has placed Israel on the wrong side of international law. Human

Rights Watch refers to it as "blatantly unlawful". The Fourth Geneva Convention prohibits home demolitions except where "rendered absolutely necessary by military operations", but the Israeli High Court ruled in both 1979 and 1982 that they were an acceptable punishment.

A key justification for the punitive home demolitions is that families, knowing their homes will be destroyed, will opt to turn in their relatives willingly before the family member can carry out an attack. However, the Shani commission found only about twenty cases where that actually happened, out of more than 660 demolitions. And that modest benefit was outweighed, it concluded, by the anger created amongst Palestinians, and the damage to Israel's diplomatic reputation. Ironically, it was none other than Defense Minister Moshe Ya'alon who appointed the commission in 2004 during his stint as army chief.

Six weeks before Shalloudi's house was blown up, on the other side of the ravine, a group of Jewish families moved into seven buildings in the dead of night. The homes were purchased by a pro-settler group called the City of David Foundation, commonly known by its Hebrew acronym Elad. They were outfitted with metal gates and security cameras; armed guards lingered outside, and accompanied the settlers whenever they left.

Elad, and a second group called Ateret Cohanim ("Crown of the Priests"), have spent years trying to "Judaize" Silwan. Sometimes they go to court to have Palestinians evicted from their homes, on the basis of Ottoman-era land deeds (Silwan once had a sizable Jewish population, and is home to an important Jewish religious site). In 2014 they tried a new tactic, approaching homeowners through straw buyers and offering exorbitant sums for their properties. "A broker came to me two months ago, a Palestinian guy, and he offered to pay me full price for my house," said Mahmoud Abdel Qader, who lives near the base of the hill. "One million shekels! He said we could go to the municipality immediately and do the paperwork."

One million shekels, roughly $250,000, is a steep price for an aging flat adjacent to a makeshift garbage dump. But several other Silwan residents had similar experiences, as did a man from Jabal al-Mukaber, a similarly grim neighborhood further south. In each case, they said, the brokers were Palestinians claiming to be affiliated with the Islamic Movement, a religious and social organization.

Naftali Bennett, then the economy minister, explained the effort in a cheerful video released after the settlers moved in. "About twenty-five years ago, a wonderful organization decided to return the City of David to Jewish hands," he said. "Slowly, and with patience, it started purchasing homes at full price, and populated them with Jewish families." Bennett went on to explain that the previous week's purchases "doubled" the Jewish population in the area. "[Now] there is a Jewish majority," he claimed. In fact there is no such thing in Silwan, even in the small area designated as the "City of David," where Jews now make up perhaps 20 per cent of the population. But the latest wave of settlement was another obstacle to a future division of Jerusalem.

There is a view, prevalent on the far right, that Netanyahu is a sort of crypto-leftist, secretly plotting to divide the city. The settlers in Silwan view themselves as a sort of beachhead, making it impossible to sever the neighborhood. "The objective, yes, it's to strengthen the Jewish presence in all areas of East Jerusalem," said Aryeh King, a member of the Jerusalem city council and right-wing activist who founded an organization devoted to settling Jews in East Jerusalem. "This way we can stop, or at least delay, Bibi's idea of dividing the city, and wait for the right political leadership that won't think about this." And so they continue to move in, many of them families with young children, even though they are seen as unwelcome interlopers; with their security details, and their ideological motives, bits of the neighborhood feel almost like Hebron. In 2016, the government approved construction of a new three-story building in the district, earmarked for Israeli Jews.

"It contains the seeds of the Hebronisation of Jerusalem," said Daniel Seidemann, an Israeli lawyer and Jerusalem expert. "[It] morphs the conflict from a political one, which can be solved, to a religious conflict that cannot."

"Second-class citizens"

A few days after Shalloudi's hit-and-run attack, I was in Kafr Kanna, a Palestinian village of 20,000 people in the northern Galilee with a rich history. Christians believe it is built on the ruins of Cana, where Jesus transformed water to wine. Two millennia later, it is largely indistinguishable from the other villages that line the highways in northern Israel, a sleepy place filled with furniture stores and automotive repair shops.

But it erupted in November 2014 after police killed a 21-year-old resident named Khair al-Din Hamdan. They said he was shot after trying to stab a group of officers; Luba Samri, a spokeswoman, said the police first fired in the air, and only shot Hamdan when they continued to "face undeterred danger". A surveillance video quickly disproved the official narrative. It showed Hamdan banging on the windows of the police van with an object in his hands—perhaps a knife, though it was impossible to tell. He turned and started to walk away, but an officer soon emerged and shot him multiple times in the back. Two others dragged Hamdan's limp body into the van and shut the doors before it sped away.

For days after the shooting, young men from the village had been blocking a major roadway with burning tires and throwing stones at the police. The mood was deeply insular and hostile, something of a rarity at protests here, where even the most violent participants typically allow journalists to work unmolested. (I was punched in the face at one point amidst a crowd of rioters who thought I was a Jewish Israeli.)

"We're second-class citizens, and we have politicians like [Foreign Minister Avigdor] Lieberman who think even that is too good," said Faris Mahrous, an older Kafr Kanna resident who spent the week trying to calm the rioters. "And these boys see the crimes in Jerusalem, in the West Bank, in Gaza. What do you expect?"

The shooting drew comparisons to what Israelis call the "October 2000 events", ten days of heavy rioting that ended with twelve Israeli Arabs and one resident of Gaza killed by the police. The protests, which coincided with the start of the Second Intifada, came immediately after Ariel Sharon's controversial visit to the Temple Mount. (In Arabic the riots are known as *hibat October*, the "October outburst".) A Jewish Israeli was also killed when a stone hit his car on the highway between Haifa and Tel Aviv.

A month later the government named a commission of inquiry to investigate the violence, led by Theodore Or, a former high court justice. The panel, known as the Or Commission, took nearly three years to publish its 800-page report; it ultimately laid blame on both the police, for their heavy-handed approach to the protests, and the leadership of the Arab community, for inciting them.

More significantly, though, the Or Commission also described the background to the riots—a clear acknowledgment that the Arab community had faced decades of official discrimination. "The state, and generations of governments, failed to deal in a thorough and comprehensive way with the serious problems that were created by the existence of a large Arab minority within a Jewish state," the authors said in their executive summary. "The government's handling of the Arab sector has been largely neglectful and discriminatory... the state has not done enough, and not made a sufficient effort, in order to create equality for its Arab citizens and to remove discrimination and injustice."

The inequality goes far beyond interactions with the police. The employment rate for Arab men in 2015 was 75 per cent, compared to 86 per cent for Jewish men. (It was a meager 33 per cent for Arab women, but cultural norms deserve a share of the blame, not just discrimination.) More than half of Arab families live below the poverty line, twice the national rate. While Jewish schools have slightly fewer students per classroom than their Arab counterparts, they get vastly more money from the state: high schools receive at least a 35 per cent premium, according to 2013–14 data from the education ministry.

Since 1948, the Arab and Jewish populations in Israel have both grown tenfold. The government has established more than 600 new Jewish cities and towns, but not a single Arab community. A 2006 Knesset report found that Arab towns were almost twice as crowded as Jewish ones, with 1.4 people per room versus 0.86 people. Jisr az-Zarqa, an impoverished town next to the wealthy resort of Caesarea, is more densely populated than Tel Aviv. In theory, of course, Palestinian citizens of Israel are free to move anywhere in the country. But hundreds of small communities have "admissions committees", which screen out Arabs and other undesirables (like Mizrahi Jews and homosexuals). The Supreme Court upheld the legality of these committees in 2014.

The report even touched on the issue of "collective rights" for minority groups within a Jewish state (which will be explored in greater depth later). "The authorities must find ways to enable Arab citizens to express their culture and identity in a dignified fashion within the public sphere," it noted.

"Injustice applied by the state to its Arab citizens, and the discrimination against them in all areas of life, produced pent-up rage and frustration that created a convenient climate and atmosphere for the outbreak of those violent events," Hashim Khatib, a member of the commission and a district court judge from Nazareth, summarized later. "The violent explosion of the frustration and rage lacked only the spark to ignite the flame."[5]

Very little of this pent-up rage has been addressed. Both the police and the attorney general decided not to pursue any charges against the officers involved in the October events. Or would later criticize the government for failing to implement his recommendations: "The writing is still on the wall," he said.

The police continue to use heavy-handed tactics against Arab protesters. During an anti-war rally in Nazareth over the summer, they doused entire streets with foul-smelling "skunk water," laced with a noxious chemical that lingers for days on clothing and skin. The water is also frequently used against Palestinians in the West Bank and East Jerusalem, even during relatively peaceful protests; I've only seen it deployed once against a Jewish demonstration. But they neglect to do basic law-and-order policing in Arab towns, where the crime rate is consequently much higher. "Before this, I can't remember the last time I saw the police in our town," Mahrous said.

Out of Africa

Months later, members of another disenfranchised group would hold their own protest against police brutality—but this time in Tel Aviv, normally an oasis of calm. They shut the Ayalon, the main urban freeway, at the height of the afternoon rush. Toward sunset they moved to city hall, where some protesters threw stones and bottles at the police, who fired tear gas and stun grenades in response. Dozens of people were hurt.

The proximate cause for all of this was a two-minute video that showed a uniformed Israeli soldier, Damas Pakada, standing with his bicycle on a street in Holon, a southern suburb of Tel Aviv. A police officer approached and, seemingly without any provocation, began shoving and punching Pakada. Several others joined the fray and detained Pakada for alleged assault.

Pakada had arrived from Ethiopia seven years earlier, one of about 130,000 Ethiopian Jews who live here, accounting for slightly less than 2 per cent of the population. While there are no hard statistics, the community has long complained of brutal and unfair treatment at the hands of police; a local activist group says that nearly one-third of the minors in Israeli prisons are of Ethiopian descent. "There's been police violence against the Ethiopian community for many years, but it's been very, very difficult to prove," said Fentahun Assefa-Dawit, the director of Tebeka, an NGO that advocates on behalf of Ethiopian Israelis. "What's different this time is the footage."

Most of the Ethiopian Jews arrived in two major waves of immigration in the 1980s and early 1990s, during the long civil war in their native country. The government forbade Jews from emigrating, so the Israeli army and intelligence services smuggled them out on a series of clandestine flights. The journey was a culture shock—from rural poverty to a modern country. The immigrants were initially housed in trailer homes, and faced a humiliating ritual upon arrival. When the first big wave arrived in the mid-1980s, the chief rabbis required them to undergo a symbolic *mikvah*, a ritual immersion required for converts. They were the only Jews forced to do so, and hundreds of them marched on the airport in protest, threatening to leave the country. The rabbinate eventually relented.

"Every white person who wants to immigrate is welcome. Every Ethiopian person, regardless of how they practiced Judaism, has been suspect," said Shula Mola, the chair of the Israeli Association for Ethiopian Jews. "I can't explain it any other way. It's about their color."

Decades later, many of them continue to live in grim conditions. Just half of Ethiopian high school students passed their matriculation exams in 2013, compared to 63 per cent of the general population, according to Israel's Central Bureau of Statistics. Mola said many Ethiopian teenagers are pushed into vocational programs instead of university. Salaries for Ethiopian families are one-third lower than the national average. "It's not just a gap between the police and the Ethiopian community," said Assefa-Dawit. "When an Ethiopian applies for a job, as impressive as his CV might be, he's not going to be invited for an interview because he has an Ethiopian name."

Racism in Israel is not limited to Ethiopians, of course. Indeed, some of the protesters in Tel Aviv chanted slogans like "we aren't Arabs!" Ahmad Tibi, a Palestinian member of the Knesset, argued that the police were relatively restrained, compared to how they deal with protests within his own community. "Every Arab wishes to be Ethiopian for a few hours," he said.

There is a long history of intra-Jewish discrimination. The first Zionist leaders were Europeans, and they regarded their Arab counterparts as backwards. David Ben-Gurion called them "rabble", a "generation of the desert" that lacked "a trace of Jewish or human education." He warned in 1949 about the prospect of Israelis becoming Arabs. "It is incumbent upon us to struggle against the spirit of the Levant, which corrupts individuals and societies." Abba Eban, the legendary Israeli diplomat, expressed a desire to "infuse them with an Occidental spirit, rather than allow them to drag us into an unnatural Orientalism." Golda Meir wondered if Israel could raise them to "a suitable level of civilization." For decades, there have been suspicions that the children of Mizrahi immigrants (mostly from Yemen) were systematically kidnapped and given to Ashkenazi families. The state appointed three separate commissions to investigate the claims. Their findings were finally declassified in 2016, but they offered few definite answers. Some doctors testified that many of the children had died in hospital, amidst a widespread polio epidemic; other medical staff reported seeing children handed over for adoption, without their parents' consent. (Whatever really happened, the fact that the rumor persisted for half a century speaks volumes about the level of communal distrust.)

They were discriminated against in the army, often humiliated by Ashkenazi officers who viewed them as "primitive". They were relocated to poor development towns on the northern and southern peripheries, with poor housing and lousy public services, located close to Israel's dangerous borders. Their story was largely ignored in the official Israeli curriculum, a problem that persists to this day. In 1971, the widespread discrimination drove the descendants of Mizrahi immigrants to found a local wing of the Black Panthers.

Russians faced their own prejudice during the mass wave of *aliyah* in the late 1980s and early 1990s. The worst of it came from the rabbinate, which often doubted their Jewishness. They were not asked to dunk in ritual baths like the Ethiopians—but an estimated 200,000 of them are officially listed in the population registry as "other", rather than "Jewish", which makes it impossible to get married in Israel. An adviser to the Jewish Agency noted in 2012 that these Russian immigrants made up an overwhelming share of the Israelis leaving the country for good. "Because they are not considered Jewish here, it is much more difficult for them to feel a part of the country," he said.[6]

The gaps have shrunk over the years, partly due to affirmative action programs (which are class- rather than race-based), partly due to marriage between Ashkenazi and Mizrahi Jews. But they remain stark. The curriculum is deeply skewed towards European history. A state commission that issued a 360-page report in 2016 offered some bleak conclusions. "The dominant stream in Israeli life still does not know the Mizrahi identity." A high school student could graduate, it noted, without "being exposed to the Mizrahi voice at all, except for the poetry of the Golden Age in Spain." Most of the prisoners in Israeli jails are Mizrahi. Among the judges who sentence them, 90 per cent are Ashkenazi.

But perhaps the starkest gap is economic: Seventy years after Israel was founded, the average city-dwelling Ashkenazi still earns 30 per cent more than his Mizrahi neighbor, a difference of more than $9,000 per year. Even for the comparatively well-off Ashkenazim in Tel Aviv, however, Israel is still a difficult place to earn a living.

A nation of immigrants

The thousands of mourners gathered under a clear blue sky in Jerusalem in January 2015 were given a stark and seemingly contradictory message. European Jews shouldn't be forced to flee their countries, but they probably should flee anyway.

President Rivlin was the first to speak at the funeral of four Jews who had been gunned down at a kosher supermarket in Paris. The shooting had shocked France's Jewish community, the largest in Europe and the third-largest in the world. It had followed a steadily intensifying spate of anti-Semitic acts over the previous few years: synagogues and Jewish-owned businesses firebombed, families in religious garb attacked on the streets. In a grim coincidence, the victims of the attack at the Hyper Cacher market were buried in the same cemetery as the four people killed in a 2012 shooting at a Jewish day school in Toulouse.

Rivlin implored France to do more to protect its Jewish citizens, and spoke powerfully about the right of Jews to live in any country, in peace. "Returning to your ancestral home need not be due to distress, out of desperation, because of destruction, or in the throes of terror and fear," Rivlin said. He was followed at the pulpit by Prime Minister Netanyahu, who quickly contradicted him. "Our president was right when he said that Jews have the right to live in many countries," Netanyahu said. "But I believe they know deep in their hearts that they have only one country, the state of Israel, the historic homeland that will accept them with open arms."

This sort of language was a constant source of friction with the Soviet Union. More recently, Ariel Sharon sparked a diplomatic crisis in 2004 when he told French Jews to flee a country plagued by what he called "the wildest anti-Semitism". Then-president Jacques Chirac told Sharon he was not welcome to visit France until he explained his comments. The controversy didn't stop Netanyahu from echoing him.

Yet the fact is that Israel is a nation of immigrants. Since the country was founded in 1948, some 2.7 million Jews have made *aliyah*, a Hebrew word that literally means "to ascend". They came in waves: hundreds of thousands of Holocaust survivors who left the ruins of Europe; more than half a million Arab and North African Jews who fled, or were expelled; and then the great exodus of nearly a million Soviet Jews after Mikhail Gorbachev finally opened the borders. Today, however, the great waves of immigration seem to be finished.

Scholars describe two sets of reasons why people migrate, separating them into "push" and "pull" factors. The former are external crises like war, discrimination, and economic collapse, which drive people involuntarily from their homelands. For perhaps the first time in history, those factors are irrelevant to the vast majority of diaspora Jews, who are concentrated in stable Western democracies, particularly the United States, France, Canada and Great Britain. Anti-Semitism still exists, of course, but Jewish communities have the political and cultural clout to fight it effectively. (The late Edgar Bronfman, Sr, a prominent businessman and a former president of the World Jewish Congress, once told David Ben-Gurion why he wouldn't make *aliyah*: "We Jews have found our Zion," he said. "It is America.")

Annual immigration dipped as low as 16,884 in 2013, roughly two-tenths of a per cent of Israel's population. It climbed markedly over the next two years, because of the war in Ukraine and fears of terrorism and anti-Semitism in Europe, but its peak in 2015 was still slightly below 30,000, or 0.35 per cent of the population. That puts Israel roughly on par with other developed countries. (The level of immigration to the US in 2015, as a share of population, was 0.31 per cent; in the UK, it was 0.51 per cent.) Amongst American Jews—who make up fully three-quarters of the diaspora—the annual *aliyah* figures have hovered around a paltry 2,000 for decades.

As for the "pull" factors, the most common is economic opportunity, but here Israel has little to offer. It does boast a relatively low unemployment rate, but also higher prices and significantly lower wages than many other advanced economies. The gap is especially stark for professionals: a doctor can earn five times more in Paris than she does in Jerusalem. The average Israeli family needs 191 monthly salaries to buy a five-room apartment, versus just 71 in Britain. *Aliyah* from the United States spiked by about 25 per cent during the Great Recession of 2008–2010, which Israel weathered better than most countries, but it quickly returned to the trend line as the economy recovered.

Avigdor Lieberman, during his stint as foreign minister, thought he could jump all of these hurdles. He told a surprised audience that Israel could bring in 3.5 million Jews—nearly half of the diaspora—over the next decade, about a twenty-fold increase over immigration levels at the time. (To put this in perspective: if Lieberman lured every single non-American Jew to Israel, he would still fall 1 million people short, and would need all of Los Angeles and Miami to hit his quota.) "I know this might sound unrealistic to some, and others will say that it is merely a slogan," he said. Then he echoed Theodor Herzl's quote about the founding of a Jewish state. "However, I say, 'If you will it, it is no dream.'"

For a couple of years, Israeli officials anticipated a major influx of French immigrants. Their numbers had long hovered around 2,000, many of them older people who wanted to retire in Israel. But the tally surged in 2014, and peaked at around 7,900 in 2015, making France the largest source of new arrivals. The demographics shifted as well, with young people and families joining the retirees. Many of them settled in Ra'anana, a suburb north of Tel Aviv that has long been a magnet for new immigrants, first from English-speaking countries, then Latin America. In recent years, it has acquired a slightly Parisian feel. Many shops advertise their wares in French alongside Hebrew and English, and the language can often be heard in cafés and parks. Imported products like wine and cheese are readily available. Schoolchildren stop at bakeries for croissants on their way home instead of falafel.

But many of them found living in Israel a struggle: the new language, the high cost of living, the scarcity of good French cheeses (a complaint I heard several times). One of the most common gripes was the difficulty in transferring their qualifications—in getting a French doctor licensed to practice medicine in Israel, for example. "You work longer hours for less money here," said Rachel Kakon, a hairdresser, over coffee and chouquettes at a patisserie on Ben Gurion Street. "It's an easier life in France, the schools, child care, everything is easier." Many left to escape a stagnant economy, where the jobless rate stands at 10 per cent, and nearly 25 per cent for the young, but Israel offered its own set of economic problems. "It's a very complicated scenario. You have to remember, the Jews aren't the only ones leaving France. There's a general pattern of emigration," said Yigal Palmor, a spokesman for the Jewish Agency. "And the Jews who leave, not all of them are going to Israel. It's not their only option."

The pudding crisis

Israelis traveling abroad occasionally post photos of Tnuva cheeses or Golan wines in Western grocery stores. They are, inevitably and inexplicably, cheaper than back home. These humorous posts became a source of national angst in 2014, when a former army intelligence officer named Naor Narkis shared a German supermarket receipt on Facebook. It listed, among other things, a cup of chocolate pudding for 19 cents, roughly three-quarters of a shekel. The Israeli equivalent, a popular dessert called Milky, costs nearly four shekels. "We challenge somebody to buy the same [items] wherever they choose in Israel," wrote Narkis, who started the page anonymously. He asked them to list the local prices, which were higher. He called the group it *Olim l'Berlin*. (The word *olim* is a collective noun for people who have made *aliyah*.)

81

Thousands of people joined his Facebook group. Few of them actually decamped for Germany. But his posts prompted a furious reaction from Israel's political class. Yair Lapid, the finance minister, called him "anti-Zionist." The agriculture minister said he "pities the Israelis who don't remember the Holocaust and abandon Israel for a pudding."

Yet none of them had any solutions for the problem. Three years earlier, Israel saw its largest protests in nearly two decades, since the era of the Oslo Accords—but this time, over cottage cheese. Itzik Elrov, a young ultra-Orthodox man from Bnei Brak, came home furious after a June visit to his neighborhood grocery. He had paid 6.90 shekels (then about $2) for a nine-ounce tub of the stuff, a popular staple in Ashkenazi kitchens (Israelis spend hundreds of millions of dollars on it annually). The price had gone up roughly 40 per cent over the past five years—at a time when annual inflation was below 2 per cent. "Don't buy it this month," he wrote, urging Israelis to boycott the product "until it spoils on the shelves."

For decades, the prices of cottage cheese and other dairy staples were controlled by the government, adjusted every year based on the inflation rate and the cost of raw materials. The government began to phase out the controls in 2006, part of a broader push toward deregulation, and the price quickly soared, even during a period when the price of milk dropped. "Only part of the price increase of cottage cheese after deregulation can be attributed to increases in input prices," three scholars concluded in a 2016 study of the stuff (some academics, it seems, get all the fun assignments).[7] Elrov's post struck a nerve: by the end of June, more than 100,000 people had joined his group calling for a boycott. Major supermarket chains, sensing an opportunity for some good PR, quickly dropped their prices.

Around the same time, a film editor from Tel Aviv named Daphne Leef had to vacate her apartment because of major renovations. She found herself priced out of the market, because rental prices had also gone up by more than 40 per cent. In fact, compared to average wages, they were at their highest level since the late 1990s. And buying an apartment was out of the question for many young Israelis: even modest properties in Tel Aviv doubled in value during the 2000s.

Leef decided to pitch a tent in HaBima Square, and invited other Israelis to join her. The national student union quickly joined her protest, along with other youth groups, and by mid-July there were hundreds of tents along Rothschild Boulevard, one of the city's most upscale thoroughfares. Tens of thousands of people took part in a demonstration in Tel Aviv on 23 July, and the protests continued across the country the following week. In a nod to the Arab Spring, the demonstrators chanted *"ha'am doresh tzedek chevrati"*, "the people demand social justice". Rallies continued throughout the summer, with the high point on 3 September, billed by organizers as a "million-man march". The actual turnout was closer to 450,000, still a very impressive figure— the largest protest in Israel's history, larger than even the mass rallies after the Sabra and Shatila massacres in 1982.

The rallies grew to include a wide range of movements from across Israeli society: animal rights campaigners, dairy farmers, gay rights activists. All of them joined the "million-man march", and all of them had different demands. Dairy farmers would have been happy with a reasonable price for their products. Hadash, the Communist party, wanted a more fundamental overhaul of the economy. The leaders of the movement came to embrace a fairly radical agenda, with calls for overhauling the tax system, major investments in public housing, and free early education.

"What's scary is that some of the groups are going to get what they want and go home," Doron Ya'akov, a protester, told me in 2011. "People have been talking about how this movement is united. But now it's going to break apart."

Netanyahu, momentarily concerned, named a committee to study Israel's socioeconomic problems and propose a set of solutions. The group was led by Manuel Trajtenberg, one of Israel's top economists. It was due to present its recommendations later in September. Trajtenberg told activists that the government would listen to him, but the committee's recommendations were non-binding, and many feared that Netanyahu would simply ignore them.

Several days after the final march, Tel Aviv decided to dismantle the tent city, and municipal officials were sent to serve notice. At first they came bearing flowers, but they returned the next morning with pickup trucks, and hauled away the tents and the accumulated trash. The protesters called them "Nazis in municipal uniforms" (a surprisingly tame insult in Israel—it is also deployed in supermarket checkout lines).

Activists made a few half-hearted attempts to restart the protests, but none of them were successful.

Three years later, Ya'akov's prediction seemed accurate. The government did take a few steps to lower the cost of living. The mobile phone industry was opened to competition in 2012, which sent prices tumbling. An unlimited monthly package now costs less than it does in America. The communications ministry estimated in 2013 that the average family saves nearly $500 per year because of the reforms. Israel is taking steps to privatize the ports in Haifa and Ashdod, a major obstacle to lowering prices in a heavily import-dependent country: the unionized dockworkers are among the country's highest-paid workers, with some hauling in close to $10,000 per month. And the price of cottage cheese has remained relatively low.

But the overall picture is still bleak. The Taub Center, an economic think tank, reported in 2016 that food prices had increased by 53 per cent over the previous decade. In the United States, during the same period, they climbed by just 27 per cent. Housing prices more than doubled, and by 2014 the average one-bedroom rental in Tel Aviv cost nearly 4,000 shekels, roughly half the median after-tax salary. Wages have been basically flat, which has pushed down home ownership rates: about half of young Israelis owned a home in 2006, but less than 40 per cent do today. A 2015 survey found that two in five Israeli bank accounts are "regularly overdrawn". Most have an overdraft of more than 5,000 shekels, and they have been in debt for more than a year.

The events of 2011 led to the rise of Lapid's socioeconomic party in 2013, and drove several prominent activists, like Stav Shaffir, into the Knesset with the Labor Party. Little had improved two years later, and a drip of corruption stories made the prime minister look like a latter-day Marie Antoinette. Most Israelis expected that these issues would decide the looming election.

They were wrong. After a tumultuous three-month campaign, one analyst would dub it the "Seinfeld election". In other words it was about nothing at all—except, perhaps, for the social and cultural schisms between Israelis, and the political system's inability to resolve them.

INEQUALITY

Religion and state

A few years ago, in a Middle Eastern country, the conservative-led government was debating a fundamental change in the state's founding document, a constitutional amendment that would have subjugated civil law to religion, forcing judges and legislators to consider ancient texts in their debates over, say, the rights of women. The debate over the measure was so fierce that it eventually brought down the government.

This was Egypt in 2012, when the Muslim Brotherhood was in power. Then it happened again, two years later—in Benjamin Netanyahu's Israel.

Israel has long defined itself as a "Jewish and democratic state", a concept enshrined in several of the country's "basic laws", which serve as a *de facto* constitution. The idea has always been riddled with contradictions. Until 1966 the Arab minority lived under martial law (though it was also allowed to vote, and to field candidates for the Knesset). Civil marriage is still forbidden, which clearly privileges the Jewish over the democratic, even though a solid majority of Israelis support it.[8]

The contradiction stems in part from Judaism's unique status as both a national identity and a religion. Some supporters argue that a Jewish and democratic state is no different than a French and democratic one: both grant equal rights to all citizens, but reserve certain privileges (like immigration) to members of a particular group. Yet in the Western world that Israel often cites as a model, national identities are becoming more malleable. An Algerian Muslim will find systemic discrimination in France, and a German immigrant in Paris might find it awkward to sing *La Marseillaise*, a strident anthem about "soaking our fields" in Prussian blood. But both can become French in a way they cannot become Jewish.

"How can Israel say that everyone is equal before the law, that you're equal before the law, when the law defines Judaism as the cultural, national and legislative basis for the state?" asked Yair Lapid at a 2013 conference on Arab participation in the economy. He called the rift between Jewish and democratic an unsolvable problem. "We all pretend that if there's a successful Arab soccer player, then we don't have a problem. But we have a problem," Lapid added.

Israel skirted the problem for decades by leaving the law deliberately vague. A Jewish state should observe the Sabbath, so public transporta-

tion halts on Friday evening, and the prime minister avoids publicly desecrating the day of rest, no matter what he does in private. But a democratic state should not force its citizens to sit at home, so it allows local
governments to enforce their own Shabbat laws. In secular Tel Aviv, a
supermarket that opens on Saturday receives a fine of just $200—and
only when one of the city's handful of overworked inspectors happens to
pay a visit. Bars and cafes are packed. In ultra-Orthodox communities,
meanwhile, nobody would think of working on the sabbath.

In 2014, though, Netanyahu decided to end the ambiguity. He first
proposed a "nation-state bill" in May, but the initiative quickly stalled
along with the rest of the Knesset's business: the kidnapping and murder of three Israeli teens in the West Bank, then the Gaza war, overshadowed all policymaking. The prime minister revived the idea six
months later, after Palestinian gunmen attacked the Har Nof synagogue. He announced his plan in mid-November, and introduced a
formal draft at a cabinet meeting on 26 November. "[Israel] has equal
individual rights for every citizen and we insist on this. But only the
Jewish people have national rights: A flag, an anthem, the right of every
Jew to immigrate to the country, and other national symbols," he said
at the meeting. "These are granted only to our people, in its one and
only state."

His vague announcement was widely seen as a sop to the conservative elements in his coalition, particularly Bennett, who was vying to
position himself as the next leader of the Israeli right. It was met with
trepidation by Israeli liberals. "Is this an empty slogan? Then I'm for it.
If it includes specific changes in our life, in order to minimize our liberal public sphere, then I'm against it," said Yedidia Stern, a vice president at the Israel Democracy Institute, a group that is one of Israel's
most principled voices for equality.

Stern offered a few examples of what might make the law objection-
able: if it designated Hebrew as the only official language, or if it
directed judges to interpret Israeli law according to "*halakhic* values",
or Jewish religious law.

The bill that was introduced for discussion was actually three bills,
one drafted by Netanyahu, and the other two by his more right-wing
coalition partners. The drafts were similar in many ways, reaffirming
banal facets of Israel's identity like the national anthem or the design of

the flag. But the right-wing versions went a few steps further. One demoted Arabic from its status as an official language, and encouraged Israel to expand its settlements in the occupied territories; both defined the country as having only a "democratic *form* of government" (emphasis mine), rather than explicitly labeling it a "Jewish and democratic state." All three also stated that Jewish law would be "a source of inspiration" for the Knesset and the courts. It was more or less the language that Stern warned about six months earlier.

"Your father was a hero"

In the middle of all this, I went back up to the Galilee, this time to meet the relatives of an Israeli policeman who had given his life for a state that was debating whether to label him a second-class citizen.

Zidan Seif, a traffic cop, was one of the first officers to arrive at the Har Nof synagogue. The police said he had played a key role in stopping the attack. In a video of the incident later aired on Channel 2, it appeared that Seif had wounded one of the two Palestinian attackers before he was shot in the head at close range.

Thousands of Israelis of all ethnicities and religions attended his funeral in Yanuh-Jat. President Rivlin delivered a powerful eulogy, addressing some of his words to Seif's four-month-old daughter. "We will tell her that her father heroically defended Jerusalem," he said. "Your father was a hero, whose death meant that many others lived." Both Israelis and diaspora Jews rallied behind the surviving family members, raising tens of thousands of dollars in donations in a matter of weeks.

But these gestures did not blunt a sense of betrayal in the Druze community. They have sent their sons to the army, often in combat roles, for more than half a century. Ayoub Kara, a Druze lawmaker from Likud, said that about 85 per cent of their men perform military service—compared to 75 per cent of Jewish men. Jewish politicians often talk of a "covenant of blood" (*brit dam*) between the two communities. The Druze commander of the army's elite Golani brigade, Col Ghassan Alian, was injured by a rocket-propelled grenade during the 2014 Gaza war, and won praise for quickly returning to the front lines.

Yet once they take off their uniforms, many complain of widespread discrimination in everything from jobs to housing. Their crowded towns are underdeveloped, and they often struggle to receive construction permits from the state, which forces them to build illegally and risk their homes and businesses being demolished. These are problems shared by Israel's entire Arab minority. But the Druze, who have served the state loyally for decades, are particularly resentful. The covenant, they argue, ends when they remove their military uniforms. They saw the nation-state bill as a deeply personal affront. "We come back to our villages, and we have no opportunities," said a resident of Beit Jann, the hometown of another police officer killed in the Jerusalem violence.

A few weeks before Seif's death, a riot erupted between Druze and Muslim youth in Abu Snan, a mixed village not far from Yanuh-Jat. At least forty people were hurt after someone threw a hand grenade into the fray. The proximate cause, as ever, was girls. But it came a few days after a schoolyard brawl between *keffiyeh*-wearing Muslim students and their Druze classmates. Residents later said that the violence in Jerusalem had pushed communal tensions to a boiling point.

And yet the Druze, Arabs in language and culture, also face discrimination from the Jewish community. Around the same time as the riots, two Druze soldiers—one a wounded veteran of the Gaza war—were refused entry to a nightclub. They said it was because of their Arabic names. Over the next few months, in Jerusalem and a kibbutz outside of Haifa, two different Druze soldiers were beaten up in bars after Jews overheard them speaking in Arabic. One of them, Tommy Hasson, had done his military service in the president's office—Rivlin posted a photo of them together on Facebook. (To add insult to injury, the hospital in Jerusalem later tried to bill Hasson for his ambulance.)

Scholars have warned for years of growing frustration within the community. A 2009 Haifa University poll found that two-thirds of Druze oppose mandatory conscription. The small but growing number of conscientious objectors includes Omar Sa'ad, a resident of the northern village of al-Mughar who spent more than five months in jail for refusing the draft. "I couldn't imagine myself wearing a military uniform and participating in the suppression of my Palestinian people," he wrote in a letter to Netanyahu.[9]

Netanyahu tried to calm the furor in a November 2014 meeting with Druze leaders. "You are our very flesh. You are an organic part of

Israeli society. Your heroic policemen and soldiers have fallen in order to defend the state and all its citizens, but we will defend your rights and your security," he said. Soon afterward, he announced a $500 million plan to improve infrastructure and create jobs in Druze communities. Again, though, the nation-state bill overshadowed his efforts. Bahij Mansour, the Israeli ambassador to the Dominican Republic and a member of the Druze community, denounced it in a sharp editorial for *Ha'aretz*, a highly unusual step for a civil servant. "This law sends a sharp and clear message to the Druze of Israel, 'You are not our allies,'" he wrote.

Seif's parents, grief-stricken and exhausted, tried to be diplomatic with the parade of journalists who tramped through their modest home. "We're not angry," said his father Nohad. "We all sacrifice for this state, and we all support this state." By contrast his brother Murad said the nation-state bill was an insult, one that would do real damage to the long-standing alliance between the Druze and the state. "There are already people in the community who don't want to enlist, and that is a source of anger," he said. "What am I supposed to tell them now?"

Regional integration

There had been an ironic parallel some months earlier in Egypt, a neighboring country that seems worlds apart from Israel. The Muslim Brotherhood had recently swept the first-ever democratic elections, with a plurality in the parliament and Mohamed Morsi in the presidential palace. After several false starts, Islamists and secular politicians appointed a 100-member committee to amend the constitution. They held a thoughtful, fascinating public debate, the kind which is unlikely to be repeated in Egyptian politics anytime soon. (Mohamed Beltagy, the Brotherhood politician who led the committee, is now serving a 20-year prison sentence.)

Nothing was more controversial than Article 2, which sought to define the identity of the Egyptian state: "Islam is the religion of the state, and the Arabic language is its official language, and the principles of Islamic shari'a are the primary source of legislation."

The previous constitution, drafted in 1971, included an identical article. It originally proclaimed *shari'a* to be only "a" source of legislation, not "the" source, but Mubarak had it amended in 1980 to placate Islamists. Morsi went a step further. He added Article 219, which tried to define the "principles of *shari'a*", a concept that had been left intentionally vague in previous constitutions. The amendment was pushed by salafi politicians, ultraconservative Muslims who were both allies and rivals of the Muslim Brotherhood. Its wording was highly technical, largely unintelligible to anyone without a background in Islamic jurisprudence. Suffice it to say, though, that the article would have changed the way Egyptian judges and legislators interpreted the law, restricting their previously freewheeling and dismissive approach to the "principles of *shari'a*".

Yuval Diskin, a former Shin Bet chief, drew the parallel in a thoughtful Facebook post in November. Both the Egyptian and Israeli laws, he argued, were the start of a "slippery slope", an effort aimed at "creating a large and significant crack that will bring out the opposite of democracy… by setting the order of priority for the values that will guide the courts, and in fact our life."[10]

For Netanyahu, as ever, the decision had more to do with politics than ideology. He had never tried to promote such a law before 2014. But his right-wing coalition partners saw it as an opportunity to advance a longtime goal. "If the bill doesn't pass, we don't have a coalition; everything will fall apart," Bennett warned. He said in a Facebook video that the bill was needed to block the Supreme Court's looming effort "to apply the law of return to non-Jews" and open the floodgates to mass immigration, something that was not, in fact, happening.

The cabinet convened in early December to vote on a vague "statement of principles", which endorsed the legislation and urged the Knesset to reconcile the various drafts into a single bill. Netanyahu also put his liberal coalition partners on notice. "I hear ultimatums, *diktat* and threats of quitting from various parts of the coalition. A country cannot be run this way," he warned.

Indeed, it could not. A stormy four-hour debate ensued, closed to the press, but raucous enough that reporters gathered outside heard lawmakers banging on tables and shouting at each other. The bill was eventually approved, 15–6; the dissenting votes came from center-left members of the coalition. Netanyahu fired Lapid and Tzipi Livni the following week, after both said they could not support the legislation before the full

Knesset. Four other ministers from Lapid's party followed him out the door, and Israel headed for early elections. "We had no choice but to join the finance minister and the justice minister, because there is no point in a belligerent government, a government without a future, without hope," said Shai Piron, the education minister.

"Faith unites us"

Sitting on the sidelines, and watching all of this with interest, were Israel's two ultra-Orthodox parties. They had just spent two long years outside the government, their first stint in the opposition since the 1990s. It was a difficult time: as mentioned earlier, the Knesset passed a 2014 law that would have required some *haredi* men to perform army service; those who refused would face jail time like their non-Orthodox compatriots. It also slashed the state stipends paid to young men studying in *yeshivot*. The community blamed much of this on Lapid, and shortly after the election it vowed never to sit in a coalition with him. (They wouldn't have to. Netanyahu would go with his base, forming a right/religious coalition, while Lapid went to the opposition, and the ultra-Orthodox quickly set to work undoing the accomplishments of the past government.)

The *haredim* (literally, those who "tremble" at God's word) have always had a complicated relationship with Zionism. In the late nineteenth century, many of Europe's leading rabbis were overtly anti-Zionist, because they believed that only divine intervention and not human endeavor should recreate a Jewish state in Palestine. Some regarded Zionism as a false messianic movement—a sort of cult. "The Torah obliges us, further, to allow our longing for the far-off land to express itself only in mourning, in wishing and hoping; and only through the honest fulfillment of all Jewish duties to await the realization of this hope. But it forbids us to strive for the reunion or possession of the land by any but spiritual means," wrote Samson Raphael Hirsch of Germany.

Aside from the scriptural problems, many ultra-Orthodox leaders were also deeply skeptical about what form the state would take. The early Zionist leaders, the descendants of the Jewish enlightenment, were secular men. Theodor Herzl, Max Nordau, Chaim Weizmann, even Ze'ev Jabotinsky, the founder of the Revisionist school—all fell somewhere between agnosticism and militant atheism. "Faith unites us, knowledge gives us freedom. We shall therefore prevent any theocratic tendencies from coming to the fore on the part of our priesthood. We shall keep our priests within the confines of their temples," Herzl wrote in *Der Judenstaat*, his 1896 pamphlet on the planned Jewish state.

In 1912, hundreds of rabbis met in the German town of Kattowitz (now Katowice, in modern-day Poland) to found Agudat Israel ("Union of Israel"), an umbrella movement for anti-Zionist Jews. It was a powerful force until World War II, when much of European Jewry was wiped out. By 1948, the remaining leaders of the Agudah had moderated their anti-Zionism, opting instead for a sort of non-Zionism, since the state of Israel might be useful as a shelter for the remnants of their community.

Their opposition was still a problem for David Ben-Gurion and the other early leaders of Israel. It looked bad, of course: Jewish divisions over the Jewish state would undermine Israel's legitimacy. But there was also a more pragmatic consideration, one that remains valid today. He thought the ultra-Orthodox could make good coalition partners. They didn't have a position on the fierce debates over how to organize the new state and its economy. By appeasing them, Ben-Gurion could help to secure a majority in the first Knesset. "If he'd fought on all fronts simultaneously and with the same passion—socialism versus communism, secularism versus religion, a free-market economy versus a centrally directed economy—he'd have united all of them against him and remained in the minority," Shimon Peres recalled.

A year before Israel declared independence, Ben-Gurion, then the chairman of the Jewish Agency, sent a letter to Agudat Israel. He outlined an arrangement now referred to as the "status quo" (a phrase that gets a lot of use in Israel). The letter made four pledges on key questions of religion and state. Shabbat would be the official day of rest for Jews. The state would offer kosher food in official dining facilities. A single authority would oversee personal-status issues like marriage, which meant, in practice, that the Orthodox would control such matters for Jews (non-Jews have their own parallel structures). And religious communities would have the right to manage their own schools, albeit with certain minimum standards for language, science, and other secular fields. The following year, he agreed to the Council of Yeshivot's demand that "Torah scholars" be excluded from the army draft.

The *haredim* were a tiny minority, too small to impose their religious views on the general public. The draft exemption only applied to 400 young men. For Ben-Gurion, this seemed a low price to pay for Jewish unity and a sturdy coalition. He also believed the whole debate would soon be irrelevant. Like many of his contemporaries, he saw the ultra-Orthodox community as an oddity, a dusty curio from the centuries of Jewish exile. Freed from the *shtetl*, they would soon adopt a new Hebrew identity and become Israeli.

Peres was a longtime friend of Israel's founder, and helped him negotiate the army exemption. He wrote a biography of Ben-Gurion in 2011 with the late David Landau, *The Economist*'s longtime Jerusalem correspondent. At one point, in a dialogue between the authors, Landau asked Peres whether Ben-Gurion thought "the number of traditionally observant Jews would decline." Peres, ever the politician, tried to dodge the question, but his answer left little doubt: Ben-Gurion indeed thought that the last adherents of European Orthodoxy would wither on the vine. "We believed that the Diasporic version of Judaism was transient," Peres said. "Ben-Gurion's objection was not to the religion but to the organized 'church'. He maintained that pristine Judaism had no hierarchy, no God's deputy, no bishops... but Ben-Gurion decided not to fight this ideological battle."[11]

In 1952, Ben-Gurion paid a visit to the home of Avraham Yeshaya Karelitz, a *haredi* religious leader better known as the "Chazon Ish" ("Vision of Man"). The prime minister wanted to discuss a program of national service for religious women, as an alternative to conscription. Much of the ultra-Orthodox community was horrified by the proposal. Karelitz, however, was an authority on reconciling Jewish law with the demands of a modern state. He came up with a *halakhic* solution that allowed observant dairy farmers to milk their cows on Shabbat, without which they would have quickly gone out of business. The prime minister thought he was the best man to approach about the national-service bill.

The meeting didn't go well. At the time, neither man said much about their conversation, so it became the subject of extensive speculation in the *haredi* press. One columnist reported that the near-sighted *rebbe* had removed his trademark round glasses, so he wouldn't have to "look in the villain's face."

Ben-Gurion recorded only a few details in his personal diary. Aside from the two interlocutors, however, a third man was present at the meeting: Yitzhak Navon, the prime minister's aide and a future president of Israel. A few years before his death in 2015, Navon published his memories of the meeting. Ben-Gurion started by asking Karelitz how religious and secular Jews could live together in Israel. He responded with a parable from the Talmud. When two camels meet on a road, one carrying a load, the other unburdened, the latter must yield. "We, the religious Jews, are like the camel with the load. We carry a burden of hundreds of *mitzvot*," he explained. "You have to give way."

Ben-Gurion, the secular camel, tapped himself on the shoulder. "Do you think this camel has no load?" he asked, listing his responsibilities: working the land, absorbing hundreds of thousands of immigrants. "These aren't *mitzvot*?"

The conversation quickly devolved into a sort of chicken-and-egg argument. The prime minister mentioned the secular soldiers who guarded the borders and protected the religious Jews studying Torah, who would otherwise be "slaughtered". Again, he asked, weren't they performing a *mitzvah*? No, Karelitz replied, the soldiers were only there because of the devout young men in their *yeshivot*. Maybe so, Ben-Gurion answered, but what good is learning Torah if everyone gets killed? Karelitz wasn't worried. The Torah, he explained, was *etz chaim*, a "tree of life".

Then the *rebbe* complained about the widespread desecration of Shabbat in Israel, the secular youths who went to the beach instead of learning Torah. "You can't force them," Ben-Gurion said. "And if they don't go to the beach, you think they'll go to synagogue?" Again, Karelitz was unconcerned. "I believe that one day, everyone will keep the Sabbath and pray."

A monolith?

The ultra-Orthodox are often presented as a monolith—a sea of men in uniform black coats. A visit to a *yeshiva* might reinforce this image: endless rows of young men wearing identical clothes, studying the same page of a religious text. But the community is quite diverse, with numerous divisions between sects and ethnicities. Some of them already share the burden: most *haredi* men do not work, but 46 per cent of them do, along with 71 per cent of women; about 2,000 men voluntarily enlist in the army each year. Overwhelmingly, however, they do not. The employment figure for men is far below the national average of 60 per cent. The only group with a lower rate of labor force participation is Arab women. And army enlistment represents roughly 20 per cent of the possible conscripts each year.

It's impossible to say what fraction of the *haredi* community supports the status quo. Indeed, this is arguably the community's biggest problem. Rabbis and politicians set the agenda; everyone else is expected to fall in line. Those who don't are often subjected to harassment. Children in ultra-Orthodox neighborhoods routinely spit on uniformed soldiers, or throw stones at them. A young conscript once explained to me how he stops in a secular part of Jerusalem whenever he goes home for leave. He ducks into a hotel or cafe, doffs his uniform in the bathroom, and puts on traditional garb. "I'd like to encourage other guys to enlist," he said. "But you can't in our community, because the extremists will come after you."

A poster campaign in ultra-Orthodox neighborhoods a few years ago called conscripts *hardakim*, a portmanteau of *haredi* and *herek*, the Hebrew word for "insect". Another one portrayed them as pigs. A few months after the 2015 election, activists started circulating a pamphlet entitled "Soul Hunters", which published the personal details—names, photos, even home addresses—of *haredi* men who work as army recruiters. It called them "professional missionaries" who "sold their souls to the devil for financial gain."

More troubling for Israel's future is the issue of education. Thousands of *haredi* students graduate each year without learning basic math, science, and English. A law passed under Netanyahu's third government offered a small fix: it required schools to teach at least ten hours of secular studies each week; those that refused would lose one-third of their state funding. But the law was quickly canceled once the ultra-Orthodox parties returned to power. Some *haredi* men would like to work—but they finish school totally unprepared to find a job. "That's why I enlisted," said another soldier, who hoped to work in the high-tech sector after his service. "I'm not going to learn computer programming in Bnei Brak." (Dozens of ultra-Orthodox men have sued the state, claiming they were "abandoned" and left to graduate without a secular education.)

It isn't just the ultra-Orthodox parties who are complicit. A recent study of developed countries found that Israeli students had fallen from seventh place to sixteenth in maths, and from thirteenth to nineteenth in science. Naftali Bennett called the findings a "national emergency", which is not an overstatement: Israel does not have many natural resources, and as a small country it will never be a manufacturing powerhouse; its prosperity is closely linked to having an educated workforce. (The results, notably, did not include boys in ultra-Orthodox schools, which would undoubtedly have pushed Israel's score much lower.)

The next day, though, Bennett's education ministry announced a plan to invest 136 million shekels over four years to teach students about Judaism—in foreign countries. He said that the programs, to be offered across Europe, would "strengthen Jewish identity and connection to Israel on the part of students at Jewish schools around the world." The sum is a drop in the bucket, less than tenth of a per cent of the education ministry's annual budget. But it was a revealing sign of priorities. "Learning about Judaism and excellence in the subject is more important in my eyes than mathematics and the sciences," Bennett said at a conference in 2016.

Some *haredim* have rebelled against these strictures from within: there are business incubators that cater to the community, and job training programs aimed at closing the educational gaps. Moshe Friedman founded a company called KamaTech in Tel Aviv that matches ultra-Orthodox applicants with high-tech employers. Friedman, a self-taught programmer, predicted that the rabbis would one day "catch up" with younger people frustrated with a life of poverty and isolation. But it is a slow process—so others take more dramatic steps.

Dasi and Ya'akov

Esti Weinstein's suicide note was 183 pages long. It was a novel, really, the story of Dasi and Ya'akov, a young couple from one of the largest Hasidic sects. They married when Dasi was seventeen—an arranged union, of course, as was the custom in their community. They met only once before the wedding, two young people on the cusp of adulthood, and yet still children in so many ways. Ya'akov gave "the speech", as Dasi called it, the awkward mumblings about how difficult it was to follow the rules of their order, the restrictions on sex and intimacy. "I pitied the thin boy in front of me, sitting with drooped shoulders, his hands together in front of his body, and him swaying uncomfortably," Dasi recalled. "His overall appearance was far from being perfect but, touching in his humiliation, it caused me to feel relaxed next to him."

And yet the marriage was anything but comfortable. He never called her by her first name. They had sex twice a month; when she asked for more, he asked his rabbi for permission. It wasn't forthcoming. "The *rebbe* said this month we should not do it again, and added and instructed that if you accept my pronouncement, that is great! And if not, that I should sleep in the living room," Ya'akov explained sheepishly. As the unhappy union wore on, though, he developed increasingly strange fetishes. Dasi would later recount how Ya'akov had forced her to have sex with other men while he watched. Eventually, her husband's predilections drove her to attempt suicide. The manuscript, fittingly enough, was called "Doing His Will".

Weinstein disappeared from her home in Azor, a small town outside of Tel Aviv. She looked much younger than her fifty years on the missing poster circulated by police—a woman with a welcoming smile, wavy locks flowing past her shoulders. Her Facebook page, too, was filled with happy moments, photos of her posing by the Sea of Galilee or a waterfront restaurant, a carefree grin on her face.

Her car was found six days later, parked near a beach in Ashdod. Her body was inside, along with a brief note to her family. "In this city I gave birth to my daughters, and in this city I died because of my daughters," it read.

The book she left behind was a *roman à clef*, the story of her own life as a Gur, the largest Hasidic community in Israel, with more than 10,000 families. (Small groups also live in North America and England.) Weinstein was married to "Ya'akov", whose real name was never mentioned. They had seven daughters together. Like "Dasi", though, Weinstein eventually reached a breaking point—when she was 42, she ran away from the community. Thousands of others have made the same journey. While there are no firm statistics, activists believe the numbers have increased in recent years. Modern technology, in particular, makes it difficult to maintain a closed community.

A few days after Weinstein's body was found, another ex-Gur named Israel Greenhouse posted two lists of the community's regulations on Facebook. The rules, he said, were never written down; instead they were passed via word of mouth, from teacher to student. He started with 104 of them, which applied to unmarried men studying in *yeshiva*. "A preliminary list, and only a partial one," he noted. Two men were forbidden from sitting on the same bed, or being alone in a room together. Combing your hair was banned. So was looking in a mirror. Boys should not be awake after 10 pm. Even saying the words "woman" or "girl" was prohibited. The list of rules for women was even longer: going to the beach alone, owning a mobile phone, looking men in the eye, walking down the street with their father, wearing sneakers—all were forbidden.

This sort of extremism is often swept under the rug, particularly when it relates to sex. There are widespread allegations of child sexual abuse in *haredi* communities, but they often go unreported. Again, there are a few hopeful signs: a new victims' center in Beit Shemesh has counseled 600 children over the past five years, nearly one-third of them in 2015 alone. Activists, filmmakers and journalists have tried to challenge the taboo. But the rabbis and politicians often duck the issue.

The following summer, an ultra-Orthodox man named Yishai Shlissel would stab six people at the annual gay pride parade in Jerusalem. One of his victims, a 16-year-old girl named Shira Banki, died from her wounds. Shlissel had recently been released from prison after carrying out a similar attack. Inexplicably, the police did not have him under surveillance, even though he had spoken publicly about his plans to carry out another attack against the "abomination".

A few ultra-Orthodox lawmakers condemned the attack, but others kept silent, and none mentioned the widespread homophobia that caused it. Days later, a *haredi* school in Jerusalem uninvited President Rivlin from a ceremony marking the first day of school because he had strongly condemned the stabbing. And in December, when the Likud swore in its first openly gay Knesset member, none of his ultra-Orthodox coalition partners sat in the plenum to hear his speech. Instead they held a boycott.

Less than the sum of its parts

Race, religion, economics: these are not usually the subjects that make the foreign media headlines about Israel. And yet they are perhaps a greater long-term challenge than the stagnant Israeli-Palestinian conflict.

Modern-day Israel often seems less like a state and more like an unhappy amalgamation of tribes (which will be discussed later in the book). The rifts are particularly stark between Jews and Arabs. In the eyes of the Jewish state, the Druze are an ideal minority. They serve loyally in the army, they overwhelmingly identify as Israeli, and often even as Zionists. (I've met young Druze who are more comfortable speaking in Hebrew than Arabic.) And yet even a brief tour around their villages demonstrates that they do not receive commensurate benefits. A 2013 study found that Druze schools receive, on average, 5,000 shekels less per pupil than their state-run Jewish counterparts.[12]

The same could be said of the tiny Circassian minority, which is concentrated in two relatively poor towns in the north. Or the Bedouin, who often serve with distinction in the army—they man an elite unit of trackers, guarding the borders—and then return home to poverty and dispossession, and the ever-present threat of eviction by the state. But they also exist within the Jewish majority. The Ethiopians emigrated to Israel decades ago, yet many of them still feel somewhat less than full citizens. Amongst Ashkenazim and Mizrahim the schism is less stark, but it still rears its head. (A Western-educated friend with the surname Mizrahi once told me about her struggle to find a job— "We thought you were from Holon," one relieved interviewer told her, referring to a predominantly Mizrahi suburb of Tel Aviv.)

The *haredim* present a particular set of challenges. On a practical level, Israeli governments depend on their support. Even when a cabinet manages to pass reforms, as it did during Netanyahu's third, they can be quickly undone, as would happen during his fourth. And they present a symbolic dilemma: how can the Jewish state fight with a group of people who seem the most fervently, outwardly "Jewish"?

This same dilemma underlies the broader tension between Israel's Jewish and democratic identity. In their efforts to portray Israel as a liberal country, politicians and propagandists often focus on a set of cultural issues, the most common of which is gay rights. In 2014, the *hasbara* group StandWithUs ran a splashy ad campaign in the *New York Times*. "Hamas, ISIS and Iran kill gays like me," read one full-page advertisement, illustrated with a black-and-white photo of a gay American named Rennick Remley. "In Israel, I am free."

It is, to an extent, a fair argument. Gays and lesbians have more rights under Israeli law than in some Western countries, let alone elsewhere in the Middle East. The state recognizes same-sex marriages performed abroad; gay couples can adopt children; discrimination based on sexual orientation has been illegal since the 1990s. When the Israeli military started allowing gays to serve openly, the US hadn't even issued the "don't ask, don't tell" regulation. Abortion is widely available, and the state health care program provides it for free. Visitors are often surprised at the number of armed Israelis on the streets, but buying a gun is actually far more difficult than in the United States. While marijuana is technically illegal, you wouldn't know it from sitting in a Tel Aviv cafe. The list goes on. All of these are largely settled issues. Israel has its share of anti-gay demagogues, like one member of the Jewish Home who calls himself a "proud homophobe". But there is no serious talk of changing the status quo.

On the other hand, Israel still lacks civil marriage. Gay Israelis cannot marry in their own country. Nor can mixed-faith couples. Public transportation is largely unavailable on Shabbat—an inconvenience to middle-class Israelis, and a serious financial burden for impoverished ones. The Orthodox rabbinate has a monopoly on issuing *kashrut* certifications, a stricture that drives up costs for locals and tourists alike. (By one estimate, about 10 per cent of hotel and restaurant bills go directly to the rabbinate.) These are not simply abstract questions of identity; they have a tangible impact on millions of people.

Few prominent Israeli politicians seem prepared to resolve them. As the next chapter details, Netanyahu's party would win a plurality despite not even bothering to draft an economic platform. Many commentators would chalk this up to security concerns: regardless of what Israelis tell pollsters during the campaign, they ultimately cast a ballot based on their most fundamental fears.

But his victory would also demonstrate how Israelis vote based on, for lack of a better term, their tribal identity. Left-leaning parties like Labor and Meretz are seen as catering to European Jews; one Ashkenazi artist's racist comments at a campaign rally would quickly become a central piece of electoral propaganda. Unhappy Mizrahi voters would "come home" to Likud because they could not imagine voting for any party except the one that first gave them a political voice in the 1970s. Lapid, cast into the opposition, would prepare himself for a run at the premiership by embracing the same *haredim* he attacked a few years earlier.

The Knesset is somewhat unique among industrialized democracies in that it has no constituencies. The entire country is one big electoral district. This was a sensible arrangement when Israel was sparsely populated and relatively homogeneous. Today, though, it is a recipe for polarization, especially when coupled with the relatively low threshold for entering parliament. It also leads to certain areas of the country being over- or under-represented: only seven lawmakers (6 per cent) hail from the southern periphery, which has 1.2 million residents (15 per cent of the population). A system of single-member districts might be too parochial for a small country, and it would create a number of permanently uncompetitive constituencies in ultra-Orthodox and Arab areas. But multiple-member districts could help to reduce the clout of small, sectoral parties.

Ha'aretz periodically floats a plan to go much further and divide Israel into cantons, an idea modeled on Switzerland, of all places. The Swiss confederation was created to avoid conflict between various ethnic and religious groups. On the surface, at least, this principle seems applicable to Israel, populated by groups with deeply incompatible visions of what it means to be an Israeli or a Jew.

"Imagine if in one Israeli province, you could get legally married under a rainbow chuppah, shop till you drop on Saturdays, not to mention visit any number of licensed cannabis cafes? Horrified at the thought? Then try neighboring 'Judah province', where cars on Shabbat, pork-serving eateries and flesh-revealing billboards could all be outlawed," the newspaper mused in 2014.[13]

One can see the appeal of this idea, particularly for the sorts of people who read *Ha'aretz*. But tens of thousands of secular Israelis live in Jerusalem, along with 300,000 Palestinians. A hypothetical coastal province south of Tel Aviv would include right-wing Likud supporters, ultra-Orthodox residents of Ashdod, *kibbutzniks*, and young families priced out of the commercial capital. The geographic divisions in Israel do not lend themselves readily to such a decentralized system. And yet, as the forthcoming election would demonstrate, the idea has a grain of merit: how can the Israeli political system possibly represent millions of people with fundamentally incompatible visions of what it means to live together?

4

THE ELECTION

*

"Put three Zionists in a room and they will form four political parties."
Levi Eshkol

Benjamin Netanyahu was in a tailspin. It was the eve of a closely-fought election, a ballot that he had once seemed the clear favorite to win, but months of bad press and personal scandals had chipped away at this sense of inevitability. Israelis were tired of their leader, already the country's second longest-serving prime minister. Suddenly the man dubbed "King Bibi" seemed in real danger of losing his throne.

The election was on a Tuesday. The final round of pre-election polls, published on Friday—Israeli law prohibits releasing polls in the last four days—showed his Likud party trailing its main center-left challenger, the Zionist Camp, by four seats. One survey had them dipping as low as twenty mandates in the 120-member Knesset, a damning indictment of the ruling party.

So he panicked. On Friday night he logged on to Facebook and posted a long screed against Noni Mozes, the wealthy publisher of *Yediot Aharonot*, Israel's largest paid daily (and no fan of the prime minister). "The public needs to know the truth," he said. "Noni Mozes is leading a timed and orchestrated campaign against the Likud, and against me." Hours earlier, during a public question-and-answer session, he warned that "the governments of Western Europe, especially

103

in Scandinavia, are funding the campaign that is designed to oust me from power." The self-proclaimed leader of the Jewish people seemingly missed the irony of accusing wealthy businessmen and sinister media barons of organizing a global conspiracy against him.

Notoriously media-averse—he once went 411 days without speaking to Israeli journalists—Netanyahu suddenly organized a last-minute media blitz. He was everywhere, on the radio, on television, and in the pages of prominent newspapers. He had refused to debate Isaac Herzog, the head of the Zionist Camp, fearing it would boost his challenger's profile, but Channel 2 managed to bring them together for a few minutes on Saturday night. Netanyahu had dark bags under his eyes, looking as if he hadn't slept in a week. "How are you?" asked the interviewer, Rima Matzliach. "I'm good. I'm more concerned with the well-being of the country," he replied, before he launched into his talking points.

Everywhere he went, the message was the same: right-wing governance, and therefore the state of Israel, was in danger. The *Jerusalem Post* asked Netanyahu if his loss at the polls could mean the country's destruction. He didn't contest the proposition.

On Sunday night, with thirty-six hours to go, tens of thousands of right-wing Israelis gathered for a rally in Tel Aviv's Rabin Square. A giant banner demanding the death penalty for terrorists loomed over the crowd. Supporters were taking photos next to cardboard cutouts of Naftali Bennett, the head of the religious-settler Jewish Home party. Bennett himself broke out a guitar and sang "Jerusalem of Gold". A group of young men taunted a woman watching from her balcony, where she had hung a poster for the liberal Meretz party, asking her to "Come down here and face us!" Someone handed out glow sticks. It had the atmosphere of some strange post-apocalyptic street fair.

Netanyahu was the keynote speaker, and he urged voters to "come home" to Likud from other conservative parties. "Our rivals are investing in a huge effort to harm me and the Likud, to open a gap between my party, the Likud, and our enemies, and if we don't close this gap, there is a real danger that a left-wing government will come to power," he warned.

The following day he toured Har Homa, a settlement in occupied East Jerusalem, and promised a major wave of new construction if re-elected. Then he disavowed the two-state solution, something he had publicly endorsed in a landmark 2009 speech at Bar-Ilan University. "If you are prime minister, you will not establish a Palestinian state?" asked an interviewer from NRG, a news site owned by Sheldon Adelson, the American casino mogul who is Netanyahu's main patron. "Indeed," the prime minister replied.

The coup de grace came around noon on election day. Netanyahu posted a video to his Facebook page, saying "Arab voters are coming out in droves to the polls. Left-wing organizations are busing them." The same warning was blasted out to Likud supporters via SMS throughout the day. It was a naked, ugly appeal to racism. In fact there was no evidence of overwhelming voter turnout among Israel's Arab minority.

Netanyahu prides himself on his image as a pragmatic conservative, and a worldly one, a politician who knows how to represent Israel on the international stage. He has beaten back primary challenges from far-right Likud figures like Danny Danon and Moshe Feiglin by portraying himself as a more sensible, steady choice. Yet he discarded all of that in the waning hours of the campaign, channeling the worst elements of Israel's political culture. It earned him days of public rebuke from the White House, and scorn from his political opponents.

Yet it would also prove tremendously effective.

Netanyahu, the gambler

None of this should have been necessary, not when Netanyahu decided in December to dissolve his government and call for early elections.

The prime minister had been less than two years into his four-year term. He was not especially unpopular. His approval ratings were in the mid-thirties—unimpressive, compared to their wartime highs in the 70s, but also in line with his average. His coalition was an awkward mix of far-right and center-left parties, but it looked reasonably stable. Even his unhappiest partners seemed to lack the political courage to bolt the cabinet. But he took a gamble anyway with the nation-state law.

Even this shouldn't have demanded such drastic measures. Lapid and Livni had offered to back a revised bill that had removed some of the most offensive provisions (like the bit that stripped Arabic of its status as an official language). The prime minister refused. "They were merely the excuse for dissolving this Knesset. No one in Israel knows what this law is about," said Amit Segal, the chief political correspondent for Channel 2. "Netanyahu was the prime minister for six years, and he never took a step to promote these laws. So one can infer that this was merely an excuse for dissolving the Knesset."

Why did he need this excuse? Because of the fractious nature of Israel's political system. Lapid had become a problematic member of the coalition, sparring with Netanyahu over the budget and a plan to exempt first-time homebuyers from tax. The latter was Lapid's flagship economic initiative. It was widely panned by Israeli economists, who said it would do nothing to alleviate the country's housing crisis, which is caused mainly by a shortage of new apartments. Netanyahu opposed it, partly because he feared a political victory would boost Lapid's standing.

Rumors had also swirled for weeks that Lapid and Herzog were trying to cobble together an alternative coalition, marrying the center-left and ultra-Orthodox parties. It was an unlikely scenario, to say the least. Lapid had spent the past two years portraying the ultra-Orthodox as the enemy. But Netanyahu saw a looming coup—a "putsch" as he personally called it. Lieberman, the foreign minister, had abrogated his party's unity pact with Likud months earlier, creating a threat from the right. Even his own party was restive: Likud members had selected a far-right slate of candidates in their 2012 primary election, turning the prime minister into one of the most liberal members of his own faction.

So Netanyahu was herding cats. From his office on Balfour Street, early elections seemed a necessary bet, and a safe one. The polls showed Likud with a strong plurality. The prime minister figured that he could return to power with a more amenable coalition.

Yet by election day he seemed in real danger of losing his throne in a ballot that had become largely a personal referendum. His face was everywhere, on billboards, bumper stickers, social media, often next to the slogan "nine years of nothing". Despite the apparent stability in Israel, voters were deeply unsettled—about the unsustainable cost of living, their increasingly fractious society, a deepening strain of nationalism and racism, and Israel's growing isolation from its historic allies in the West. Netanyahu's tenure had begun to look like something of a lost decade, a period of prolonged drift. And yet his challengers were mostly unable to articulate an alternative, offering few solutions during what was a deeply personalized, ugly campaign.

One campaign ad asked, "Who did Bibi hurt for nine years?" A succession of ordinary Israelis—students, soldiers, pensioners—faced the camera and answered "*bi*", (which means "me" as well as playing on the prime minister's nickname). "Bibi hurt each one of us," the ad concluded.

Weathering the storm

Seen from afar, this might have appeared an odd claim. When Netanyahu started his second term in early 2009, the world economy was deep in recession, and Israel had just finished its first ruinous war against Hamas in Gaza. Soon Egypt would plunge into revolution and years of political chaos. A catastrophic civil war would erupt across the northern border in Syria, giving rise to extremist groups and pushing the region into turmoil unprecedented in modern times.

Israel had weathered all of this fairly well. The economy had kept growing, by 5 per cent in 2010, and 4.6 per cent in 2011, despite stagnation among its largest trading partners. Unemployment had hovered around 6.5 per cent, lower than many other advanced economies. On the security front, the army had fought two more wars in Gaza, Palestinians had carried out around of "lone wolf" attacks, and there had been occasional flare-ups of violence on the northern borders. It may not have been quiet, but in relative terms it was peaceful, given the ominous constellation of forces gathering all around: the Islamic State, al-Qaeda, jihadists on the Sinai Peninsula, and a strengthened Hezbollah.

Netanyahu, in other words, could plausibly claim to have steered Israel through a turbulent time in relative peace and prosperity. Yet more than half of the country wanted him gone.

The economy was an oft-cited reason, because years of strong macroeconomic growth had not helped most Israelis. Average wages in 2013 stood at about $28,800, more than $10,000 below the median in the Organization for Economic Cooperation and Development (OECD). But it is far more expensive to live in Israel than in other OECD countries. The price of basic consumer goods is 12 per cent higher than the average, for instance.

Likud offered little to such voters. The party didn't even bother to publish an economic program before the election. On 25 February the state comptroller, the government's top auditor, blamed the high cost of housing partly on Netanyahu: the government, he said, had failed to come up with a long-term strategy to lower prices. Netanyahu stepped before the cameras to deliver an outlandish response. "When we talk about housing prices, about the cost of living, I do not for a second forget about life itself," he said. "The biggest threat to our life at the moment is a nuclear-armed Iran." (It called to mind Joe Biden's famous quip about former New York mayor Rudy Giuliani: "There's only three things he mentions in a sentence: a noun, a verb, and 9/11.")

Reports of the Netanyahus' personal corruption also fueled the perception that he was indifferent to the economic concerns of regular Israelis. A separate comptroller's report, also released in February, found that the first couple's expenses at the official residence were beyond "proportionality and reason". The Netanyahus had spent two-and-a-half times the amount budgeted for hairstylists and makeup, and tens of thousands of shekels to clean their private home in Caesarea, where they spend only a few days each month. (Police would eventually question the prime minister's wife Sara about suspicions that she had stolen patio furniture, among other things.)

"Trust me, I know what happens next. They'll start buying golden toilets," an Iraqi Jew in southern Israel told me. The allusion to Saddam Hussein was only half in jest.

It wasn't only economics that divided the Israeli electorate—it was also dueling views about Israel's place in the world. On the campaign trail, center-left voters fretted about Israel's deteriorating image in Europe and the United States, and its growing religiosity. "I can't travel abroad without feeling embarrassed," one woman told me.

The right feared the opposite, that Israel was too deferential to world powers, and that the judiciary had blocked the Knesset from imposing religious and nationalist legislation. "The State Department is breathing down our necks," a man complained at a Jerusalem campaign event for Bennett's party.

Is Israel Jewish, democratic, or both? Is the Palestinian minority equal to the Jewish majority, or is it a dangerous fifth column? Should Israel patch up its relations with the West, or go it alone? Netanyahu could not answer these questions; indeed, he didn't even try. He barely even ran a campaign, appearing only with pre-selected audiences of sympathetic Likud activists. He spoke only about Iran and security matters.

THE ELECTION

"The debate has gained a new feature, which I would say is universal values, the way Israel is connected to the world,"Tamar Hermann, the polling director at the non-partisan Israel Democracy Institute, said in the run-up to the vote. "Is it important for Israel to be part of the democratic, liberal world? Or should it look for its identity in Jewish morality? It's not about specific issues, but about which kind of society we want to see."

The issues

On an unseasonably warm March evening in Tel Aviv, an hour after Shabbat, the cafés and restaurants along fashionable Rothschild Boulevard were overflowing. Further down the road, in stark contrast, a few dozen Israelis were camped in the median, trying to recreate the tent city that became the nucleus of the 2011 socioeconomic protests.

The largest crowds were streaming into Rabin Square for an anti-Netanyahu rally. It would be the city's largest political demonstration in four years. The keynote speaker was Meir Dagan, a former Mossad chief who seemed out of place amidst a sea of Meretz flags. Ariel Sharon, after all, once said that "Dagan's speciality is separating an Arab from his head."

But Dagan had become a savage critic of the prime minister since he had left the agency in 2011. Days earlier, he denounced part of Netanyahu's speech to Congress about the nuclear deal with Iran as "bullshit". On this Saturday evening, he warned the crowd that Israel would become an apartheid state if it did not reach an agreement with the Palestinians. He looked frail, and choked back tears as he spoke. (He had been battling liver cancer, and would die the following March, exactly one year after the election.)

"Israel is surrounded by enemies. Our enemies do not scare me; I'm worried about our leadership," he said. "The crisis we are experiencing today is the worst I can remember since the founding of the state." He was the most prominent face in an unprecedented generals' revolt, with hundreds of retired commanders joining a vocal coalition against Netanyahu.

Hermann has long conducted a monthly survey called the "Peace Index."The first campaign-season survey, conducted in late December, found 56 per cent of Israeli Jews "strongly" or "moderately" in favor of negotiations with the Palestinians. Ten years earlier, it was 75 per cent. Meanwhile, only 30 per cent of the Jewish public believed that negotiations between Israel and the Palestinians would lead to peace in the coming years—down from 46 per cent a decade ago.

Put those numbers together, in other words, and less than one-third of Jewish Israelis support negotiations and actually believe a two-state solution is possible. A solid majority think—for better or worse—that the status quo cannot be changed.

The Zionist Camp had promised to renew negotiations with the Palestinians. In that sense, it did offer a contrast with Netanyahu. But Herzog himself did not seem to think the negotiations would succeed. "I don't want to build expectations," he said at a campaign stop. He vowed that Jerusalem "must remain united as Israel's capital," and promised not to concede the Jordan Valley, both deal-breakers for the Palestinians. His nebulous peace plan envisioned at least five years of talks—longer than the term of an Israeli government. The Oslo Accords, which were meant to be a five-year interim measure, had recently turned twenty-one. Herzog's plan was to create another five-year plan. The differences between Netanyahu and Herzog, as the journalist Barak Ravid summarized in a column for *Ha'aretz*, were more style than substance.

A month before the rally, a few hundred people had packed into a hangar at Tel Aviv's old port for a debate on foreign policy and security issues. It had covered the breadth of Israel's main Zionist parties, from Meretz to Jewish Home. It was also conducted in English—a hint as to the intended audience.

Michael Oren, Israel's former ambassador to Washington and a candidate with the centrist Kulanu party, told the audience it might take "two or three generations for a Palestinian leader to emerge and sign a deal with us." Hilik Bar, the Labor party's secretary-general, joked about a recent trip to Northern Ireland. "They told us it took 700 years to resolve their conflict," he said.

This accounts to some degree for the 25 per cent of Israeli Jews who want to talk for the sake of talking. The peace process has not brought peace, but the process itself pays dividends, helping to shield Israel from international criticism. "We have to be convincing when we say we have no desire to continue ruling over 2.5 million Palestinians," Oren said. It has similar psychological benefits for Israeli voters, replacing the prospect of permanent occupation with one of indeterminate negotiations. Practically speaking, the two are the same, but the latter is easier to stomach.

"This is not a parameter that differentiates between the parties, because Israelis understand that whoever is prime minister, nothing will change with the Palestinians," said Dani Dayan, the former director of the Yesha Council, the main settler lobby group.

There is similarly little daylight between them on other security issues. Netanyahu's opponents panned his controversial Iran speech in Washington, even though they broadly agreed with the prime minister's Iran policy. In January, when Israel and Hezbollah seemed close to a war, Herzog rushed before the cameras to announce his support for Netanyahu. "There is no coalition and no opposition," he declared.

Indeed, by the end of the debate, the audience had grown bored. Attendees started asking questions about gay marriage, the cost of living, the status of asylum-seekers from Africa—anything but security. The issue was raised only rarely during the final month of the campaign. In February, the heads of eight major political parties agreed to a two-and-a-half-hour televised debate on Channel 2. Netanyahu refused to participate, which compelled Herzog to withdraw, and the leader of the ultra-Orthodox United Torah Judaism also stayed away, presumably because his religious supporters are not meant to watch television. Still, the debate covered the full spectrum from right to left. And the word "peace" was mentioned exactly five times—three of them by Ayman Odeh, the leader of the Joint List, a coalition of parties representing Palestinian citizens of Israel.

"In this election, in this campaign, I think it's the first time that the word peace doesn't exist, in any party's slogan. No one talks about peace," said Ayelet Shaked, a prominent member of the right-wing Jewish Home party. "And I think that, in reality, most of the public acknowledges that we cannot make peace, even in the far future."

Fatigue

Sderot translates as "boulevards", but the city of 24,000 in southern Israel is better known for the bomb shelters that line the boulevards. It becomes a focal point for the media every few years when Israel goes to war against Hamas. The city sits just a few kilometers from the border with Gaza. More than 8,000 rockets have landed there over the past decade, according to the mayor.

In peacetime it is just another working-class locale on what Israelis call the periphery, the underdeveloped regions away from Jerusalem and the coastal plain. More than half of Sderot's residents live below the poverty line; salaries are well below the national average.

It is also a Likud stronghold. Among Sderot voters, 37 per cent opted for Likud in 2013, compared to 23 per cent nationwide. Like many towns in the Negev, it was built to absorb the waves of new immigrants—first *mizrahim*, Jews of Arab descent, and then Russians in the 1990s—who would go on to form Likud's base. They faced endemic discrimination from the country's Labor-dominated elite, but Likud, under the savvy leadership of Menachem Begin, gave them a political home.

Oddly, given Netanyahu's mid-30s approval rating, Likud presented the prime minister as almost the sole face of its campaign. He usually appeared alone on advertisements, alongside the slogan "only Likud, only Netanyahu." It was an attitude that seemed destined to hurt the party. On a visit to Sderot five days before the election, many lifelong Likudniks told me they planned to vote for Kulanu, led by a popular ex-Likud minister, Moshe Kahlon, or simply not vote at all. "I've always voted for Likud. My parents voted for Likud," said one man. "But he hasn't done anything for us. Six years, and it's all words. He says he's a strong leader, but he's just verbally strong."

A week before the election, Netanyahu toured Mahane Yehuda, a teeming market in Jerusalem that traditionally votes Likud. Visits to the *shuk* are a rite of passage in Israeli politics, akin to eating corn dogs at the Iowa state fair. But Netanyahu didn't take the media along. He cited security concerns. There were none. The real worry was political; vendors in the *shuk* said they were also leaning towards Kulanu. Netanyahu had to cancel a rally in Ashdod, another Likud stronghold, when party activists could not find enough bodies to fill the event hall.

For all the fatigue and confusion, however, right-wing voters were clear about one thing: they were not crossing the divide to back the Zionist Camp. The party plateaued in most surveys at around twenty-four seats, just one-fifth of the Knesset. Herzog cut a bland and professorial figure, despite hiring a coach to work on his reedy voice. The

Ha'aretz columnist Ari Shavit wrote a fawning profile that—even so—described him as a "bar mitzvah boy". His running mate, former justice minister Tzipi Livni, is one of Israel's least popular politicians. Many judge her as a self-interested carpetbagger, and by 2015 she was on her fourth political home. Even the unpopular President Obama had a higher favorable rating among Israelis than she did.

With eleven parties poised to enter the next Knesset, the campaign became intensely personal. At one point or another, it seems, every party leader attacked the other ten. Candidates accused each other of racism, corruption, terrorism. The average voter was often hard-pressed to explain why, exactly, they supported a particular party, beyond the individual appeal of its leader. "I've covered eight elections in Israel, and this is by far the weirdest one," said Dana Weiss, a presenter on Israel's Channel 2. "Nobody has any idea what this is about."

The confusion had helped to resurrect a number of politicians who had been left for dead. Yair Lapid, the dark horse of the 2013 election, had been performing poorly at the start of the campaign after two largely unproductive years as finance minister. In the final weeks of the campaign, however, he received a surge in support, even though he did not have any concrete policies.

Outside the Zionist Camp headquarters in Sderot there was a large poster of Amir Peretz, the former defense minister. He is deeply unpopular in Israel, seen as the man responsible for the disastrous strategy in the 2006 Lebanon war. He once managed to be photographed reviewing troops on the Golan Heights through a pair of binoculars with their lens caps on. But the Moroccan-born Peretz grew up in Sderot, and the party figured a personal appeal couldn't hurt. "We're hoping people will vote for us because of Amir," admitted Melania Shkolnik, a campaigner.

Several parties were still struggling just to survive. Foreign Minister Avigdor Lieberman, once a kingmaker—"the real Frank Underwood of Israel politics", one strategist quipped in reference to *House of Cards*—imploded amid a massive corruption scandal. Members of his Yisrael Beiteinu party resigned, or were hauled off by police. His frantic search for new candidates went as far as scooping up a 24-year-old student union president who had once posted on Facebook about "smelly Arabs."

The ultra-Orthodox Shas, which caters to religious *mizrahi* Jews, faced its own crisis. Two men, Aryeh Deri and Eli Yishai, have long battled to lead the party. Yishai took over for a spell after his rival was convicted on corruption charges, but Deri regained control in 2012.

In December of 2014, shortly after the Knesset was dissolved, Yishai decided he'd had enough. He broke away from Shas to form a new party, Yachad, and announced a merger with Jewish Power, a far-right faction that counts among its candidates a onetime member of Kach, the banned Jewish terrorist organization. In a surreal moment, Israeli politics were roiled by a leaked video of Rabbi Ovadia Yosef, the vaunted spiritual leader of Shas. In an attack on Deri, in which he argued that he should not lead the party, he said, "He was judged in court. Why take someone who's a thief? Why take someone who accepts bribes?"

Rabbis set the agenda for ultra-Orthodox parties, but they rarely do so from beyond the grave. Yosef died in 2013. No one took credit for the leak, but it was believed to have come from Yishai. Deri briefly stepped down, a political stunt that ended when the Shas "council of sages" begged him to return. The party rebounded in the polls after that, focusing its outreach on what it called "the transparent" working-class Israelis who felt ignored in the socioeconomic debate. There was no small irony in this, since Deri is a convicted felon worth about a million dollars.

"People are confused with their options," Tal Schneider, an Israeli political analyst, predicted before the vote. "Voter turnout is going to be lower than usual because of the general sentiment of disgust." (It would actually be the highest since 1999, but much of the enthusiasm materialized at the last minute, a dynamic that would serve Netanyahu well.)

"They marginalize our vote"

The sun was setting over Yarka, a Druze village in the northern Galilee, and hundreds of people—local politicians, religious leaders, ordinary residents—were thronged outside a wedding hall to welcome a man most hadn't even heard of before January.

He was the one fresh face in the 2015 election, Ayman Odeh, a 41-year-old lawyer and activist from Haifa. He had previously been a city councilman and a low-ranking candidate with Hadash, the joint Jewish-Arab communist party. Suddenly, though, he had been catapulted onto the national stage. He had been chosen to head the Joint List, a coalition of the four parties that traditionally represent Israel's Palestinian minority, which makes up one-fifth of the population.

On the Friday before the election, he was criss-crossing the Galilee. His campaign managers, in an endearing bit of naïveté, scheduled four rallies in four hours. (The Yarka event alone ran for almost three.)

The List was born out of necessity. In 2014 the Knesset passed a "governance bill", promoted heavily by Lieberman, that raised the electoral threshold from 2 per cent to 3.25 per cent. The Arab parties rarely cleared that line; some, if not all, would have been forced out of government. (In a profound bit of irony, Lieberman himself spent several weeks polling near the higher threshold, though he eventually won 5 per cent of the vote.)

So they joined forces—an unwieldy marriage, as Odeh and other parliamentarians freely admitted. The list's candidates covered the spectrum from communists to Islamists; it included a women's rights activist, and a practicing polygamist. Some of them had not spoken in years owing to longtime rivalries. Still, the Joint List injected a degree of enthusiasm into Israel's Palestinian politics. Voting has always been a fraught issue in the Arab sector: activists call for a boycott ahead of every election, arguing that their participation lends implicit approval to Zionism. About 55 per cent of the community voted during the 2013 election, well below the nationwide figure of 68 per cent.

In the run-up to the election, party strategists predicted turnout would hit 60 per cent. They underestimated: 63.5 per cent of Palestinian citizens of Israel voted in 2015. Odeh's campaign events in the north were consistently packed, many with a sizable number of first-time voters. Tamer Nafar, one of the founders of the popular Palestinian rap group DAM, released a song shortly before the election announcing that he would vote for the first time. "Across the Arab world, sectarianism is raging, so we, the Muslims, and the Christians, and the Druze, we're joining hands in one home," he sang.

"The Israeli establishment has tried to negate us, to divide us. They split us between Arab and Druze, and they marginalize our vote," said Hana Sweid, a longtime parliamentarian from Hadash. "This is the last time."

In a strange way, Odeh ended up owing some of his popularity to Lieberman. Palestinians often cited the foreign minister's overt racism as a reason for voting. His campaign slogan, "Ariel to Israel, Umm al-Fahm to Palestine," was a blunt call for ethnic cleansing, "swapping" the Arab city into a future Palestinian state, in exchange for a Jewish settlement in the West Bank. He once proposed beheading "disloyal" Arab citizens with axes. Perhaps the ugliest moment, though, was a single word he muttered during the televised February debate. He launched a personal attack on Odeh, calling him a terrorist and asking why he wasn't debating from "a studio in Gaza." Odeh responded calmly, pointing out that Arabs make up one-fifth of the population. *Baintayyam*, Lieberman responded: "For now."

Netanyahu had spoken out in the past against anti-Arab racism. However, he embraced it during the campaign, chastizing Palestinians who "shout against Israel and demonstrate against it, [that] you are welcome to move to the Palestinian Authority or to Gaza." He warned repeatedly that the Zionist Camp was looking to form a government with "the Arabs".

"In the last three months, he's been worse than Lieberman," Ahmad Tibi, the head of the secular Ta'al party, told me at a rally in Jaffa on the eve of the vote. "We're talking about a prime minister here. It's hard to believe. For the first time, a prime minister is telling his citizens to leave the state."

In this fraught climate, Odeh was managing to appeal to Jews as well, saying he hoped to win at least one seat's worth of votes from them. He cultivated a mild-mannered, friendly image, and avoided controversial issues. Asked about Hamas, for example, he stressed the need for Palestinian unity, asking why, "Sixty-six years after the *nakba*, we're still divided between Hamas and Fatah." He also chose to focus on the economy, an issue that resonates with everyone, and about equality, often citing Martin Luther King Jr in speeches (a photo of King would later hang in his Knesset office). He released a kitschy but well-received campaign video that showed him winning over voters at a Shabbat lunch in Tel Aviv. When Amos Biderman, the *Ha'aretz* cartoonist, drew a caricature of the candidates dressed in costume for Purim—the Israeli equivalent of Halloween—Odeh was Mickey Mouse.

Many Jewish Israelis, perhaps a bit patronizingly, described him as likable, surprising, "the guy next door." They contrasted him with outspoken Arab parliamentarians like Tibi and Hanin Zoabi, the latter of whom was suspended from the Knesset in 2014 because she refused to describe the kidnapping and murder of three Jewish teenagers in the West Bank as "terrorism". Judy Shalom Nir-Mozes, the wife of a Likud minister, fretted that Odeh was "a very dangerous person in my eyes, because he conveys a message to which you can connect as an Israeli."

Historically, Arab parties have refused to sit in the government, arguing that they cannot join a Zionist cabinet, cannot be responsible for settlement construction or another war in Gaza. "Every Israeli government, from Buji (the nickname for Herzog) to Bibi, they're all the same thing," said Abdullah Abu Ma'arouf, a Joint List candidate. The most they would do, Odeh and others said, would be to provide backing from outside the government. There was historical precedent for this. After then-Prime Minister Yitzhak Rabin had signed the Oslo Accords in 1993, support from the Arab parties allowed him to survive a no-confidence motion.

If Netanyahu and Herzog had been forced to form a unity government, Odeh could have become Israel's first Palestinian opposition leader. He downplayed that, too. "We shouldn't be talking about Arab or Jewish," he said. "We should be talking about citizens."

What is Zionism?

One night in early January, with the snow still melting from the year's first winter storm, voters schlepped into a religious seminary in Jerusalem to hear a succession of right-wing candidates warn that the Supreme Court and the US State Department were conspiring to destroy Israel.

The leaders of most political parties in Israel choose their candidates by fiat. Jewish Home is one of the few that holds primaries. The party's leader, Naftali Bennett, seems in many ways like an Israeli dispatched straight from central casting: an officer in the elite Sayeret Matkal commando unit, then a millionaire high-tech entrepreneur, and finally a charismatic politician who speaks fluent English. He took over the creaky half-century-old National Religious Party in late 2012 and, within one election cycle, raised it from three seats to twelve.

It was still widely seen, however, as a far-right faction for religious settlers. Bennett wanted to change that. He had an eye on the prime minister's office, and to get there he needed to transform Jewish Home into a broader right-wing party. So he recruited a handful of secular candidates, most notably Eli Ohana, a popular football star whose support for the 2005 Gaza disengagement was anathema to the party faithful. Activists joked that Bennett had stuffed the rabbis and settlers in the closet until after the primary. Instead he released photos from a paintballing trip with two secular candidates from Tel Aviv.

It was an ambitious ploy, and a well-timed one, with so many disenchanted Likudniks. But the thing about democracy, as Bennett once said, is that it lets the people decide—and his people were still on the far right. At the primary event in Jerusalem, one prospective candidate promised to gut Israel's high court, saying that the liberal justices "make it very difficult to strengthen the Jewish identity of the state… they always come and cancel the laws." Another questioned Lieberman's right-wing credentials, and vowed to "Judaize" occupied East Jerusalem, "putting more and more Jews in and breaking up the continuity that the Arabs have." A third, a longtime settler activist, talked about his efforts to buy up land in the West Bank and sell it to Jews. Someone in the audience asked if he had "any connections to Christians." He said no. The crowd applauded.

Little surprise, then, that Bennett's plan backfired. Ohana dropped out of the race within days, and only two secular candidates were elected to realistic spots. "It was the biggest gaffe anyone has made in Israeli politics in a long time," Bennett admitted.

Less embarrassing, but more telling, was the case of Dani Dayan, a man sometimes described as the "settler foreign minister." He traveled often to Europe and the United States to lobby on their behalf, and was well received by diplomats; he lives in Ma'ale Shomron, a settlement in the northern West Bank, and is a vocal opponent of the two-state solution. Bennett personally recruited him to run with the party.

But these right-wing credentials were not enough for the Jewish Home faithful, because Dayan is also secular. He once refused to tell an interviewer whether he believes in God. He grew tired of questions about his faith, or whether he observes Shabbat, and left the party after a poor showing in the primaries. "I understood quite early that I don't suit them, they don't suit me," he said later over coffee at a Jerusalem hotel. (The Argentine-born Dayan would soon be appointed ambassador to Brazil, only to have his nomination blocked when Brasilia refused to accredit a settler as Israel's chief envoy; Netanyahu eventually tapped him to be the consul-general in New York.)

The national-religious, as mentioned earlier, comprise nearly one-fourth of the Jewish population, much higher than previously thought, and they are gradually gaining prominent roles in politics, the army, and other institutions. But the community holds a number of views that are well outside the consensus, which puts a ceiling on the popularity of a party like the Jewish Home. Gay rights, for example, are something of a settled issue in Israeli society. Bennett faced almost universal criticism for his party's stance—though he himself supports equal benefits for same-sex couples (but not formal marriage), one of his candidates proclaimed himself "a proud homophobe." Dozens of gay soldiers responded by posting photos of themselves with their partners on Bennett's Facebook page. "You cannot be a nationwide leader in Israel in 2015 and be perceived as homophobic," said Dayan, who is a vocal supporter of gay rights.

The bar mitzvah

A small crowd of party activists, many barely out of their teens, clustered around the stage, dancing awkwardly to the pumping music. A boyish, smiling Herzog and a stern Livni stared down from the Jumbotron, superimposed on a fluttering Israeli flag. Bored and exhausted journalists mobbed the concession stand for $5 hot dogs, waiting for the guests of honor to arrive.

The Zionist Camp's election-night party, at a mostly empty sports arena in Tel Aviv, felt more like a low-rent bar mitzvah than the coronation of a new prime minister.

There were hints, throughout the day, that the coronation might not even take place. Down in the south, in the Likud strongholds, voters were holding their noses and casting ballots for Netanyahu. You could spot them immediately: they admitted to doing the deed, then rushed away when asked why, seemingly embarrassed by their actions. Outside a polling station in Ashdod, the pavement littered with mock ballots for

Likud, Natan Ben Dror lit a cigarette and pondered what he'd done. "I don't know why I did it, really," he admitted. "I guess because I'm a Likudnik," the Hebrew word for a Likud supporter.

It was the same in Sderot, despite the skepticism I had encountered on a trip to the city just a few days earlier. None of their explanations were enthusiastic. *"He's a strong man." "I always vote Likud." "Who else would I vote for?"* But they did it, nonetheless. Some pointed to their phones, to the text messages warning them about the "droves", the mythical high Arab turnout. "We need a right-wing government, or Buji (Herzog) is going to let the Arabs run wild in the Knesset," said Dvir Amar, a student.

"This part of the country, it's a right-wing place," said Moshe Solomon, an Ethiopian Jew working as a security guard outside a Sderot polling station. "The people don't like him. But they'll do it anyway." Some of them, at least. Solomon, another Likudnik, hadn't made up his mind about whether to vote yet. "Maybe after work," he laughed.

Even in the settlements, where voters lean further to the right, it seemed many were acceding to Netanyahu's request that they "come home" to Likud.

There was equally no last-minute surge toward Herzog. Polling places in Tel Aviv and the kibbutzim, the bastions of the Israeli left, were busy, but voters were split, between Herzog, Lapid, and the liberal Meretz party. A handful gave their votes to the Joint List—though the party won only a few thousand Jewish votes, far short of the 35,000, one seat's worth, that it had hoped to win.

So the mood at the Zionist Camp's party was oddly subdued. It turned grim around 9.30 pm, half an hour before the polls closed, when exit polls from Israel's three main television networks began to leak out. Producers from Army Radio whispered about a survey that showed Likud in a dead heat with the Zionist Camp. Outside the arena, an ashen-faced staffer pulled aside one of the party's top parliamentarians. "We didn't pull it off," she said, downcast.

There was a brief cheer inside the arena when the official exit polls were broadcast at 10 pm. None were good. Two showed a tie, the third a one-seat advantage for Likud. All showed the Zionist Camp with twenty-seven seats, the party's best showing in sixteen years, but without a clear path to coalition. It was hard to mask the sense of disappointment. The best that Herzog could hope for was an unwieldy unity government, rotating the premiership with a resurrected Netanyahu.

When Herzog finally appeared to speak, well after midnight, he told the crowd to leave. "You can all go home now and get some sleep," he told his supporters, who dutifully complied. "There won't be any decisions made tonight."

"Simmering from within"

In 1996 Israel had started a short-lived political experiment, allowing voters to elect a candidate directly for prime minister. The exit polls on election night had shown a victory for the Labor Party's Shimon Peres. But the polls had got it wrong. He had lost the election by less than 30,000 votes, giving Netanyahu his first term as premier. A phrase entered the political lexicon. "We went to bed with Peres, and woke up with Netanyahu."

Nineteen years later, we went to bed with Netanyahu, but a chastened Netanyahu, one who might have to share power. We woke up to a triumphant Netanyahu: with 99 per cent of the ballots counted, he suddenly had thirty seats, compared to the Zionist Camp's twenty-four. The exit polls had missed a last-minute surge in Likud votes, which gave him the closest thing to a commanding victory that is possible in Israel's fractious political system. Herzog himself was taken aback. He learned about the shift in a grim early-morning phone call from Livni, and soon called Netanyahu from his north Tel Aviv home to concede defeat.

Nearly a year after the election, Amit Segal produced a telling report for Channel 2, based on interviews with Netanyahu's campaign managers. It opened with footage from a Likud focus group, where the party faithful admitted they were exhausted with the prime minister. "How many times can you vote for Bibi?" asked one young woman. "He's worn out. He should take a sabbatical," said another. But then the consultants asked their subjects to imagine Election Day. "You're lying under the blanket, the weather is terrible, you don't feel like going out to vote—but the race is close, and a left-wing government is possible. Who would you vote for?" Everyone sitting around the table gave the same answer. "Likud."

The campaign knew it couldn't win on the issues, so it didn't even try. Instead it focused on identity. It relentlessly portrayed Herzog and Livni (both bland centrists) as "the left," and reminded supporters that the Labor party had a long history of insulting *mizrahim*. It played off the excitement over the Joint List, with anonymous text messages that falsely claimed Herzog had promised to appoint an Arab minister. (I showed one to Tibi, who laughed: "Tell them I have no plans to become defense minister.")

And then it broadcast a sense of panic: come home to Likud, voters were warned, or right-wing rule will end, a message drummed home (again, via a text-message salvo) even as late as the afternoon of the vote. The strategy worked to perfection. Nearly 600,000 voters, fully 14 per cent of total turnout, came to the polls in the final two hours, compared to just 6 per cent in the previous election.

So, after a grueling three-month campaign, almost nothing had changed. Netanyahu would remain in office. The balance of power within the Knesset barely shifted. The "battle for Israel's soul" ended, like so many of Israel's recent battles, with an inconclusive ceasefire.

For all the events, the media appearances and get-out-the-vote campaigns, Herzog's strategy had ultimately been a simple one: he had tried to be the antithesis of Benjamin Netanyahu. Some of that was genetic. His demeanor was quiet and reserved, his voice nasal. After some coaching he tried to perk up his delivery, striding around the stage and punctuating his words with chopping gestures, but his style could still best be described as on the soporific side. He had barely mentioned Iran. There had been no talk of existential threats or the Holocaust, no rhetorical bombast. He had talked about gay marriage, solar energy and making it easier to get a mortgage.

The Palestinians had been courted, albeit skeptically. "I do not know what kind of mood I will be faced with from the Palestinian leadership, because they have fallen in love with unilateralism, but I believe Livni and I are the only ones who can rally the international community behind us," he had told prospective voters in Tel Aviv. He had even offered an olive branch to the Jewish diaspora, which had found supporting Israel increasingly troublesome in recent years. "The impact on the Jewish community is not discussed enough in the corridors and halls of power in Israel. I think it should be taken into account," he had promised.

He had also spent much of the campaign trying to reclaim "Zionism" from the right—rejecting their exceptionalist, messianic view, and portraying Israel as a sort of Switzerland on the Mediterranean. The problem for Herzog, of course, is that it is not. It is a country with no fixed borders; it has nonexistent relations with many of its neighbors, and a seemingly permanent domination over another people. It is slowly becoming a pariah in the West. The "peace camp" is a shell of its former self; poll after poll shows that younger Israelis hold more hawkish and nationalist views than their parents. Herzog lost, but even if he had won, it seems doubtful that he could have addressed these issues. "The fear is that he will dilute his views, blur his views, to act like a prime minister for all Israelis, and this will lead to a further deterioration in the legitimacy of the political system," Hermann said before the vote. "People will feel betrayed, especially those who crossed the lines."

Almost everyone agreed that tossing out King Bibi would have been a breath of fresh air. Two days before the election, atop a Vietnamese restaurant on Rothschild Boulevard, the offices of V15 were buzzing. It was a grassroots organization, born in December of 2014 with a single Facebook post, that went on to recruit tens of thousands of volunteers to mount the largest get-out-the-vote operation in Israeli history. Campaigners had knocked on more than 150,000 doors before the vote, urging voters to change the government, and returned to each one on election day.

"He's done nothing on the economy, he ignores the Palestinians, he tells us there's no solution to Gaza, that we just have to accept another war every two years," said Nimrod Dweck—one of the co-founders—of Netanyahu. "He's had nine years. It's enough. If you have no ideas, it's time to step aside."

Herzog did have economic ideas, which called for billions of dollars of additional spending and an expanded role for government. On the deeper issues, though, he spoke only in generalities, largely ignoring the Palestinians, offering no plan for Gaza. He seemed like a vestige of an older Israel, when the political consensus was both more settled and more liberal. Had he won, he would have taken over a country that has moved sharply to the right, and one that fractured during Netanyahu's tenure. He would have ushered in a rhetorical change, a sense of normalcy—but little more.

"All parts of our society are simmering from within," he said at one campaign event during his closing argument. "My role as a leader is to unite everybody... if I'm strong enough, I'll be able to lower everyone's prices, and move toward a coalition that will move Israel in the right direction. And that's all I can say."

The tribes of Israel

The outcome was seen in the West as further evidence of Israel's drift to the right. "We've also seen reports from Israel describing it as the most right-wing coalition in Israel's history," said Mark Toner, the State Department spokesman, at a press briefing in late May, after Netanyahu cobbled together his coalition. "And we also know that many of its ministers have said they opposed a two-state solution. This raises legitimate questions about the direction it may be headed in."

Over the seven-decade sweep of Israel's political history, it is fair to say the country as a whole has become more conservative. The first half of that history was dominated entirely by the center-left predecessors of the Labor party. Likud didn't win its first election until 1977. Since then, however, the left has struggled to regain power: right-wing prime ministers have ruled for twenty-nine of the past forty years.

Yet by the same count, those electoral results also suggest that the right-wing camp has hit a ceiling. In 1981, the right/religious bloc won 64 seats; the Zionist left/center-left won 52; and Hadash, a Jewish-Palestinian Communist party, won 4. Fast forward to 2015: voters gave 67 seats to the right/religious bloc; 40 to the left/center-left; and 13 to the Palestinians. The left ceded a lot of ground—but largely to the Arab parties, which came into existence in the 1990s. So the size of the right/religious bloc has remained fairly constant for a generation.

The real shift is found within the blocs. In 1981, the two largest parties—Likud and Alignment, a forerunner of Labor—won 95 seats, nearly four-fifths of the Knesset. No other party won more than 5 per cent of the vote. In the last election, though, Labor and the Zionist Union won just 54 seats. If they had agreed to form a unity government, they wouldn't have had a majority. Seven other parties cleared the five per cent mark.

Even more significantly, within the conservative camp, the political spectrum has shifted to the right. The 2015 coalition was the first in decades not to include a single centrist or center-left party, even a small one as a fig leaf. The members of the coalition, particularly from the Likud, were more conservative than in previous years. When journalists from Walla polled the cabinet, just four ministers were willing to publicly endorse the two-state solution, the official policy of the Israeli government (and the Palestinians, and much of the international community). Outsiders often view Netanyahu as a right-wing ideologue; he's actually one of the more liberal members of his own government.

The Israeli electorate, in other words, isn't moving right so much as moving apart. This phenomenon is not unique to Israel: political polarization in the United States, for example, is at its highest level since World War II, a rift caused mostly by the Republican party's hard-right turn. But it is particularly stark here. The "effective number of parties" in the Knesset, a metric based on the number of parties and their shares of the vote, has increased from 3.13 in 1981 to 6.94 today. Compared to European parliaments, only Belgium has a more fractious political system.[1] Not coincidentally, Belgium broke a world record in 2011 for going the longest time without a government.

This is a symptom of the wider polarization in Israeli society, and the growth of narrow tribal identities. Aside from Labor and Likud, each of the parties in the Knesset appeals to a closely-targeted segment of the Israeli electorate: Jewish Home to settlers; Yisrael Beiteinu to Russian emigres; Meretz to leftists in Tel Aviv. Yesh Atid had a lock on the socioeconomic vote in 2013, but two years later it had to compete with Kulanu, which ran on a similar message, albeit calibrated to a narrower audience. "By the second year of a Knesset, the different parties are already beginning to think about how to position themselves," said Yohanan Plesner, the president of the Israel Democracy Institute. "Because of the unstable nature of our coalition politics, the level of fragmentation, these processes have started earlier and earlier."

This was President Rivlin's theme when he took the stage at the annual Herzliya conference in June, two-and-a-half months after the vote. The previous gathering had featured the spat between Lapid and Bennett, and was quickly overshadowed by a bloody summer. Rivlin would steal the stage in 2015. "In the 1990s... Israeli society comprised a clear and firm majority, with minority groups alongside it," he began. "A large secular Zionist majority, and beside it three minority groups: a national-religious minority, an Arab minority, and a *haredi* minority. Although this pattern remains frozen in the minds of much of the Israeli public, in the press, in the political system, all the while, the reality has totally changed."

There were twelve tribes of Israel in antiquity. Today there are four, the groups Rivlin mentioned above. And none of them can claim a majority. He illustrated this point with two simple pie charts. In 1990, 52 per cent of elementary school students were enrolled in *mamlachti* schools—secular state-run institutions. The other 48 per cent was divided between state-run religious (16 per cent) *haredi* (9 per cent and Arab (23 per cent) schools. By 2018, he projected, just 38 per cent of pupils would be studying in the *mamlachti* schools. Ultra-Orthodox enrollment would jump to 22 per cent, while Arab schools would experience slight growth to 25 per cent. The religious schools would remain nearly flat, at 15 per cent.

Israeli society has many other divides, of course. Jews are split between Ashkenazi, Mizrahi, Ethiopian, Russian; Arabs, between Muslim, Christian and Druze. Everyone is divided along political and socioeconomic lines. But these four "tribes" are separated by the deepest chasms. Their children attend different schools. They consume different media. Only two of the four groups regularly serve in the army. "In the past, the IDF served as a central tool for fashioning the Israeli character," Rivlin said. "However, in the emerging Israeli order, more than half of the population does not serve in the military." To a large extent, they are even divided by geography, with the ultra-Orthodox cloistered in homogeneous communities and "acceptance committees" in hundreds of towns and *kibbutzim*.

Academics and analysts had been making these points for years. Rivlin was the first Israeli politician to express them so clearly, and in such a high-profile forum. In hindsight, his speech was a warning, one that has gone largely unheeded by the rest of the government. From religion to education to culture, the disagreements would only grow worse over the next two years, amplified by an increasingly short-sighted and authoritarian prime minister.

"Israeli politics, to a great extent, is built as an inter-tribal zero sum game. One tribe, the Arabs, whether or not by its own choice, is not really a partner in the game," Rivlin said. "The other three, it seems, are absorbed by a struggle for survival, a struggle over budgets and resources for education, housing, or infrastructure, each on behalf of their own sector."

5

THE DIVIDE

"America is something that can be easily moved."

Benjamin Netanyahu

In the basement of Jerusalem's posh Inbal Hotel, hundreds of American rabbis were gathered. They had flown in for the annual gathering of the Central Conference of American Rabbis (CCAR), the umbrella organization for Reform Jewry in the United States and Canada, the largest community in North America, with some 1.5 million members. Its rabbis hold their conference in Jerusalem once every seven years.

Their 2016 visit, in many ways, had a celebratory feel. Three weeks earlier, the Israeli cabinet had decided to create an egalitarian prayer space at the Western Wall, the holiest site where Jews are allowed to worship. It was seen as a hard-fought victory for activists who had worked for decades to challenge the gender segregation enforced by the ultra-Orthodox rabbinate. They had been further heartened by a 11 February High Court decision that required public *mikvot*, or ritual baths, to open their doors for non-Orthodox converts. "It's an incredibly significant moment for our community," said Steven Fox, a Los Angeles native who serves as CCAR's chief executive.

But it wasn't all a victory lap. Midway through the first day of the conference, a staff member took to the podium with the warning that the rabbis should prepare themselves for some heckling in the Knesset later in the week. They were due to address a session of the parliament's immigration committee, which also handles relations with the Jewish diaspora. A few days earlier, however, a *haredi* lawmaker had described the Reform community as "mentally ill". David Yosef, a member of the ultra-Orthodox Shas party's Council of Sages, called them "literally idolators". The rabbis were told to expect a warm welcome from the committee leadership—but insults from some of the other Knesset members.

Around the same time, the Israeli government held a secret conference in Jerusalem to discuss the boycott movement.[1] One of the attendees was Frank Luntz, the American political operative who helped develop Newt Gingrich's "Contract with America". Luntz is a wordsmith, a consultant who tests individual phrases on hundreds of focus groups, searching for language that provokes the right emotional response from voters. Thus oil drilling (negative, dirty) became "energy exploration" (positive, evokes a frontier spirit); the estate tax became the "death tax". In a 2007 interview with NPR he even redefined the word "Orwellian": it was a positive concept, he explained, "to speak with absolute clarity, to be succinct", an interpretation that surely sent the author spinning in his grave.[2]

While he does not work for the Israeli government, Luntz has often used his focus groups to test pro-Israel messaging, usually with the goal of selling the Western world on right-wing Israeli policies. He drafted a handbook in 2009 that explained, among other things, how to justify the steady expansion of settlements in the occupied territories. *Newsweek* summarized his findings: "Be positive. Turn the issue away from settlements and toward peace. Invoke ethnic cleansing."[3] (Netanyahu sometimes seems to follow his advice, not least in a much-maligned 2016 YouTube video that cast the Palestinian refusal to accept settlers in their future state as a sort of modern-day *Judenrein*.)

In recent years, though, his focus groups have demonstrated a steady decline in American support for Israel. Luntz sounded an alarm bell in 2015 after he surveyed "opinion elites"—highly-educated, high-earning, politically active members of the establishment. Three-quarters of the Democrats thought Israel had too much influence over US foreign policy. From the same sample, 47 per cent described it as a racist country. An overwhelming majority thought settlements were an "impediment to peace", despite his rebranding efforts. "Israel can no longer claim to have the bipartisan support of America," Luntz said.[4]

The attendees at the closed Jerusalem conference heard a similar warning. Luntz had done a survey of Jewish students in the US, asking if they believed that Israel wanted peace, and if they viewed it as a "civilized and Western country". Most did not. Perhaps most striking, only 31 per cent agreed that Israel was a true democracy. "The ministry of tourism came out very bad in the data presented at the conference," an attendee told the news website NRG. "They sell Israel in this way, 'we have girls in bikinis, we have beaches, we have beer and bars; come to us.' And it doesn't work."

"Welcome to Israel's Vietnam"

In the winter of 1987 and 1988, as the first intifada erupted in Israel and the occupied territories, Albert Vorspan wrote a series of notes in his diary. Vorspan was the senior vice president of the Union of American Hebrew Congregations (now the Union for Reform Judaism), and a committed Zionist. But he was deeply troubled by what he called the "harvest of rage" on his television screen each night, an eruption that revealed the "political and moral bankruptcy of Israeli policy." It also revealed something else to Vorspan: the extent to which support for Israel had become, in his words, a "surrogate faith" for American Jews.

> This is the downside of the euphoric mood after the Six-Day War, when we felt ten feet tall. Now, suffering under the shame and stress of pictures of Israeli brutality televised nightly, we want to crawl into a hole. This is the price we pay for having made of Israel an icon—a surrogate faith, surrogate synagogue, surrogate God. Israel could not withstand our romantic idealization.[5]

It is a myth that American Jews are a monolithic bloc when it comes to Israel, though they used to be. Before 1967, the community's attitude could be best characterized as indifferent. Only a few hundred people emigrated each year, and financial support for the newly-established state quickly dried up, dropping by more than half by the end of Israel's first decade. The 1967 war changed that. It brought a sense of pride over Israel's overwhelming victory—along with, ironically, a paralyzing fear over Israel's perceived vulnerability. J. J. Goldberg, the editor of *The Forward*, noted the paradox in his 1997 book *Jewish Power*. "The Six-Day War demonstrated that Israel was more secure than anyone had dreamed," he wrote. "What the American Jewish community learned from the war was the reverse: that Israel might be destroyed at any moment." Support for pro-Israel groups surged, and tens of thousands of American Jews voted with their feet; immigration to Israel from North America climbed from 826 people in 1968 to 8,122 three years later, a tenfold increase.

But the unanimity was short-lived. The Likud party came to power in 1977, and liberal American Jews quickly began to criticize its policy of expanding settlements in the occupied territories. Then came the first Lebanon war (particularly the Sabra and Shatila massacre) and the first intifada, shattering what Vorspan called the "romantic idealization" of Israel. "Now Israel reveals itself, a nation like all the others," he added in his diary. "Welcome to Israel's Vietnam, Kent State and Watts rolled into one. What did we expect? An eternity of Golda Meir and 'the woman of valor,' *kibbutzniks* dancing the *hora* around bonfires?" *Aliyah* rates fell, and eventually settled around 2,500 people per year, less than a tenth of a per cent of the population. The formal Jewish and pro-Israel community fragmented, with the rise of groups like J Street, the center-left alternative to AIPAC, and Jewish Voice for Peace, which supports a boycott of Israeli settlements.

As Dov Waxman wrote in *Trouble in the Tribe*, his 2016 survey of the relationship, "the consensus about Israel that prevailed within the American Jewish community in the 1960s and 1970s has long since disappeared."

Another myth—in essence a canard, repeated by both anti-Semites and some of Israel's strongest advocates—is that American Jews consider Israel a political issue of paramount importance. A 2016 survey by the American Jewish Committee found that just 10 per cent of American Jews chose foreign policy as the most important issue in the presidential election. Some 12 per cent ranked it as the second-most important. The economy, health care, and national security all received a larger share of the vote.

Still, we can make two sweeping generalizations about American Jewish attitudes toward Israel. The first is that, for all the talk of growing alienation, most American Jews still retain warm feelings for the Jewish state. A wide-ranging 2013 Pew poll found that 69 per cent of American Jews feel an emotional attachment to Israel. There is a notable generation gap—60 per cent of millennial Jews answered yes, compared to 79 per cent of senior citizens—but a majority from almost every Jewish demographic feels that connection.[6]

The survey also found, however, that 57 per cent of American Jews have never been to the country. Few of those who do visit can fully engage with the culture, since 83 per cent cannot hold a conversation in Hebrew. Which leads to the second conclusion: most American Jews are attached to an imaginary Israel.

The average American Jew, after all, is a secular liberal. They vote Democratic in larger numbers than almost any other demographic group; they overwhelmingly support liberal social causes and economic policies. And so they view Israel as an extension of their own community—the Upper West Side with better weather and inferior bagels, if you will. Needless to say, in a country where the right has held power for roughly three of the past four decades, this is a misreading of the political map. But the disconnect goes further. The community directs its activism toward issues which are, in a sense, parochial: of great concern to American Jews, but far less import to the people who actually live in Israel, who would prefer civil marriage to a mixed-gender prayer space. The peace process, a source of so much angst in New York and Washington, is not a pressing day-to-day concern to the majority of Israelis.

To take a concrete example, in September 2016, Pew conducted another survey, this time a twin poll of Israeli and American Jews. The pollsters asked both groups to identify the most important long-term problem facing Israel. Two-thirds of American Jews cited security and terrorism. Only 38 per cent of Israeli Jews agreed. They were more concerned about economic problems—which received just one per cent of the vote from American Jews.

Boycott, Divestment, Sanctions (BDS)

On a rainy winter morning, hundreds of people, including the president and four cabinet members, packed a Jerusalem conference center for an anti-BDS summit sponsored by *Yediot Aharonot*, the country's largest paid daily newspaper. This would be an odd scene in many countries, akin, say, to the *New York Times* hosting a summit to help the Bush administration combat international criticism of the Iraq war.

One by one, guests took the stage and described the Palestinian-led boycott as Israel's greatest threat. Gilad Erdan, the minister in charge of fighting BDS, warned that campaigners would be made to "pay a very high price," though he quickly clarified that he wasn't planning to assassinate anyone. Another minister called for the "targeted civil elimination" of boycott activists. Isaac Herzog, the opposition leader, predicted that the movement could soon "spiral into a catastrophic situation" for Israel. The somewhat inexplicable keynote speaker, comedian Roseanne Barr, explained that the movement was full of "rich, privileged feudalists promoting ethnic strife to divide the working class," in a speech that evoked no small measure of sympathy for whoever was doing the simultaneous translation.

The only discordant note came from Moshe Kahlon, the finance minister. "A threat is a threat," he said, noting that his office was prepared to help Israeli businesses hurt by boycotts. But he went on to explain that he hadn't received many phone calls. "I don't think there's something that you can specifically call a detrimental effect, or some kind of damage" to the economy, he said.

BDS activists are much better at self-promotion than they are at causing economic pain. A decade after the campaign started, it has had almost no discernible impact. Foreign investments in Israel hit a record high of $285 billion in 2015, a threefold increase since the BDS movement started. Exports to the European Union, its largest trading partner, were up more than 30 per cent during that period. Western embassies host never-ending delegations of business executives, eager to talk high-tech in Tel Aviv and agriculture in the Negev. And Israel's emerging allies in Asia and Africa literally laugh when asked about pressure from the BDS campaign. "We view it as a fad on your college campuses," one Asian diplomat in Tel Aviv told me.

The movement insists otherwise. It has a long list of "successes" on its website. Yet it can rarely prove that these victories resulted from political pressure and not ordinary market forces. One of the prime BDS targets is Alstom, a French conglomerate that helped to build the

Jerusalem light rail, which cuts through the occupied eastern half of the city. The campaign demanded that it withdraw from the project, and declared victory in 2011 when the firm lost its bid to develop a railway in Saudi Arabia, calling it a first step toward "kicking Alstom out of the Arab world". A year later, though, the kingdom awarded it more than $1 billion worth of contracts to develop power plants— hardly a sign of a boycott. In 2016, a seemingly not-at-all-chastened Alstom accepted a $395 million offer to extend the light rail into yet another settlement in East Jerusalem.

And yet Israel continues to treat BDS as an existential threat. Politicians (and *Yediot Aharonot*) have declared "war" on it. The government has allocated $26 million to fight the movement, a figure that some lawmakers would like to increase exponentially. When Erdan took office in 2015, he said he accepted the job with a sense of "holy dread." All of this for a campaign that, by one 2014 estimate, had caused about $30 million in damage, 0.01 per cent of Israel's annual GDP—roughly fifty-two minutes worth of economic activity.

"If I were them, I'd be very happy, because it gives me all the legitimacy," said Gideon Meir. "It tells me that the Israelis are afraid, that we created a big problem for them... we're helping them to become legitimate." Meir would know: he ran the foreign ministry's public affairs department before he retired from the civil service in 2014.

At a time of growing division in Israel, the anti-boycott campaign offers politicians a chance to wave the flag. The European Union opposes BDS, but it did decide in November 2015 to require labels on packaged food and cosmetics produced in Israeli settlements. Diplomats counseled a measured response, because it was a trivial move; none of the products were pulled off the shelves, and the consumers inclined to boycott already know the provenance of Psagot wines and Ahava exfoliators. David Simha, the head of the Israeli-Palestinian chamber of commerce, said the goods in question accounted for less than 0.01 per cent of Israel's $30 billion in annual exports to Europe.

The response from politicians was anything but measured. "The European Union should be ashamed," said Prime Minister Benjamin Netanyahu. The right-wing justice minister, Ayelet Shaked, threatened to sue the EU. Michael Oren, a former ambassador to Washington-turned-lawmaker, printed up a batch of "made in Europe" stickers and wandered through a supermarket slapping them on bags of Italian wafer cookies—with a photographer in tow, of course. "We want to show that we are doing a lot," Meir said. "So we're doing a terrible job, because we're treating BDS as a domestic political issue."

Bricks in the Wall

The Western Wall is under the supervision of Israel's ultra-Orthodox chief rabbinate, which believes in strict gender segregation. Thus most of it is reserved for men, with women crammed into a small space at the far end of the plaza, hidden behind a screen. For decades, there was no mixed-gender area. Female worshippers were forbidden to read from the Torah or wear *tallit*, the ritual prayer shawl.

A group called Women of the Wall started challenging this policy in 1988. Activists would gather each month to sing, read from the Torah, and otherwise offend ultra-Orthodox sensibilities. Most times they would be dragged away by police, arrested, occasionally even attacked. A 2013 poll found that a plurality of Israelis—and a narrow majority of Israeli men—supported their campaign, but successive Israeli governments, always fearful of offending the crucial *haredi* parties, made little effort to change policy.

Three years after that survey, though, Israel's most conservative and religious government in decades finally appeared to accede to their demands—in essence by meeting them half way. The wall's main plaza, the iconic 21,500-square-foot backdrop for national ceremonies and visits by foreign dignitaries, would remain segregated and under Orthodox control. But the cabinet established a new mixed-gender area that sits further south, amidst an archaeological site called Robinson's Arch. It is less than half the size of the Orthodox section, and only a narrow portion actually touches the wall, which is largely blocked by piles of millennia-old rubble. The decision was Solomonic. The response was Monty Python: A breakaway group called Original Women of the Wall rejected it, saying they would accept nothing less than full equality.

Still, the Reform rabbis viewed it as a major victory, as they did the high court's ruling on *mikvot*. All strains of Judaism, from Reform to Orthodox, require would-be converts to immerse themselves in a bath. Since the chief rabbinate only recognizes Orthodox conversions, however, the religious services ministry, which oversees the baths, forbade other denominations from using them. The ministry argued in court that non-Orthodox converts could be excluded since they were not legally Jewish. (The court's response was masterful: since no prospective converts are legally Jewish until they finish the process, judges ruled the policy was discriminatory.)

The religious right was furious. One politician, from United Torah Judaism, argued that the supreme court had "no authority to enforce Jewish law." And he singled out the Reform movement for particular criticism. "Not every mentally ill person can come to the operating room, and decide the rules of medicine, and force the hospital to have an operation by whatever way works," said the lawmaker, Israel Eichler. "And so it is intolerable that the directors of ritual baths will have to allow organizers of Reform religion-changing ceremonies into a Jewish ritual bath."[7]

The vitriol continued for weeks, long after the Reform rabbis packed their bags and returned to the United States. David Azoulay, the ultra-Orthodox religious services minister, refused to sign off on the Western Wall compromise, saying that Reform Jews "must not be given a foothold among the people of Israel." He described the issue in the starkest terms, calling it *yehareg v'al ya'avor*, a cardinal sin, which an observant Jew should die rather than commit. (The Talmud describes just three such sins: idolatry, murder, and sexual immorality.) Another ultra-Orthodox lawmaker, Health Minister Ya'akov Litzman, threatened to resign unless the government moved to "reduce the reformists". Channel 20, a right-wing television network launched in 2014 to offer programming about Jewish culture, described members of the Reform movement as the bootleg sneakers and fake Rolexes of the Jewish world.

"That's the disconnect for our young people," said Denise L. Eger, the president of CCAR. "They hear about Israel and they think science, hi-tech, life-saving medical advancements. And then they hear this other piece, and something doesn't add up for them."

One participant made this point to Netanyahu himself during a meeting with the Israeli prime minister. He briefed the rabbis on the regional situation, describing the threats that Israel faced from "medieval" groups like the Islamic State and Hamas. "And I told him, 'Mr Prime Minister, we have medieval Jews as well,'" the rabbi recalled. "He was silent for a moment. I think he was taken aback slightly."

Only slightly, though. Tellingly, the meeting with the Reform rabbis was conducted in near-secrecy. Netanyahu met during the same week with the prime minister of Bulgaria and the CEO of Microsoft. He released videos of both. But the prime minister didn't even issue a written statement about his meeting with the leaders of the largest Jewish community in the diaspora.

Netanyahu decided to postpone implementing the cabinet's decision, pending further discussion. He convened a group of non-Orthodox rabbis in June; they left disappointed, without any firm commitments from the prime minister. In September the issue went to the supreme court, which heard follow-up arguments to its January ruling. The justices berated the government for "dragging things out endlessly," and wondered if Netanyahu was hoping for a new decision that would force him to act. "Enough is enough," said Miriam Naor, the chief justice. "Do you expect us to pull your chestnuts out of the fire for you?"

As this book went to press, more than a year after the cabinet decision, the prayer area still hadn't been opened. During the High Holidays in 2016, a group of Orthodox Jews even erected a curtain in the mixed-gender area and started conducting segregated prayers there, creating their own "facts on the ground". Lawmakers also introduced a bill to impose criminal penalties on women who tried to read from the Torah at the Wall. Far from offering religious equality, the Knesset was contemplating whether to throw Reform Jews in jail.

Little Jew boy

A few weeks before the rabbis were warned about the Knesset, Dan Shapiro found himself on the receiving end of a different insult. The US ambassador was a popular figure in Israel, a fluent Hebrew speaker who appeared often on local television and radio. His role was often a ceremonial one: Secretary of State John Kerry and other senior officials handled the serious diplomacy, while Shapiro spent much of his time visiting schools and high-tech companies.

But he found himself staring across the intra-communal divide in early 2016 after he addressed the annual conference of the Institute for National Security Studies, a high-profile confab in Tel Aviv. His speech was mostly diplomatic boilerplate about Iran's nuclear program and the peace process, the sort of text an ambassador reads dozens of times each year, to no real reaction. Towards the end, though, Shapiro allowed himself a few critical paragraphs. He said the State Department was "concerned and perplexed by Israel's strategy on settlements" in the occupied West Bank. And he accused authorities of being too lax about the hundreds of anti-Palestinian attacks carried out by settlers each year. "Too many attacks on Palestinians lack a vigorous investigation or response by Israeli authorities; too much vigilantism goes unchecked; and at times there seem to be two standards of adherence to the rule of law: one for Israelis and another for Palestinians."[8]

On the one hand, this was a simple restatement of longstanding American policy. "There's really nothing new here in what he said," John Kirby, the State Department spokesman, said the following afternoon.[9] Yet it was also an unusually strong statement from Shapiro. The British ambassador, no stranger to American diplomatic pablum, later called his comments "unprecedented" for a US envoy in Tel Aviv.

So he was fiercely criticized by the Israeli right—particularly by one former aide to Prime Minister Netanyahu. "It was a statement typical of a *yehudon*", the ex-aide, Aviv Bushinsky, said in a debate on Channel 2. The word, a diminutive of the Hebrew for "Jew", could be variously translated as "little Jew boy", or as "kike". "It's the behavior of Jews who are trying to show that they are extra left-wing, more liberal and more balanced," Bushinsky added. Shapiro was the third US ambassador to earn the sobriquet, alongside Daniel Kurtzer and Martin Indyk, the latter of whom was once an executive at AIPAC. An Israeli diplomat described it as "the worst slur a Jew can use against another Jew."

Bushinsky had been out of politics for a decade. He was speaking as a media commentator, a private individual, not on behalf of the prime minister. His comments would not have merited a mention, were it not for the torrent of vitriol directed at President Obama a year later after he abstained from vetoing a symbolic Security Council resolution that reiterated long-standing criticism of Israeli settlements. Far from being an outlier, it proved that Bushinsky's remark was really a leading indicator.

Israelis, unsurprisingly, stereotype American Jews: the overly-exuberant kids with bad Hebrew stumbling off the Birthright buses; the pasty beachgoers cowering under umbrellas to avoid the Mediterranean sun. For a section of the Israeli right, though, there is also a genuine hostility toward the American Jewish community, at least when it comes to issues of war and peace. Over the past seventy years, the United States has given Israel close to a quarter-trillion dollars in military aid, constant diplomatic support, and the highest level of intelligence sharing and cooperation granted to a non-NATO state. Even so half of Israeli Jews, and 62 per cent of those who identify as right-wing, feel the US is insufficiently supportive of Israel.

This is, on the merits, an absurd argument. But it has nothing to do with the merits. The Israeli right resents the fact that the American government occasionally complains about its half-century occupation of the Palestinians, and it has become increasingly forthright about that resentment. "Nobody was standing there with a hammer forcing him to say it," Bushinsky added.

"Worse than kapos"

In August, an unusual press release popped up in my inbox. A big red headline blared, "for the first time, the Trump campaign goes into Israeli territory". He planned to open five campaign offices in Israel (two of them in settlements), something no candidate had done before.

Israel doesn't have any votes in the Electoral College, nor does it have a large population of American expats. Tzvika Brot, the director of the campaign team, estimated that 300,000 Israeli citizens were eligible to vote in the US election, though non-partisan surveys put the figure closer to 200,000. Either way, they were a tiny fraction of the 136 million Americans who voted. If Israel were a state, it would be smaller than Rhode Island. But the campaign believed they could play a useful role. A 2012 exit poll found that 10 per cent of American Israeli voters were registered in the key swing state of Florida, for example, where Trump ultimately won by less than 113,000 votes.

The American Jews living in Israel, unlike their counterparts back home, are a reliably Republican voting bloc. John McCain won just 21 per cent of the US Jewish vote in 2008, according to exit polls, and

Mitt Romney picked up only 30 per cent in 2012. Trump was polling worse than either of them. His brand of white nationalism and his flirtations with anti-Semites earned him few Jewish admirers.

In Israel, however, exit polls found that 85 per cent of 2012 voters opted for Romney, and just 14 per cent for President Obama. McCain won by a similarly lopsided margin. Trump's aides hoped that his embrace of Israel, and his pledge to tear up the nuclear accord with Iran, would add some votes to his column. The campaign offices were shambolic. They hung red-white-and-blue posters across the country, and offered some help on obtaining absentee ballots, but mostly they were a symbol, a low-cost way for Trump to affirm his pro-Israel bona fides.

In the end he only won 49 per cent of the Israeli vote, against 44 per cent for Hillary Clinton, according to exit polls. Turnout was also down sharply compared to the previous two elections. Still, for a historically unpopular candidate like Trump, it counted as a victory. His share of the Jewish vote was twice as large in Israel than in the United States.

During the campaign, he promised to be Israel's "best friend" in Washington, and gave regular interviews to *Israel HaYom*, the Sheldon Adelson-owned newspaper that serves as a mouthpiece for Netanyahu. His rhetoric created meteoric expectations on the Israeli right: one ultra-Orthodox lawmaker went as far as to say that his election heralded the coming of the Messiah. So did his earliest moves, particularly his choice of David Friedman as ambassador, a man who would probably agree with Bushinsky's criticism.

The new ambassador has no diplomatic experience. He worked as Trump's bankruptcy lawyer, and then served as a quasi-official Middle East adviser during the campaign. He supports Israeli settlements in the occupied territories, and not just rhetorically—he was the president of a foundation that donated millions of dollars to a yeshiva in Beit El, outside of Ramallah. In a private 2016 meeting with a group of settler leaders, he argued that Israel could annex the entire West Bank while retaining its Jewish identity.

President Obama, he said, was an anti-Semite. Huma Abedin, one of Hillary Clinton's top aides (and a Muslim), was a secret member of the Muslim Brotherhood. Perhaps the most jarring slur, though, was directed at American Jews who support a two-state solution, particularly the lobby group J Street. He compared them to *kapos*, the prisoners in Nazi concentration camps who were put in charge of other inmates. "They are far worse than *kapos*", he wrote in a commentary for *Arutz Sheva*, a right-wing Israeli website affiliated with the settler movement. "The *kapos* faced extraordinary cruelty and who knows what any of us would have done under those circumstances to save a loved one? But J Street? They are just smug advocates of Israel's destruction delivered from the comfort of their secure American sofas."

"A United States that no longer exists"

Donald Trump will be the president who breaks the pro-Israel lobby in the United States. It sounds absurd, of course. Aside from Friedman, his Israel advisers also include his son-in-law, Jared Kushner, whose family runs a foundation that funnels tens of thousands of dollars to West Bank settlements (including at least one extremist *yeshiva*). Steve Bannon, his top adviser, was invited to speak at a far-right Zionist Organization of America dinner just days after the election. The Israel lobby seems to be on good terms with the new administration. And it is—but only a part of it.

The Brookings Institution, one of the more staid think tanks in DC, hosts an event called the Saban Forum, a yearly affirmation of the US–Israel relationship. (It is named after Haim Saban, the Israeli-American billionaire and Power Rangers producer who is a top donor to the Democratic Party.) Each year, they present a survey on American attitudes toward the Israeli-Palestinian conflict. In 2014, the pollsters found that a surprising 38 per cent of Americans supported imposing economic sanctions on Israel over its illegal settlements. Two years later, the number jumped to 46 per cent. Within those figures was a striking partisan gap: Democratic support for sanctions jumped by a quarter, from 48 per cent to 60 per cent, while Republican support stayed flat: 32 per cent in 2014, and 31 per cent in 2016. Similarly, the number of Democrats who thought Israel had too much influence on US policy rose from 49 per cent in 2015 to 55 per cent the following year. The number of Republicans who felt that way actually dipped, from 25 per cent to 22 per cent.

"There's been a change in the Democratic party, and it goes beyond Obama, or this administration. They're demographic changes," said

Zalman Shoval, a former Israeli ambassador in Washington. "And we really should take this into account."

It's not hard to see why. Netanyahu went to war against Obama's signature foreign policy initiative, the Iran deal, and renounced the two-state solution. His government has done little to address the pet issues of many American Jews, like the Western Wall or Israel's refusal to accept many foreign conversions to Judaism. (In one of 2016's more extraordinary moments, a rabbinical court ruled that Ivanka Trump, the future president's daughter, was not really Jewish because her conversion was performed by an unapproved rabbi.) The Israeli ambassador in Washington, Ron Dermer, refuses to meet with groups to the left of AIPAC, like J Street. "Bibi is like that friend who only calls when he needs something," quipped one of the rabbis at the Jerusalem conference.

"Suddenly we were expecting the Jewish community to become Republicans," said Meir. "The government of Israel talks to Republicans. It almost doesn't have any dialogue with the Democratic party, and especially not with the liberal Jewish community."

A few weeks after the election, Dermer was feted the Israeli ambassador in Washington, Ron Dermer, was feted at the Center for Security Policy, a far-right "think tank." The group's founder, Frank Gaffney, is a conspiracy theorist who believes that Obama is part of a secret Muslim Brotherhood plot to infiltrate the US government, a scheme that also involves anti-tax activist Grover Norquist. The proof for this, he believes, can be found in the new logo for the Pentagon's missile defense agency, which features a vaguely crescent-shaped object. He has been denounced by the Anti-Defamation League for peddling "anti-Muslim bigotry."

Gaffney's views have a following in Trump Tower. Bannon hosted Gaffney on his radio show dozens of times, and there were reports that he was brought in to advise the transition (though Trump's team denied it). And Dermer praised him warmly, calling him a steadfast friend of Israel. "If you have enemies, Frank, it's because you have stood up for something, many times in your life," he said, echoing Churchill.

These sorts of comments gamble with Israel's decades of unquestioned diplomatic and military support from Washington. Israel often claims that "shared values" unite it with America; its top representative in Washington thoroughly undercuts that argument by embracing far-right racists. "American Jews having that automatic connection and attachment to Israel can no longer be an operating assumption," said Fox. "The generation that lived through the miracle of 1948, the generation that saw the 1967 war, there was no question about loyalty. But today we can no longer assume that connection is there."

The tension between liberalism and Zionism, always lingering below the surface, has become more pronounced. And the Israeli government's embrace of a president (and his controversial political coterie) loathed by the vast majority of American Jews will only widen the chasm. "He thinks that he knows the United States better than anybody else in this country," said Efraim Halevy, a former Mossad director who became a fierce Netanyahu critic. "What he doesn't know is that he knew a United States that no longer exists today."

6

DEMOCRACY

"If a problem has no solution, it may not be a problem, but a fact—not to be solved, but to be coped with over time."

Shimon Peres

It was not yet dawn on 31 July when 18-month-old Ali Dawabsheh was burned to death. His family had gone to visit relatives the night before, returning at around 1 am to their home in Douma, a Palestinian village outside of Nablus. They went to bed. Sometime later, a group of masked men smashed the windows and tossed Molotov cocktails inside. They had already torched one house, only to find it empty, so they moved on to the Dawabsheh residence.

Ali's parents Riham and Saad managed to escape the house, their clothes engulfed in flames; both would die from their wounds in the coming weeks. Only his brother Ahmed, four, survived the attack, with burns over nearly two-thirds of his body.

Before they fled, the arsonists took the time to spray-paint two short messages on the walls: the single word *nekamah*, "revenge", beneath a star of David; and the phrase *yechai hamelech hamashiach*, "long live the king, the Messiah," a slogan associated with a branch of the ultra-Orthodox Chabad movement. The attack, reminiscent of Mohammed Abu Khdair's murder a year earlier, was thought to be the work of Jewish militants, and it was widely condemned in Israel. "A nation whose children were burned in the Holocaust needs to do a lot of soul-searching if it bred people who burn other human beings," said Gilad Erdan, the public security minister. President Rivlin and Prime Minister Netanyahu both paid a visit to Ahmed in the hospital (though the latter was given a chilly reception).

Not everyone was convinced, though. On the far right, activists speculated that the arson was the result of a village feud, not the work of Jewish militants. The graffiti looked too stylized, they said, not like the rough cursive Hebrew hastily scrawled at the scene of other arsons. "Something here is very fishy," one settler told *Arutz Sheva* after he joined a left-wing group for a condolence visit to the village.[1] This was reminiscent of the rumor-mongering that followed Abu Khdair's murder, when voices on the right suggested that it was an "honor killing"— that his family murdered him for being gay. (This was nonsense: after a long investigation, the police indicted two Israeli Jews for the attack.)

As Israeli society has become more nationalist and religious, it has given rise to several extremist groups that deliberately work to fan the flames of Jewish-Arab hatred. One of the most notorious is Lehava. The group's name is an acronym for *LeMeniat Hitbolelut B'eretz HaKodesh* (For the Prevention of Assimilation in the Holy Land) though the word *lehava* also means "flame" or "blaze" in Hebrew. The Knesset has debated whether to ban Lehava as a terrorist organization, with one lawmaker comparing it to the so-called Islamic State. Its main focus is miscegenation: marriage between Jews and Arabs. Even if you believe this is a problem, it is not a significant one. In a country of 8.4 million, the number of Jewish-Arab marriages is thought to number in the hundreds. A 2016 Pew poll found that 98 per cent of married Jewish Israelis have Jewish spouses. 89 per cent said they were uncomfortable with the idea of their children marrying a Christian, and 97 per cent with a Muslim. Nonetheless, the group operates a hotline which Israelis can call to report a mixed relationship. "If you know a girl who is involved with a *goy* and want to help her, press 2."

In 2014, Lehava gathered a mob to chant "death to Arabs" outside a mixed wedding in Jaffa. On Thursday nights, dozens of Lehava activists clad in black T-shirts fan out across Jerusalem's city center. Some of them harass couples that appear "mixed" and hand out pamphlets warning about the dangers of assimilation. Others chase after Palestinians, yelling racial epithets and, occasionally, attacking them. Police have logged at least twenty such assaults over the past few years. Nobody has been arrested. The group also organized a protest at the lighting of the municipal Christmas tree in Jerusalem in 2015. "Christmas has no place in the Holy Land," said the group's leader, Bentzi Gopstein, who called Christians "blood-sucking vampires." Three members of Lehava were convicted of setting fire to a bilingual Jewish-Arab school in Jerusalem.

Liat Bar-Stav, an Israeli journalist, spent more than two months undercover with the group, and returned with a story of violence and racism. She recounted one incident in which Lehava activists were alerted to a group of Arabs talking with a Jewish girl in a public park.

> "Look at them running," one of the people with me says excitedly. "Wow! They're coming with brass knuckles and chains," adds another activist alongside me. My heart is pumping wildly, adrenaline rushes through me. Am I about to get involved in a fight just two hours after beginning my activity in Lehava? It turns out the girl isn't Jewish. Following a brief exchange of words, the two groups part ways; and I breathe a sigh of relief.[2]

While it sounds like a fringe group, it also has powerful backers in the right-wing government: Tzipi Hotevely, the deputy foreign minister, invited it to the Knesset in 2011 to discuss "procedures for preventing mixed marriages." Talk of a ban went nowhere. In 2016 Lehava proudly announced that it had completed its fifth annual summer camp, to train the next generation of ideologues.

Hilltop youth

The national-religious movement, as mentioned earlier, is divided between those who accept the legitimacy of the state and those who do not. The former is a much larger group. But, as the history of the Middle East amply demonstrates, it does not take many extremists to start a fire.

Some of them are known as the "Hilltop Youth," because they live in the most remote parts of the West Bank, in isolated settlements or in the "illegal outposts," the term for settlements built without approval from the Israeli government. Some outposts are little more than a ring of trailers, others rough dwellings inside of caves. Most of the activists are in their late teens and early twenties. They came of age during the *hitnat-kut*, the 2005 "disengagement" from Gaza. Prime Minister Ariel Sharon unilaterally decided to dismantle two dozen settlements in the strip and expel the 9,000 Israeli citizens living there. Four isolated settlements in the West Bank were also demolished. Polls at the time suggested that a plurality of Israelis, from 45 to 54 per cent, supported the decision. (They feel differently in hindsight: in 2015, on the tenth anniversary of the disengagement, 59 per cent of Israelis said they had opposed it.)

Over the past decade, Israeli security officials believe they have carried out hundreds of "price tag" attacks, burning homes and olive groves, vandalizing churches and mosques. Two members of the group were indicted in 2015 for torching an historic church on the Sea of Galilee. Many other crimes go unsolved; they are notoriously hard to prosecute. Indeed, they are a group only in the loosest sense of the word. "[They] are working in groups of two to three activists, max," said Lior Akerman, a former head of the Shin Bet's Jewish division. "They are not in contact with other gangs. They do not receive instructions from a leader, and they do not hear any guidelines."

The teenagers arrested in December for the Douma attack were also thought to be Hilltop Youth sympathizers. Investigators spent nearly a week questioning them. But their efforts typically yield little evidence, not least because the detainees have a handbook on how to outsmart the Shin Bet. The manual was written by Noam Federman, a far-right activist who once served as a leader of the Kach party, the political wing of the Kahanist movement. Kach was banned in 1994 and labeled a terrorist organization, but Federman stayed active in extremist circles, and was arrested numerous times on charges of attacking Palestinians. Most of the charges were eventually dropped for lack of evidence.

In his manual, Federman advises his compatriots to ignore summonses for as long as possible, and to choose their words carefully in the interrogation room. Detainees should spend their free time in prayer or studying. "Every person goes to reserve duty or to the army, and that is how you should regard arrest, too," he wrote. Much of the handbook is devoted to explaining how the Shin Bet uses informants to trick detainees. In one case, he wrote, a jailhouse janitor offered to pass notes between two suspects, only to turn them over to authorities.

Other employees have been shown forged newspaper articles claiming that their friends confessed to a crime. "There have been cases in which the Shin Bet brought in a well-known radio announcer and faked news broadcasts," he added.

Again, their numbers are small, a tiny fraction of Israel's Jewish population. But their existence underscores Israel's longtime failure to take seriously the threat of Jewish extremism.

The most prominent member of the Hilltop Youth is Meir Ettinger, 24, the grandson of Meir Kahane, the American-born rabbi whose Kach movement was banned in Israel. He helped to found Ramat Migron, an illegal outpost of another illegal outpost, which was eventually demolished by the government. He then spent the next few years moving from settlement to settlement, eventually ending up in Yitzhar and studying at Od Yosef Chai, the extremist *yeshiva* shuttered by the army in 2014 for its connection to the attacks on soldiers posted there. By the time of the Douma arson, he was the top suspect on the Shin Bet's list of Jewish extremists.

Ettinger does not give interviews, but he used to blog regularly on *HaKol HaYehudi*, "The Jewish Voice", a portal that mixes news with far-right political and religious commentary. He also wrote a private document that the Shin Bet describes as his "plan for rebellion", a plot to topple the state.

At first glance it seems outlandish, the ramblings of an angry, messianic youth. And yet, on reflection, there was a logic to it. Communists once spoke of "heightening the contradictions", trying to intensify the problems in capitalist society to produce a revolution—making things worse before they get better. Ettinger simply adapted that argument to a Jewish state. "The goal is disturbing the foundations of the state until the point where the Jews are forced to decide whether they want to take part in the revolution or in suppressing the revolt, because it will not be possible to ignore it or continue to sit and do nothing," he wrote.

Will Ettinger overthrow the state and replace it with a Jewish kingdom? No. His movement is small, and the state is powerful. But his writings, extreme as they are, touch on a valid point: there are indeed contradictions between being Jewish and democratic. From an army that increasingly worries about dissent in the ranks, to a cabinet that appeases the sensitivities of its most religious members, these inconsistencies are at the core of Israel's contemporary problems.

"The idea of the revolt is very simple," Ettinger added. "The state of Israel has many 'weak points', issues on which it moves on tiptoe so as not to spark riots. What we will do is simply to 'spark' all of these explosive barrels, all of these contradictions between Judaism and democracy."

"It's difficult to stop"

A pair of bodies on the pavement, covered in blood-spattered white sheets. Dozens of police officers sweeping through Jabal al-Mukaber, a rough neighborhood in East Jerusalem, searching cars and clashing with local youth. An emergency cabinet meeting to discuss home demolitions and closing the Palestinian parts of Israel's "eternally reunited" capital to traffic.

It all felt grimly familiar. Israel imposed those measures in 2014, after the assault on the Har Nof synagogue that killed six people, the apex of a month of violence. It would do the same in the winter of 2015, in response to a much more sustained intifada. The violence had started, once again, with tensions on the Temple Mount. Israeli police raided the compound on 13 September, just before Rosh Hashanah; officers said they had found pipe bombs stockpiled inside the houses of worship. Several Palestinians were injured during clashes with the police, which would continue off-and-on for several days.

On 1 October, a Palestinian gunman killed an Israeli couple, Eitam and Na'ama Henkin, while they were driving between two settlements in the occupied West Bank. The couple's four young children, in the back seat of the car, survived the shooting. Two days later, a Palestinian teenager stabbed four people in the Old City, killing two. The calls for retaliation came swiftly. Netanyahu was in New York at the time, attending the United Nations General Assembly. But his mouthpiece, *Israel HaYom*, quoted an unnamed aide talking about a "second Defensive Shield", the massive military operation launched in 2002, at the height of the second intifada.

The violence continued to metastasize: another stabbing in Jerusalem, and in the southern city of Kiryat Gat; deadly clashes on the

Gaza border; a Palestinian woman stopped at a checkpoint outside of Jerusalem, allegedly carrying a bomb in her car. The number of Israelis applying for gun permits jumped by a "double-digit percentage" in a matter of weeks. "Clearly we cannot assign a police officer to protect every citizen", said Erdan. "So self-defense is central and vital."

The general panic grew on 13 October, following a pair of seemingly coordinated attacks in Jerusalem. One Palestinian man attacked pedestrians with an ax after driving his car into a bus stop; two others shot and stabbed passengers aboard a municipal bus. Three Israelis were killed, raising October's death toll to seven, after more than twenty attacks. The next evening, an elderly woman was injured in a stabbing at Jerusalem's central bus station, and a separate attack was foiled near the Old City.

Once again, politicians and pundits debated what to call it, bringing about a rare agreement between Ismail Haniyeh, the Gaza-based leader of Hamas, and Isaac Herzog, the Israeli opposition leader: Both said that Israel was witnessing the start of a third intifada. "Whatever we're calling it, it's different than what we experienced in the past," said Michael Herzog, a retired head of the Israeli army's strategic division (and Isaac's brother). "It's carried out by young people... it's protracted, it's not really organized, and it's difficult to stop."

An intifada

"Intifada" is often translated as "uprising", though it comes from an Arabic root, *nafada*, meaning "to shake off". One of its first public appearances in the Palestinian context came in December of 1987, in the inaugural communiqué from a then-nascent Islamist group called Hamas. "The intifada of our vigilant people in the occupied territories is a resounding rejection of the occupation," it said.

The first intifada, which would continue until the early 1990s, was a grassroots movement over which the PLO had limited control. Its early leadership was a loose coalition of activists and intellectuals. They focused largely on nonviolent tactics—economic boycotts and civil disobedience. Some Palestinians also threw stones and Molotov cocktails at the Israeli army in the occupied West Bank. Compared to the second intifada, though, the Palestinian violence was limited:

there was only one suicide attack (an Islamic Jihad operative who seized the wheel of a passenger bus and drove it off a cliff) from 1989 until mid-1993.

Israel nonetheless responded harshly, with what Defense Minister Yitzhak Rabin called the "broken bones" policy, ordering security forces to shatter the limbs of protesters. More than 1,500 Palestinians were killed, tens of thousands were wounded, and some 120,000 were jailed. Israeli troops demolished homes, uprooted trees, and deported dozens of prominent Palestinian activists. These images of widespread violence, of soldiers harshly beating teenage protesters, dealt a blow to Israel's international standing. For the first (and last) time, Jerusalem was forced to respond with meaningful overtures—a 1989 peace proposal, the 1991 Madrid conference, and eventually the Oslo Accords, which afforded the Palestinians a limited degree of autonomy in the territories and promised an end to the conflict within five years.

The uprising's successor was equally momentous, though it had the opposite effect. Starting in 2000, four years of attacks killed some 1,000 Israelis, the majority of them civilians. Heavy fighting took place in the urban centers of the West Bank: Jenin was besieged for weeks in 2002, and gunmen roamed the old city of Nablus. If the first intifada gave the Palestinians fresh legitimacy on the world stage, the second stripped it away, prompting widespread condemnation. There was no formal end to the second intifada; instead it simply fizzled out in late 2004 and early 2005, after the death of Yasser Arafat, Israel's unilateral disengagement from Gaza, and the completion of large pieces of the separation barrier between Israel and the West Bank.

A decade later, conditions seemed ripe for another uprising. The Mitchell Report, a study of the Second Intifada prepared by former US senator and Dayton Accords negotiator George Mitchell, blamed the revolt on the failure of the Camp David talks in September 2000. By 2014, the "peace process" was stuck even more deeply in the mud. Bush had his "road map" and the Annapolis conference; Obama made several attempts at negotiations. None were successful. Settlements kept expanding, and the routine indignities and violence of occupation continued in the West Bank.

But those same conditions also augured against a third intifada. An exhausted and polarized Palestinian public no longer had prominent activists with enough influence to organize a grassroots uprising. The political leadership was divided, with Fatah controlling the West Bank and Hamas in charge of Gaza; both factions were seen as out-of-touch, self-interested, focused primarily on preserving their fiefdoms. Economic conditions in the West Bank had improved a bit, and Israel had relaxed some of its restrictions on internal movement, while the blockade of Gaza had turned that territory into a hermetically sealed, open-air prison.

So the topic became something of a running joke among the local press corps, the subject of breathless articles by foreign reporters parachuted into Jerusalem and Ramallah. There was no one to lead a third intifada, nor a public appetite for one. Violence was at historic lows. In the six-plus years between January 2009 and March 2015, Palestinian attackers killed fifty civilians inside Israel and the occupied territories—compared with 289 civilians in 2002 alone, at the height of the second intifada.[3]

"We live in shit already"

For a time during the winter of 2015, some residents of East Jerusalem started their mornings with a rush-hour queue at makeshift checkpoints manned by Israeli police. One woman died while waiting in line to reach a hospital. For others the day began earlier, with the sound of demolition charges blowing up a neighbor's home. Some hurried home in the evenings, fearful of working a night shift. They passed heavily armed Israeli police at seemingly every intersection.

Israeli authorities had wrestled the situation in Jerusalem under control by deploying thousands of extra police, making hundreds of arrests, setting up dozens of checkpoints and roadblocks, and even briefly building a wall around one Palestinian neighborhood. The violence did not entirely stop, and it continued in to pop up in other cities, but the breakneck pace of attacks in Jerusalem was halted.

As with the previous year, most of the attackers had no clear links to political factions, according to Israeli security officials, and no criminal records. Relatives struggled to explain what had happened. "He was a happy boy", said the uncle of a Palestinian teenager who had plunged a knife into an Israeli policeman's neck. "He had a job and a family, a decent life", said a young man whose cousin, a telephone company employee, had hacked a pedestrian to death with a meat cleaver. The crackdown brought calm, but it also reinforced the sense amongst Palestinians that Israel was encroaching ever further into their isolated city. The residents of Sur Baher, a district in the southeast, would queue each day for forty-five minutes at a checkpoint on their way to stock produce shelves and pump gas in West Jerusalem. In Shuafat, a few miles northeast of the Old City, the morning rush could take two hours.

"We live in shit already, and then they come and demolish our homes, put us out on the streets," said Mu'ataz Abu Jamal, a relative of no less than three attackers. "Why should I explain what was in my brother's head?"

The tightest closure was in Issawiya, a rough district of 14,000 people adjacent to the prestigious Hebrew University on Mt. Scopus. Only one road leading out of Issawiya was still open to traffic; the western exits were sealed with concrete blocks, where pedestrians queued for questioning and a thorough search by Israeli border policemen. At one point these restrictions on movement turned into a matter of life and death. Hoda Darwish, 65, developed breathing problems after a tear gas canister landed near her home on 18 October. Her sons tried to drive her to Hadassah hospital, normally a six-minute trip. The journey took forty-five minutes, with a lengthy stop at a checkpoint where Israeli security forces fired shots in the air to subdue the crowd, according to her sons. She died en route.

Ministers also pondered a more drastic step. At a security cabinet meeting in October, Netanyahu proposed revoking the residency of some 80,000 East Jerusalemites who live beyond the concrete-and-barbed wire "separation barrier" that Israel started to build during the Second Intifada. The idea never appeared on a formal cabinet agenda. It was frightening nonetheless to the inhabitants of places like Shuafat, a squalid refugee camp that houses some 30,000 people. Israeli police rarely venture inside, and Palestinian police have no jurisdiction, so crime and drug use are rampant. Netanyahu's proposal would isolate them further—they would lose the ID cards that allow them to cross the barrier for work or pleasure, effectively forcing them to apply for permits to visit an adjacent neighborhood.

One Shuafat resident—19-year-old Mohammed Ali—stabbed an Israeli policeman outside the old city. A CCTV video of the attack showed him sitting calmly on a ledge; one officer appeared to ask for Ali's ID, and the teenager jammed a knife into his neck. He was quickly shot dead.

On a visit a few days later, steps beyond the metal turnstile that led into the camp, there were charred dumpsters and the burned-out hulks of cars, the aftermath of almost daily clashes between Israeli security forces and local youth. Many businesses were shuttered, and the few that were open had hardly any customers. Teenagers peered down from the rooftops, jeering at the soldiers manning the checkpoint into Jerusalem proper. Ali's uncle Mahmoud gestured outside his house, where the streets were littered with trash. "This is all the incitement my nephew needed", he said. "He was angry about the settlers on Al-Aqsa [mosque], but really, it's hard to grow up with any hope here."

The violence would continue intermittently for more than six months. In March, a Palestinian from Qalandia went on a stabbing spree near my home in Jaffa, killing an American tourist and wounding ten others. In June, gunmen attacked a popular market in Tel Aviv, killing four and injuring sixteen. They ordered a leisurely dessert before the shooting spree. There were hundreds of shootings, stabbings and vehicular attacks across the country, far too many to list.

And yet this time the response was oddly subdued. There was no talk of the controversial nation-state law, which Netanyahu had described as so important during the much smaller wave of violence a year earlier. The government did not collapse. A year later, the widest violence in more than a decade had largely dropped from the public discourse—except for a single event in Hebron.

Elor Azaria, the soldier discussed at the beginning of this book, was eventually found guilty. The presiding judge, Maya Heller, spent nearly three hours reading the entirety of her lengthy verdict. She made it clear that Azaria did not act in the heat of battle; rather, he had intended to kill a Palestinian. Military prosecutors had only charged Azaria with manslaughter. Her verdict suggested that they could have tried for murder. He would later be sentenced to eighteen months in prison—a remarkably light term for an offense that carries up to twenty years. The military officers I spoke with were largely satisfied, though: Azaria was merely a grunt, they argued.

But they were less sanguine about how the trial had turned him into a right-wing icon: his face appeared on T-shirts; politicians rushed to defend him and demand a presidential pardon. Outside the heavily-guarded courtroom, hundreds of his supporters blocked roads and scuffled with police, and at least one Israeli journalist was roughed up. "Azaria got what he deserved", one officer said. "But how many other Azarias are out there?"

The generals

The men lined up along the red carpet, nearly two dozen career officers, had centuries of military experience between them. They were waiting for the guest of honor, and their new boss, who had about eighteen months of it.

The generals were silent. Most of them smiled when Avigdor Lieberman arrived in a black SUV. Still, it was hard not to imagine their inner monologues. The career officers of the Israeli army, after all, are used to serving under like-minded leaders: three of the four previous defense ministers served as army chiefs and retired with the rank of lieutenant general before they ascended to the top of the Kirya, the defense ministry in Tel Aviv. Lieberman, who was twenty years old when he made *aliyah*, did a shortened program of military service for new immigrants past the age of conscription. He moved quickly into politics, and for the next two decades he showed little interest in the nuances of Israel's security policy. Eretz Nehederet ("A Wonderful Country"), a popular satirical program, imagined his first meeting with a military aide. "From today, no more aerial photos," the Lieberman character instructed. "Why photograph the air? You should photograph things."

His appointment capped off a tumultuous period in Israeli politics. A fortnight earlier, in mid-May, commentators had been talking about a unity government. Isaac Herzog seemed ready to bring his center-left Zionist Union, or at least a chunk of it, into the coalition. He told a group of party activists that he had "identified a rare regional diplomatic opportunity" which justified joining Netanyahu's right-wing cabinet, a move that would see him assume the role of foreign minister. Herzog never actually identified this opportunity, but the talks received an unlikely boost from Abdel Fattah al-Sisi, the Egyptian president. "There is now a great opportunity for a better future and life and greater hope and stability," he said during a speech in Cairo. "Should not we seize the chance and move in that framework?" It was seemingly an important endorsement: Sisi is probably more popular with Israelis than either Netanyahu or Herzog. (I had a framed Sisi propaganda poster hanging in my apartment, a souvenir from covering the coup in 2013; pizza guys and plumbers would often nod approvingly and tell me that he should lead the Arab world.)

"Netanyahu has a need to expand his coalition," said Uzi Arad, his former national security adviser, suggesting it could purge the government of what he delicately called "hardline" elements. "It would moderate Israel's image to the world."

And then, as suddenly as the negotiations began, they ended. Lieberman announced on 18 May that he had been offered the defense ministry in exchange for bringing his party, with its paltry six Knesset seats, into the coalition. He is one of Israel's most bombastic politicians—the opposite of Herzog in both style and substance. In 1998 he even proposed bombing the Aswan High Dam (and thus killing millions of people downstream) to punish Egypt for supporting Yasser Arafat.

The prime minister continued to publicly offer Herzog a job, but the Labor leader, realizing he had been played, quickly bowed out. "Netanyahu has now turned himself into the government secretary of the far right-wing of Avigdor Naftali Smotrich," he wrote on Facebook, referring to three right-wing lawmakers (Lieberman, Naftali Bennett, and Bezalel Smotrich, the settler advocate and "proud homophobe" from the Jewish Home party). It was a brilliant tactical move on Netanyahu's part, neutralizing Herzog's ability to act as opposition leader.

On issues of diplomacy and security, Netanyahu's fourth government effectively had no opposition. The Zionist Union was busy fighting amongst itself, consumed with one of its quadrennial leadership struggles; no less than nine challengers would line up to run against Herzog in the 2017 primary. Yair Lapid, the centrist talk show host-turned-politician who hoped to become the next prime minister, tried to position himself for a future election by moving to the right and avoiding any major criticism of Netanyahu on defense issues.

The only real criticism, ironically, came from the men who once executed Netanyahu's security policy. During his four terms in power, the prime minister has worked with twenty different defense ministers, army chiefs, and directors of the Shin Bet and the Mossad. Thirteen of them have publicly attacked his policies and leadership; of the seven who haven't, three are currently in office. (Lieberman himself is among the critics.)

Their role as the loyal opposition highlights the failure of the Israeli political system to debate the country's most serious issues. It has also turned the army and the security services into a political football— perhaps one of the most dangerous trends in recent years.

The melting pot

The Israeli army, unsurprisingly, occupies an exalted place in society, and not only because the country has been almost constantly at war since it was founded. Israel's system of mandatory conscription makes it one of the few institutions that brings together young people from across ethnic, socioeconomic and religious lines. Secular middle-class kids from Tel Aviv meet religious teenagers from Jerusalem, poor soldiers from the Negev, and Druze boys from villages in the Galilee. New immigrants learn Hebrew. David Ben-Gurion, the first Israeli prime minister, referred to it as a "melting pot".

"The IDF must serve not only as a military training apparatus but also as a state school that imbues the youth entering its ranks with knowledge of the language, the country, Jewish history, the fundamentals of general education, neatness and order, and, most importantly, love of the homeland," he wrote in 1964.[4]

At the highest levels, though, the officer corps has historically been far less diverse. Its top ranks, especially in the elite combat units, were originally dominated by men from the *kibbutzim* and the Labor movement. They played a disproportionately large role even into the 1980s, with Labor out of power and the army embroiled in a controversial war in Lebanon. Back then, more than 25 per cent of army officers (and a similar share of air force pilots, another "elite" group) were kibbutzniks, at a time when they represented just 3 per cent of the Israeli population.

Rabin was the most famous example, but equally influential was Amnon Lipkin-Shahak, a fellow paratrooper and a longtime friend of the slain prime minister. He enlisted in the army in 1962. When he finished his military career thirty-six years later, he was the chief of staff; he then joined the Labor party for a brief stint in the Knesset. As a man respected by both the Israeli public and the Palestinian leadership, he played a major role in negotiating the Oslo Accords. In 1994, when the massacre at the Ibrahimi Mosque in Hebron threatened to derail peace talks, the prime minister dispatched Lipkin-Shahak to Tunis to meet with Yasser Arafat, the Palestinian leader. "Arafat so trusted Amnon... that he agreed to return to negotiations without demanding any compensation," Martin Indyk, the former US ambassador to Israel, wrote decades later.[5]

His views put him at odds with Netanyahu, the head of Likud, who was a fierce critic of both Rabin and the Oslo process. Netanyahu won the early election called in 1996, in the wake of Rabin's assassination, and quickly set about trying to undo his predecessor's efforts at peace. The climax came in September, when he and Ehud Olmert (then the mayor of Jerusalem) agreed to open a previously restricted part of the tunnels underneath the Temple Mount and Al-Aqsa Mosque. His security officials had warned that the move—like any changes in the Old City—would lead to Palestinian riots. Indeed, Rabin had considered the same proposal, but decided not to do it, according to his longtime aide, Eitan Haber. "We waited thousands of years, said Yitzhak Rabin, and we will wait a few more," he wrote in *Yediot Aharonot* after the riots. But Netanyahu went ahead anyway, to demonstrate Israel's "sovereignty over Jerusalem" to his right-wing base.

The security chiefs were correct. More than a hundred people died in the ensuing violence. Netanyahu rejected any criticism of his decision, however, and blamed the riots on Arafat. "We're in a peace process, not in a process where anyone can come and say, 'oh dear, I feel like shooting at Israeli forces,'" he said sarcastically at a news conference on the third day of unrest.[6]

Arafat indeed deserved a large share of the blame: the PLO helped to organize the riots, and his security forces joined the fighting. But so did Netanyahu, who approved the plan without notifying his generals, many of whom said they learned about it only after the tunnel was opened. Once the fighting stopped, he maneuvered to place the blame on the security services, a move which only angered them further.

Lipkin-Shahak gave his response a few weeks later, at a memorial service on the first anniversary of Rabin's murder. In an emotional speech addressed to his former commander, the general lamented the army's "fall from grace" over the past year. "Polarization, hedonism, sectarianism [and] apathy... have penetrated the nation's consciousness, and decimated consensus," he said, "transforming the IDF from one of our most hallowed institutions into a collective punching bag."[7] It was a scathing address—a direct criticism of the political establishment from a serving army chief. Ze'ev Maoz, a military analyst, started speculating publicly about a coup.

The putsch didn't happen, but a general took power nonetheless. Netanyahu's government collapsed in 1998, largely over the Wye River Memorandum, an interim agreement with the Palestinians. Lipkin-Shahak announced that he would run for office, as did Yitzhak Mordechai, who was Netanyahu's defense minister—a particularly humiliating rebuke to Bibi. Both men eventually bowed out, however, and consolidated their support behind Ehud Barak, who swept to power with 56 per cent of the popular vote.

"This is, indeed, the dawn of a new day," Barak said on election night, before a crowd of supporters in Tel Aviv's Rabin Square. "It is time to end the division and to find harmony."[8]

It would take Netanyahu a full decade to climb back to power. But he learned a lesson from his defeat, and began laying the groundwork for his second term in 2007, when he was the opposition leader. The Knesset lengthened the "cooling-off period" for security officials, barring them from politics for three years after retirement, a sixfold increase from the previous law. The bill was drafted by Yuval Steinitz, a Likud lawmaker who has long been a close Netanyahu confidante. "This is a big day for Israeli democracy," Steinitz said after the vote. "For the first time, we have positioned a wall between the IDF and politics."[9]

For twenty years, Netanyahu has made a simple pitch to Israeli voters. "In a chaotic, dangerous region, I will keep you safe." The only challengers who could effectively rebut his message are the retired generals and spies. A longer cooling-off period put them squarely on the sidelines; depending on the timing of elections, an ex-security chief with political aspirations could have to wait seven years to challenge Netanyahu—plenty of time for their stars to fade, both literally and figuratively.

The falafel story

On a gray, rainy day in March, Netanyahu drove up to northern Israel to eulogize one of his sharpest critics.

Even by the standards of the Mossad, Israel's storied spy service, Meir Dagan was a legendary figure. Under his tutelage the agency assassinated Imad Mughniyeh, one of Hezbollah's top military commanders, on the streets of Damascus. It blew up Iranian nuclear scientists commuting to work. Muhammad Suleiman, a top Syrian general, was gunned down while hosting a dinner party at his home in Tartous. In 2010 *Al-Ahram*, the largest state-run newspaper in Egypt, called him "Superman".

After his retirement, though, Dagan had only one target: his former boss. Netanyahu spent several years threatening an Israeli airstrike against Iran's nuclear program. But Dagan, like much of the Israeli intelligence community, believed that such a move was premature: the regime in Tehran was still years away from actually producing a bomb. He doubted that tiny Israel could effectively neutralize Iran's nuclear facilities, which were spread across the country, some in well-fortified bunkers. It could only deal a temporary setback—and that tactical victory would be a strategic defeat, because it would justify Iran's pursuit of nuclear weapons and accelerate the program. Along with Gabi Ashkenazi and Yuval Diskin, the heads of the army and the Shin Bet, he spent his last year in office quietly fighting Netanyahu.

In the summer of 2010, Netanyahu asked Dagan and Ashkenazi to stay for a private chat after a security cabinet meeting. He wanted to give them a shocking order: he told them to accelerate plans for a strike, so that by the end of the summer the air force would be ready to move at a few hours' notice. Ashkenazi pushed back, calling it a "strategic mistake" and warning that Iran might notice the preparations and attack preemptively. Dagan was even more blunt. "This is an illegal order," he said. Israeli law requires the security cabinet to approve a war. With his three security chiefs opposed to the move, Netanyahu doubted he would have a majority. Their opposition effectively took the issue off the table.

The argument went public the following year. "It's the stupidest thing I've ever heard," Dagan told at audience at the Hebrew University in 2011, mere months after leaving his post. "It will be followed by a war with Iran." He repeated the argument in several subsequent public appearances. In a 2012 interview on 60 Minutes, he warned that an airstrike would bring missiles raining down on Tel Aviv. "It will have a devastating impact on our ability to continue with our daily life. I think that Israel will be in a very serious situation for quite a time," he said.

Dagan, a bald man built like a fireplug, would remain one of Netanyahu's most persistent and colorful critics. A camera crew from Channel 2 sat with him in March 2015, while Netanyahu denounced the Iran deal in a controversial speech to Congress. At one point, when the prime minister was discussing Iran's progress toward a bomb, Dagan could be seen muttering "bullshit". Days later, he was the keynote speaker at the anti-Netanyahu election rally in Rabin Square. By then he was battling an advanced case of cancer; he had received a liver transplant in Belarus several years earlier.

Netanyahu ignored all of this in his eulogy. He recalled sitting with the former Mossad chief and laughing at "how daring and even rude his ideas were". In interviews shortly before his death, though, Dagan offered a different recollection of his meetings with the prime minister. He liked to tell the "falafel story". The notoriously indecisive Netanyahu would approve covert actions, then quickly change his mind, fearing the potential consequences. So instead of driving back to his apartment in Tel Aviv, after meeting Netanyahu, "I would go for falafel in Mahane Yehuda," Dagan said, referring to a popular market near the prime minister's office. He would eat, and wait for the inevitable phone call asking him to return. (For more complicated operations, which took longer to contemplate, he would drive out to Abu Ghosh, an Arab village west of Jerusalem that is famous for its hummus.) "I was never wrong," he said. "He always called me back."

He was even harsher in remarks published shortly after his death: Netanyahu was "the worst manager I know," he said, a man who didn't have the "balls" to approve daring moves.[10]

The London-born Efraim Halevy cuts a very different profile—soft-spoken, slightly rumpled, a newspaper tucked under his arm, his jowls pulled into a perpetual frown. Towards the end of our interview in a Tel Aviv cafe, he struggled to get the waitress's attention. "You see, nobody listens to me anymore," he chuckled.

He had a lengthy career in Israeli intelligence, but his best-known achievements (the public ones, at least) were as a diplomat. He forged close personal ties with King Hussein of Jordan, a relationship he used to help broker the historic 1994 peace treaty. Three years later, while Halevy was the Israeli ambassador to the European Union, Mossad tried to assassinate Hamas leader Khaled Meshaal on Jordanian soil, spraying him with poison on a busy Amman street. The bungled plot threatened to destroy the fragile agreement. Halevy was dispatched to Amman to help smooth tensions. (Again, Netanyahu sought to place the blame on his security chiefs, this time Danny Yatom, the head of Mossad; Halevy was soon brought out of retirement to head the agency.)

But for all his stylistic differences, he reached the same conclusions as Dagan. "All the time he's fighting, not only the Iranians, but fighting his base, his political base. [Netanyahu] is basically a very insecure individual," Halevy said. "He is a purveyor of fear in this country."

Indeed, he wondered if the prime minister was ever truly serious about striking Iran. As a politician, Netanyahu often proposes far-right ideas to appease his base, only to let them quietly wither—like his attempt at the "Jewish state bill", which was quickly dropped after the 2015 election. "It's unheard of that if the prime minister, the defense minster and the foreign minister together, all three of them are gunning for an operation, that all the rest would simply say no," Halevy said. "The theory which is being pushed around that, in his heart of hearts, he didn't want to do the operation, I think that's true. And therefore this whole charade, this major meeting and so forth, it was pointless."

"No daylight"

Six weeks after world powers signed the nuclear pact with Tehran, a billboard finally compelled Israelis to debate the subject. The advertisement, plastered over Rabin Square in mid-2015, announced the imminent opening of the "Iranian embassy in Israel". A phone number listed at the bottom led to a cryptic recording, which asked callers to leave a message for the nascent diplomatic mission. Curious onlookers debated in the cafes below: Was it a political statement? By the left, or the right? Could it ever come true?

In the United States, the Jewish community had spent months tearing itself apart over the agreement, which imposed restrictions on

Iran's nuclear program in exchange for sanctions relief. Congressmen who supported it were slurred as self-hating Jews, even Nazi *kapos*. One might have expected a similar level of passion in Israel, where the prime minister had spent months portraying the deal as a harbinger of the second Holocaust. Yet the most striking thing about the Iran debate in Israel was the utter lack of one. The Knesset's dysfunctional foreign affairs and defense committee did not hold a single substantive hearing after the agreement was signed in July. Politicians like Isaac Herzog, the putative head of the opposition, read from the prime minister's talking points. With a crucial vote looming in Congress, Netanyahu jetted off to an expo in Milan to discuss sustainable agriculture.

"Let me put it very simply: There has not been any real discussion in this country on the subject," said Halevy, one of the few public figures to support the deal. "At the time the Congress is looking at every full stop and comma, the Israeli Knesset is on holiday."

Henry Kissinger once remarked that Israel has no foreign policy, only a domestic one. That aphorism has never been truer than in the Netanyahu age. The prime minister's opposition to the deal was well known. He repeated it at every turn, even invoking the specter of mushroom clouds over Tel Aviv in his response to a report on the high cost of housing. But his opponents believed he would ultimately lose the fight to block the deal in Congress. They muted their criticism, hoping to win favor with skeptical center-right voters, and to use Netanyahu's inevitable defeat against him. Lapid vowed to support Netanyahu "to the outside world, in English." Herzog went even further, saying there was "no daylight" between him and the prime minister on Iran. Ironically, their cynical ploy strengthened Netanyahu's position, giving the appearance of unanimous opposition to the deal. The prime minister even cited Herzog's support in an August address to the Jewish Federations of North America. "The man who ran against me in this year's election and who works every day in the Knesset to bring down my government, Herzog, has said that there is no daylight between us when it comes to the deal with Iran," he said.

They didn't change their tone until the deal was done. Lapid launched a broadside on 20 September, weeks after Obama secured passage of the agreement in Congress. He said the prime minister had failed because he couldn't "read the map" and understand a changing

America. "He has lost by knockout," the former finance minister concluded, calling the vote "Israel's biggest foreign policy failure."

All of this was widely interpreted to mean that Israelis were united in opposition to the deal. The truth was that Israel never bothered to debate it. There were certainly reasons for skepticism. Iran, with a well-documented history of hiding its nuclear facilities, could cheat: the agreement did nothing to limit its aggressive role in the region, nor did it stop Iran from enriching uranium. But there were also reasons to support it, none of which filtered into the public discourse.

"I know Herzog very well, I have high regard for his intellectual capabilities," Halevy said. "I think on the Iranian issue, he should have taken a different stance. But suddenly it became almost unpatriotic to be not together. Netanyahu has been very successful at putting down the line: if you're not speaking the way I'm speaking... you are deviating from the interests of the state of Israel."

With politicians eying the next election, the task of promoting the pact fell to the retired leaders of Israel's security services. Dozens of them signed an open letter in *Ha'aretz* in August, urging Netanyahu to accept the deal as an "accomplished fact" and work with Washington to implement it. There was, to be sure, a degree of tokenism in the effort. Among the best-known signatories was Ami Ayalon, a former Shin Bet director who traveled to America to urge lawmakers to support the deal (and who harbors a grudge against Netanyahu dating back to the tunnel riots). His agency, however, is tasked with domestic security—keeping track of Palestinian militants, not Iranian centrifuges. Other signatories included an ex-police commissioner and the one-time head of the fire brigade, neither of them noted experts on the nuclear fuel cycle.

Halevy was somewhat harder to dismiss. So was Uzi Eilam, a former director of Israel's atomic energy commission. "I'm a bit different because I'm actually familiar with the technology," he joked.

He offered strong praise for many of its provisions, particularly the shutdown of the heavy water reactor at Arak, a step he called "quite good", effectively blocking Iran's path to a plutonium bomb. In a perfect world, he added, the agreement would also have barred Iran from producing enriched uranium. "But if it were possible, it would have been reached along these very long two years of haggling," he said. "And frankly, [among] those who oppose the agreement, I didn't see anybody that came out with a real comprehensive solution that is different. So I think that we should be realistic."

The security services are not monolithic, of course. Amos Yadlin, a former head of military intelligence and the Zionist Camp's candidate for defense minister in the 2015 election, called it a "highly problematic agreement that entails risks to Israel's national security." Still, the evidence suggested that most of Israel's generals saw the deal as an opportunity, not a disaster—a view not limited to the retired ones. In August 2015, for the first time, the army released its strategic program to the public. The document did not mention Iran as a nuclear threat. An army spokesman cautioned against reading too much into the text, but analysts quickly interpreted it as yet another sign of discord with Netanyahu.

A last mission

Two weeks after Lieberman took office, on a sweltering Thursday afternoon in June, the normally staid Herzliya conference was the hottest item on the political calendar. The keynote speaker was Ehud Barak. He was unpopular with the Israeli public, but he still had a following in the press corps, and he promised them a bombshell.

His warm-up act was the recently unemployed Moshe Ya'alon, whose typically dry cadence obscured a harsh attack on his former boss. He accused Netanyahu of "fear-mongering", of trying to convince Israelis that a "second Holocaust" was looming around the corner. Bibi had spent years warning Israelis that the Palestinians, Iran, and even the BDS movement jeopardized their very existence. Ya'alon was blunt. "At this point, and for the foreseeable future, there is no existential threat facing Israel," he said.

Barak took the stage a few hours later, and his speech didn't disappoint. The ex-commando had already prepared the ground, telling Channel 10 in May that Israel had been "infected by the seeds of fascism". He repeated that charge at Herzliya, and he elaborated on it, warning that Netanyahu's government was "eroding democracy" in Israel. "A hostile takeover has occurred," he said. "The right-wing government, especially in the past year, is no longer walking in the footsteps of Ze'ev Jabotinsky and Menachem Begin. A fanatic core with radical ideology has taken over the Likud." He went on to warn that the government's "radical, dangerous agenda" was "endangering the future of the entire Zionist project."

A central piece of his criticism, of course, was Netanyahu's failure to take bold steps to resolve the conflict with the Palestinians. Two years earlier, in a private meeting with business executives, the Mossad chief told them that it was the Palestinians, and not Iran, who posed the greatest strategic threat to Israel.[11] It was an embarrassment to Netanyahu, who had spent years arguing the exact opposite. (It wasn't the last time Tamir Pardo would humiliate his boss. A few months later, he warned a group of US senators not to impose new economic sanctions on Iran, saying it would "throw a hand grenade" into the delicate nuclear negotiations.)

But the prime minister stuck to his argument. In late 2015, when he addressed the Knesset's foreign affairs and defense committee, he explained that—while he did not want Israel to become a binational state—he saw no solution in the near future. "You think there is a magic wand here, but I disagree," he told opposition lawmakers. "I'm asked if we will forever live by the sword: yes."

Barak once dressed up as a woman to sneak into Beirut and kill PLO members. Yitzhak Rabin oversaw the ethnic cleansing of Lydda (now Lod). Ariel Sharon's military activities sparked international outrage. Yet all of them eventually decided that it was essential for Israel to make peace with the Palestinians, and that doing so would require Israel to relinquish territory. Even setting aside morals and geopolitics, there was a sound military logic for doing so. A two-state solution would make the army's job immeasurably easier. It could get out of the business of occupation—the checkpoints, the nightly raids, the endless clashes at Qalandia and Bil'in. It could focus its resources on defending a clearly-demarcated border, instead of devoting thousands of soldiers to protect a few hundred settlers living amidst a hostile Palestinian population. The peace process may not be an issue for most Israeli voters, but it remains a point of major friction between the army and the right-wing government.

"If you gathered in one room all the former IDF chiefs of staff, the Shin Bet's directors, the heads of military intelligences, and the directors of the Mossad, 90 per cent of them would tell you that it is way simpler to defend Israel from within borders that reflect its security interests, with a solid Jewish majority for generations, alongside a Palestinian state, than to defend 'one Jewish state' stretching from the Jordan River to the sea, with millions of Palestinians within its borders," Barak said in his speech.

Benny Gantz, the recently-retired chief of staff, made a similar point a few months earlier, at a conference of the Institute for National Security Studies. He told the audience that Israel's greatest long-term threats were inequality and the educational system, not security. And he argued in favor of a renewed diplomatic push with the Palestinians. "Even if it fails, and we'll need to continue to live by the sword, we need to be able to look at our kids in the eyes and tell them we tried," he said.

An army that had a country

Lieberman's first few months as defense minister were wholly uneventful. Israel didn't bomb the Aswan High Dam or invade Gaza City. He stopped commenting publicly on Elor Azaria, who by then was on trial for manslaughter. When it came time to implement a Supreme Court ruling and demolish Amona, an illegal outpost in the occupied West Bank, Lieberman was one of the few right-wing voices to support Netanyahu (which will be discussed later in the book). Unlike Bennett, he didn't react with glee to Trump's election as president. None of this was a great surprise: even opponents have described him to me as "the most pragmatic politician in Israel." And that was the point. By installing a hardheaded right-wing politician in the defense ministry, Netanyahu made it harder for the traditionally centrist security establishment to act as a countervailing force.

Demographic trends also tilt in his favor, as the *kibbutzniks* no longer play such an outsized role in the Israeli army. They have been eclipsed by soldiers from the national-religious community. A study by *Ma'arachot*, the defense ministry's official journal, found that they accounted for 26 per cent of the officer corps in 2008, up from just 2.5 per cent in the 1990s. That number will continue to rise: according to some researchers, more than one-third of army cadets now hail from the *dati-leumi* sector.

Over the past few years, Netanyahu has appointed an unprecedented number of religious Israelis to the top echelons of the security services.

Yoram Cohen, who led the Shin Bet from 2011 until 2016, was an observant, *kippah*-wearing Jew, the first in the agency's history. So is Roni Alsheich, the police chief. In 2016, after Pardo's retirement, Netanyahu appointed his national security adviser Yossi Cohen to run the Mossad. He was an agency veteran, certainly qualified for the job, but he was also seen as a loyalist, personally close to the prime minister and his wife Sara. And he, too, identifies as *masorti*, a traditionally observant Jew. While "religious" is not necessarily a synonym for "right-wing", polls have consistently found that religious Israeli Jews are more likely to back conservative parties than their secular counterparts.

Such a shift has been inevitable—a reflection of a changing society. Indeed, a few Israeli officers were pleased to have a civilian in the defense ministry. Shortly after Lieberman took office, a general reminisced about his childhood, when his mother would take him to see military parades in their hometown. The onlookers, he recalled, knew most of the officers by name. "When a society knows most of its generals, and not its artists, its Nobel Prize winners, it is a sick society," he said. "For a lot of years, Israel was an army that had a country."

But, as the Azaria case illustrated, the shift is not just demographic. It is also ideological. Barak alluded to this in his Herzliya speech, arguing that the Israeli right was engaged in a long-term struggle to "re-educate" the army. "They understand that it is essential gradually to undermine the sanctity of the IDF's values, its ethical code, and the healthy instincts of so many of our best commanders and fighters," he said.

In interviews over the past few years, multiple senior officers expressed the same fear: if a future government ordered, say, a large-scale evacuation of the West Bank, would the rank-and-file carry it out? The army is not just more ideological, but also more connected to the public discourse in Israel, which has become increasingly right-wing and nationalist. "When I was a young soldier, even my mother didn't know where I was, and that was a good thing," another staff officer observed. "Today they [young soldiers] bring phones… society has a much better idea about what we do. But it also means my soldiers know what's happening in society."

There have already been a few glimmers of dissent in the ranks. Elor Azaria's comrades threatened to go AWOL if he was convicted. In late

2016, as the army prepared to help raze Amona, a dozen soldiers left their posts and went to another outpost in a show of solidarity.

One case that became notorious was that of "David", a soldier from the Nahal Brigade, who was filmed in 2014 threatening to shoot a Palestinian photographer. His behavior didn't break any norms. Any journalist who works in the occupied territories, especially a Palestinian, has been caught up in similar situations. But it embarrassed the army because it was caught on camera. David was arrested. Hundreds of soldiers quickly posted photos of themselves holding signs that read, "I'm with David *HaNahalawi*" (a Hebrew word for a Nahal soldier). The photos, dubbed a "revolt" in the press, spread quickly across social media and websites like 0404, a popular right-wing portal. David was soon released.

A year later, when he passed his officer training course, the far-right activist Baruch Marzel wrote about him on Facebook. Marzel had once offered to buy pizzas for any soldier who killed a Palestinian attacker; he regularly invites the troops stationed in Hebron for Shabbat meals at his home, in an effort to spread his far-right views. (Azaria was one of his regular guests.) And he was, unsurprisingly, full of praise for David. "Good luck, hero," he wrote. "We love you."

Media and culture

Miri Regev enjoys being booed. An acrimonious populist and a rising star in the Likud party, she likes to cultivate an image as a sort of Daniel in the den of leftist lions. The gathering of artists at Tel Aviv's museum in March 2016 was, to be sure, not the friendliest audience. Regev had been named culture minister almost a year earlier, and spent much of her early tenure butting heads with the cultural establishment, which she viewed as irredeemably liberal.

When she took the stage—at a conference organized by the liberal newspaper *Ha'aretz*—she wasted little time launching into a combative routine. "I was told to always start with a quote. It makes a cultured impression," she began. "So here goes. As the famous Chinese philosopher Sun Tzu once said, 'Cut the bullshit! Cut the bullshit!'"

Her quote, delivered in English, was quickly drowned out by boos. She plowed on, promising to expose the "hypocrisy" of Israeli artists. "We will guarantee loyalty to the laws of this country!"

Regev, fifty-one, spent the first two decades of her career in the military, rising through the ranks until she became the IDF spokesperson in 2005. She left the army two years later and quickly moved into politics, entering the Knesset in 2009 and making a name for herself by inciting against Sudanese and Eritrean asylum-seekers. Calling them a "cancer in our body", she warned that they were part of a left-wing plot to destroy Israel's Jewish identity. (She later apologized, to cancer patients.) By the time Likud held primaries in the winter of 2014, Regev had risen to number five on its list, ahead of party stalwarts and respected officials like Defense Minister Moshe Ya'alon. She campaigned aggressively for the Likud during election season—not only in conservative constituencies, but again in hostile territory, like a gay bar in Tel Aviv.

Her reward was the culture ministry, which put her in charge of a small department with a roughly $119 million budget, 0.01 per cent of total state spending. The ministry distributes some of that money to hundreds of cultural institutions and art schools, which cover the rest of their budget through private donations, tuition, and ticket sales. It hardly seems like a prestigious job. Her predecessor, Limor Livnat, retired from politics in 2014 after a mostly forgettable six-year stint at the ministry. But it was a perfect fit for Regev, a politician cut from the mold of Donald Trump or Nigel Farage, since it gave her a chance to clash regularly with "the left", and to make headlines for doing it.

One of her first acts was to temporarily defund the Midan Theater in Haifa, which had put on a play about a Palestinian prisoner who killed an Israeli soldier. Regev accused the theater of trying to "undermine the state". She also asked Ayelet Shaked, the justice minister, to investigate whether the theater had any "ties to terrorism", a groundless allegation that went nowhere. The funding decision was quickly reversed, too: the attorney general at the time, Yehuda Weinstein, ruled that it would limit freedom of expression.

Still, it was an early shot across the bow. She followed up in January by trying to create a legal basis for future funding cuts, drafting a "loyalty bill" that would allow her ministry to defund artists who acted "against the principles of the state". The language was broadly worded. It would apply to performers who incited violence, a reasonable provision, but also to those who desecrated the Israeli flag or commemorated the *nakba*, the mass displacement of Palestinians that accompanied the state's founding in 1948.

Several months later, her office sent a questionnaire to cultural institutions, asking whether they performed in the Galilee and the Negev—historically underdeveloped regions of the country, referred to in Hebrew as "the periphery"—and in Jewish settlements in the West Bank. She threatened to slash their funding by one-third if they did not. Israeli artists already have an incentive to tour the country: their annual payments from the culture ministry are based on the number of performances they put on. Yet much of the country's culture is still concentrated in the major cities along the coastal plain, and in Jerusalem. Regev's effort might have seemed laudable, were it not for one additional provision she tacked on, which revealed her ideological motives: artists who performed in the West Bank stood to receive a small bonus.

Regev, the daughter of Moroccan immigrants, draws much of her appeal from ethnic resentment. She often describes herself as "Miri Regev from Kiryat Gat," a largely Mizrahi town in the south. After she was named culture minister, she gleefully denounced European culture. "I never read Chekhov," she told an interviewer from *Israel HaYom* in 2015. "I listened to Jo Amar [a Moroccan-Israeli singer] and Sephardic songs, and I'm no less cultured than all the consumers of Western culture."[12]

Amulets and idols

Culture remains one of the major gaps between Ashkenazi and Mizrahi Jews. A 2012 analysis by a Mizrahi activist group found, for example, that groups teaching Western styles of dance receive more than 95 per cent of the state funding allocated for dance programs. The orchestras in Tel Aviv and Haifa, whose programs emphasize European classical music, receive millions of shekels each year; an orchestra that performs ancient Middle Eastern music characteristic of the *mizrahim* receives about 70,000 shekels. "People on the periphery don't get money for promoting or creating their own cultural events, on the basis of their own cultural heritage," said Yossi Dahan, a professor and analyst who writes frequently about inequality in Israel.

Some of this can be explained by simple demographics: big cities have larger audiences. But the Ashkenazi left has not done much to endear itself to its critics. For many Israelis, the most memorable moment of Labor's pre-election rally in 2015 was not the ailing Meir Dagan's denunciation of the prime minister. It was the speech delivered by Yair Garbuz, a painter and art professor who railed against the "amulet kissers [and] idol worshippers". They had taken over, he warned, and the coming election offered reasonable Israelis a last chance to reclaim their country from the "freaks", the "destroyers of democracy".

It was a not-so-thinly veiled reference to Mizrahi Jews: their hand-shaped *hamsa* amulets, their saints—their "Arab" traditions. His insults were soon blasted out to supporters of the Likud party, which was worried about a low turnout; on election day, not a few right-wing voters cited Garbuz as their reason for going to the polls. "Garbuz's speech hurt us, without a shadow of a doubt," Isaac Herzog, the leader of the Labor party and Netanyahu's main challenger, acknowledged a few days after the vote.

This was fertile ground for Regev. But only to a point. In the summer of 2016, Army Radio broadcast a poem by Mahmoud Darwish as part of an educational segment. Darwish, born in the Galilee in 1941, is widely regarded as the Palestinian national poet. He spent much of his adult life in exile after joining the PLO, and gave an eloquent voice to Palestinian feelings of dispossession. So his words can be challenging to Israeli ears. The late Yossi Sarid, a left-wing former education minister, tried to introduce them into the national curriculum in 2000, but backed down after provoking a furious reaction in the Knesset.

Twelve years later, though, a successor agreed to teach Darwish to high school literature students. This meant it should have been uncontroversial when Army Radio read one of his most famous poems, "Identity Card," best known for its defiant refrain "*sajjil, ana 'arabi*", "write down, I am an Arab."

But the Israeli right was incandescent: a Palestinian national symbol on their airwaves, and on an army-run station to boot. "The IDF radio station has gone off the rails," Regev complained. Avigdor Lieberman went further, summoning the director of the station for a dressing-down, and then comparing Darwish to Hitler. "By the same logic," he argued, "[Army Radio could] broadcast a glorification of the literary marvels of Adolf Hitler's *Mein Kampf*." (Darwish, for the record, was not an anti-Semite.)

A few months later, an artistic duo read the same lines at the Ophir Awards, the Israeli equivalent of the Oscars. One of the performers was Tamer Nafar, a co-founder of DAM, the first Palestinian Israeli rap group. The other was Yossi Tzabari—a Mizrahi Jewish artist. They performed a piece called *ana mish politi*, literally "I am not political". An ironic name, of course: the title was a mix of Arabic and Hebrew, which was itself a political decision at a prestigious Israeli event. Midway through the performance, both men recited Darwish's poem, in their own native tongue. "*Tirshom, gam ani aravi*", Tzabari said, his fist raised in the air, "write down, I am also an Arab. *Aval b'negud Darwish Mahmoud, ani aravi min al-yehud.* But unlike Mahmoud Darwish, I am an Arab from the Jews."

It was all too much for Regev, who got up from her seat and stormed out early in the performance. A theatrical flourish, and one that generated the desired headlines—though had she stayed, she might have enjoyed the rest of the number, which quickly turned into a criticism of racism on the left. "The robbed Cossack who mourns in English about ethnic cleansing in the Jewish state," Tzabari continued, adding a bit of a Mizrahi accent to his Hebrew, a few guttural *ayns* and trilled *reshes*. "They speak of equality, coexistence and liberty… but fear and constantly ignore the hyphen that connects Arab to Jew."

Beat the left

In August, after a Tunisian man had got behind the wheel of a truck and killed eighty-six people on the promenade in Nice, a number of French towns decided to ban the burkini, the full-body swimsuit designed for observant Muslim women. The ban was short-lived. Photos of four French policemen ordering a woman to remove her burkini on the beach triggered worldwide outrage, and the country's top administrative court soon overturned the laws.

Israelis were mostly confused by the whole affair: the beaches here are all a mix of skimpy bikinis and conservative clothes, for Jewish and Muslim women alike. A poll by the Israel Democracy Institute found that nearly two-thirds of Israeli Jews think democratic governments have no business dictating dress codes.

Yet on 28 August, Israel had its own swimwear controversy, though it was the opposite of *l'affaire burkini*. Hanna Goor, a singer and former reality-show star, was booted off the stage at a cultural event in Ashdod, a port city south of Tel Aviv, because she was wearing a bikini top. Organizers asked her to cover up, and she refused. The culture ministry, which had sponsored the event, explained that her attire was not "respectful" of the religious Jews in attendance. "The policy of the ministry… states that festivals and events paid for with public funds will respect the public at large, which belongs to various communities and sectors," it said. Days later, the ministry said it would start drafting "modesty guidelines" for future events. The guidelines were never actually written, but the threat had an immediate effect: two weeks later, a Tel Aviv dance troupe (also funded by the ministry) removed a topless number from its latest performance.

There was a prelude of sorts to the modesty guidelines in July, when the Shenkar art and design college outside Tel Aviv hosted an exhibition. One of the paintings, drawn by a student, featured a nude woman; while it did not identify her, her face looked unmistakably like Justice Minister Ayelet Shaked. The president of the college, Yuli Tamir, quickly ordered the painting to be removed.

The artist, Yam Amrani, could not explain the painting's artistic value, beyond saying that he hoped to "induce discomfort that conveys nihilism". The editorial board at *Ha'aretz* wrote in his defense, but many of their colleagues were unconvinced. One of the paper's former correspondents called the painting "cheap and old chauvinism"; Orit Kamir, a law professor at Hebrew University, penned a critical op-ed that called it an "act of shaming". But Larry Abramson, the head of the art school, resigned in protest. "Who's to judge? You have to allow art to be seen, even if you don't like it personally," he said. "It's always dangerous when a politician with a vested interest conducts cultural criticism."

"A liberal state is supposed to be neutral concerning the content of literature, of culture," Dahan said. "When this distinction is made, it's basically used to censor, to intimidate actors and writers."

This view was once shared by the leaders of the Israeli right. Menachem Begin, the first Likud prime minister, argued back in the 1950s that the Knesset should voluntarily limit its own authority. He wanted it to pass a law that would forbid future parliaments from "limiting oral or written freedom of expression or association or other basic civil and human rights." This view, needless to say, has fallen out of favor—not only with Regev, but with many younger lawmakers and activists on the right. The education ministry (led by Bennett) banned a novel featuring an Arab-Jewish romance from schools, calling it a threat to Jewish identity. Im Tirtzu, a far-right group that has campaigned mercilessly against liberal NGOs, released a poster that called Amos Oz, David Grossman, and other celebrated Israeli icons "moles in culture", suggesting that they were foreign agents. The Knesset debated one bill to bar Breaking the Silence, the anti-occupation group led by combat veterans, from speaking in Israeli schools, and another to forbid Israeli teenagers from doing their national service with liberal NGOs like B'Tselem. "It's part of a bigger picture of nationalism—trying to beat the left and the Arabs as much as you can," said Amir Fuchs, a researcher at the Israel Democracy Institute. "It's populism, which is a popular thing right now, and not only in Israel."

The Bibiton

The early elections that propelled Regev into the culture ministry happened for a number of reasons: Netanyahu's effort to push the "Jewish state law"; aftershocks from the Gaza war; the general fragility of his coalition. But there was an additional reason, which hasn't been mentioned yet: the so-called "*Israel HaYom* bill".

The prime minister has a unique advantage over his Israeli rivals, or indeed most democratically-elected leaders. He has a popular newspaper in his back pocket. His first stint in office lasted only three years, and he blamed his 1999 defeat partly on the media, telling aides "I lost because I didn't have a newspaper." He fixed that problem before returning to office with the help of his friend and ally Sheldon Adelson, the American casino magnate, who founded *Israel HaYom* ("Israel Today") in 2007. Adelson further expanded his media empire in 2015 with the purchase of *Makor Rishon* ("Primary Source"), a flagging conservative daily that now publishes weekly.

Israel HaYom is today the country's most-read publication, with a weekday print run of 325,000, one copy for every twenty-five Israelis. It owes its wide exposure largely to the fact that it is free. You can grab a copy from the display outside your local corner store or coffee shop. If you don't, a vendor might thrust one into your hands in the shopping mall—or even through your window as you sit in Tel Aviv traffic.

Adelson calls the paper a corrective, an attempt to fix a deep bias in the Israeli media. "The newspaper [sic] there was so far to the left politically that it was misleading the public," the reclusive mogul told the *Macau Daily Times* in a rare 2015 interview.[13] (Some Israelis wonder wryly how he would know: Adelson has never lived in Israel, nor does he speak Hebrew, though his wife is Israeli.)

"Maybe you believe him, maybe you don't," said Oren Persico, a reporter for *The Seventh Eye*, a media monitor founded by the nonpartisan Israel Democracy Institute (it now publishes independently). "But he had a mission, and he did this on behalf of his close friend, the prime minister."

It was, and is, an expensive mission. *Israel HaYom* does not disclose its finances, but a former business partner revealed in a 2011 deposition that it loses $3 million per month. Adelson's generous subsidy does not just ensure positive press for the prime minister; it also allows the newspaper to kneecap its rivals, particularly *Yediot Aharonot*, which once boasted the country's largest readership (and thus its most lucrative advertising space). Since *Israel HaYom* is not subject to regular market forces, it can offer cut-price ads, driving down revenues across the industry. A 2014 report by *The Seventh Eye* found that a full-page advertisement in *Israel HaYom* could be bought for one-third of the price of a similar ad in *Yediot:* 25,000 shekels (about $6,400), compared to roughly 80,000 shekels.[14]

The paper is broadly right-wing, but not dogmatically so. One of its regular columnists is Yossi Beilin, the liberal politician who helped to negotiate the Oslo Accords. *Israel HaYom*'s only real ideology is loyalty to the prime minister. Many Israelis call it the "Bibiton", a portmonteau of Netanyahu's nickname and *eiton*, the Hebrew word for newspaper. Others are more blunt. Avigdor Lieberman, who grew up in the Soviet Union, has compared it to *Pravda*, the mouthpiece of the Communist Party. My colleague at *The Economist*, Anshel Pfeffer, reported in 2015 that its headlines are "routinely approved by the prime minister's office."

In late 2014, the Knesset began debating the loftily-named "law for the advancement and protection of written journalism in Israel." Despite the title, its purpose was quite narrow: the bill would have made it illegal to distribute free daily newspapers. Or at least some of them. Israel has a number of smaller free tabloids, like the *Post*, which is found mostly in convenience stores and gas stations. But the *Post* is only printed five days a week—so the authors of the bill defined a "daily newspaper" as one that publishes six times. Their definition also specified a minimum number of pages. The result was a bill that only affected a single newspaper, and thus quickly became known as the "*Israel HaYom* bill". It was sponsored by Eitan Cabel, a lawmaker from the opposition Labor Party, but it attracted co-sponsors from five other parties, four of which were members of the coalition: Yesh Atid, Jewish Home, HaTnuah, and Yisrael Beiteinu. The legislation was one of the few issues to attract truly cross-partisan support.

Both *Israel HaYom* and the prime minister's office deny that there is any collusion over coverage. But in its most egregious moments, the paper really does live up to the *Pravda* comparisons. On the Saturday before the election, Netanyahu and his top challenger, Isaac Herzog, faced off for a "mini-debate" on Channel 2. Herzog was in the studio, while the prime minister spoke from his residence, looming over Herzog on a giant screen.

That Sunday's *Israel HaYom* featured a photo of the debate on page three, with an accusatory red circle around the earpiece clipped to Herzog's collar. "Herzog was the only interviewee with a headset," it noted matter-of-factly, implying that someone—perhaps his campaign staff, perhaps a Channel 2 producer—was feeding him material from backstage. The incriminating "headset", of course, was the IFB earpiece that any television guest wears. Herzog couldn't hear Netanyahu without one. The prime minister surely had one of his own. But Herzog had a reputation for being indecisive and clueless. *Israel HaYom* found a way to reinforce it, to hundreds of thousands of readers, just two days before the ballot.

His finger on the button

Benjamin Netanyahu was a busy man in his fourth government. In addition to his day job as prime minister, he also served as communications minister, foreign affairs minister, economy minister, and the "minister of regional cooperation." (He briefly added the defense portfolio to that list during the interregnum between Ya'alon's resignation and Lieberman's appointment.)

He took most of those jobs in order to hold them in reserve for a potential center-left coalition partner. The foreign ministry, in particular, was seen as a lure for Isaac Herzog, a way to entice him into a unity government. But one of them was sacrosanct. During his talks with Herzog, the Labor leader asked Netanyahu to give his party the communications ministry. "I'd give you the prime minister's job before that," Netanyahu reportedly replied. With two newspapers already in hand, he wanted to use the ministry to rein in Israel's broadcast and online media.

Israel is a tiny media market, smaller than even the population of 8.4 million would suggest. One-fifth of Israeli citizens are Arabs, who speak Hebrew but often prefer to consume the news in their first language. Channel 9, a Russian-language station, serves the million-plus Israelis who emigrated from the former Soviet Union. Native English speakers can choose from a plethora of newspapers and websites, plus a new television network, i24, which also broadcasts in French and Arabic. So the Hebrew media have a limited audience at home, and almost none abroad: most Jews in the diaspora cannot speak Hebrew well enough to read *Yediot Aharonot* or watch the Israeli news.

The country's most popular network, Channel 2, is run jointly by two companies called Reshet and Keshet. The prime minister has proposed breaking it apart, arguing that a split would encourage diversity and competition. It would also force both companies to hire their own news teams, at a cost of perhaps tens of millions of dollars, and strip Channel 2 of its status as the country's leading evening news program. "Israel is a small media market, and we can't export our news," said Amit Segal, the Channel 2 political correspondent. "So it would be better to have one big channel than two smaller ones that probably wouldn't be viable."

Channel 10, the country's most liberal, narrowly escaped bankruptcy in 2015 after an arcane licensing dispute. It blamed the prime minister for its financial woes, because he blocked a deal to settle the channel's long-standing debts. The network is seen as Israel's most edgy, and a perennial thorn in Netanyahu's side: its top investigative correspondent, Raviv Drucker, has doggedly pursued stories of official corruption, and once took the prime minister to court to find out how often he speaks with Adelson. Both channels are still operating normally, but the threat lingers. "Netanyahu is almost obsessed with the media, so it's amazing he's done nothing yet," Segal told me in early 2016. "But he wants us to know that he has his finger on the button."

The specter of "reform" also hung for years over the Israel Broadcasting Authority, which operated the state-run Channel 1 and several radio stations. For decades, the IBA was funded by a license fee, charged to any household with a television—whether or not they used it to watch IBA's dated programming. The Knesset voted to abolish the fee in 2014, partly due to reports that the broadcaster had spent 30 million shekels on lawyers to chase down families who didn't pay.

Around the same time, the poorly-managed IBA was declared bankrupt. The communications minister at the time, Gilad Erdan, drew up plans to replace it with a new Israeli Broadcasting Corporation, which branded itself "Kan", a Hebrew word for "here". It was meant to be everything IBA was not: modern, relevant, and digital-savvy. (Channel 1 often looks like a public-access station in a mid-sized American city; its studios could be a broadcasting museum.) Above all, it was to be immune from political pressure. Kan would be exempt from the oversight regulations that apply to most public corporations, a move which would limit the government's ability to appoint directors or influence editorial decisions.

Netanyahu approved the plan, but in mid-2016, months before Kan was scheduled to launch, he had a change of heart. In public, he argued that scrapping the new public broadcaster would increase competition in the Israeli media. In private, though, he offered a different reason for killing it: a fear that the new broadcaster, unlike its predecessor, would become a critical, liberal voice. "What if everyone in the corporation were people from Breaking the Silence?" he asked during one closed meeting with journalists. [15]

Regev put it even more bluntly during a cabinet meeting that summer. "What's the point of the corporation if we don't control it?" she asked. "What, we'll put up the money, and then they'll broadcast whatever they want?" [16] Some of her colleagues were incredulous. Gila Gamliel, a fellow minister from Likud, said publicly that Regev's remarks "bordered on fascism… we should keep in mind that we are a democratic state," she said.

On the other hand there was Channel 20, a station launched in 2014 to offer programming about Jewish culture and heritage. It soon positioned itself as an Israeli version of Fox News, complete with a fluttering flag graphic in the lower-left corner. The channel was fined several times for airing news content, which its charter did not allow, including coverage of the big right-wing rally just days before the 2015 election. Yet it continued to push an agenda: after President Reuven Rivlin appeared at a December conference that also hosted a left-wing NGO, it accused him of "crossing a red line" and "spitting in the faces" of Israeli soldiers.

The digital media, too, came under pressure. *Ha'aretz* reported in 2015 that editors at Walla, the country's most popular news site, had been instructed to post more positive coverage of the prime minister's wife, Sara. The government does not regulate websites, of course. But Walla is owned by Bezeq, Israel's largest phone company, which was then engaged in sensitive talks with the state about reforming its lucrative landline business. Its owner, Shaul Elovitch, is thought to be close to Netanyahu. "And who's handling the negotiations? The communications minister," said one Walla journalist. "The editor in chief has asked to personally review any stories dealing with Netanyahu."

Bottles and Bibitours

It was Netanyahu's third trip to Moscow in nine months, a visit meant to highlight the deepening ties with Israel's newest neighbor in the Middle East. He reached out to Vladimir Putin after the latter sent troops to prop up the Assad regime in Syria, and the two quickly became close. "We place great importance on our relationship with Israel," said Putin, who courted the Israeli prime minister with a surprise tour of the Kremlin and tickets to the Bolshoi.

Yet the first question at their 7 June press conference, from a reporter with Israel's state-run Channel 1, was about an explosive scandal involving a French financier who has been linked to kidnapping and murder. It was the latest in months of salacious stories about Netanyahu and his wife Sara, and the prime minister could barely contain his frustration. "They trample the image of my wife and turn her into human dust," he said, accusing the media of "systemic persecution".

The interpreter at the Kremlin declined to translate the lengthy answer into Russian, saying it was about domestic issues. "But why?" Putin asked with a chuckle. "It's interesting to us, too."

If there is one man in Israeli politics who can bring down Benjamin Netanyahu, it is Benjamin Netanyahu. He has featured in a truly impressive list of corruption scandals during his eight-plus years in office. Many of them are small-time swindles—a politician taking advantage of his position to live the high life, or just to line his pockets a bit (like the absurd "Bottlegate" scandal, in which his wife pocketed the eight-cent refunds from returning empty wine bottles that were purchased by the state). But several are not. His personal lawyer, David Shimron, has been accused of a conflict of interest in Israel's $1.3 billion purchase of three submarines from Germany. Shimron also works with ThyssenKrupp, the German conglomerate that manufactures the subs. The deal was approved in 2016 after an unusually short period of discussion; Moshe Ya'alon, who was the defense minister when it was first mooted, said he "strenuously opposed" the purchase.

Then there was Arnaud Mimran, the 44-year-old French playboy accused of taking part in a vast carbon-trading fraud that may have cost European taxpayers €5 billion. French authorities called it the "heist of the century." In May 2016, Mimran told a French court that he had given €1 million to Netanyahu's reelection campaign. Apart from the ethical issues, the donation would have been a major violation of Israeli election law, which caps individual donations at about $3,000. Both men quickly changed their stories: Mimran later said the gift was actually €170,000, then just €40,000; Netanyahu initially denied receiving any money, then said it was for "public diplomacy on behalf of Israel", not his campaign. The attorney general eventually opened an investigation.

The two were undeniably friends. Mimran told the court how he brought Netanyahu into a fancy private club in Paris; the French website Mediapart turned up photos of them dining in a seaside restaurant in Monte Carlo in 2003. That was a year after Mimran and six other defendants paid $1.3 million to settle insider-trading charges with the SEC. And he seemed to graduate quickly beyond securities fraud. Authorities believe that Mimran smuggled some of his stolen money through Israeli banks. The gangster who helped launder it turned up dead in 2010. Police have also accused Mimran of kidnapping another associate, a Swiss banker, and holding him hostage until he agreed to forfeit his share in a jointly-held company. He was a dubious associate for a head of government.

A veritable shadow cabinet has done time in Israeli prisons, which is one reason why Transparency International ranks Israel as among the most corrupt countries in the developed world. Aryeh Deri was convicted of taking bribes while serving as interior minister in the 1990s; he was reappointed to the same job in 2016, and quickly fell under investigation again. The previous prime minister, Ehud Olmert, is locked up for graft. In early 2016, on his last morning as a free man, a local radio station invited a former health minister—another ex-con—to offer some advice. (The guards are "not sentimental about ministers," he noted.) Barak and Sharon were both investigated, though neither was charged.

At the center of many Netanyahu scandals is Sara—or "The Lady", as the chattering classes sometimes call her. She lost two civil lawsuits in 2016 filed by former domestic workers who accused her of verbal and emotional abuse. One employee claimed she had used racist slurs, allegedly complaining, "We are sophisticated Europeans. We don't eat as much food as you Moroccans. You are stuffing us, so that when they photograph us abroad, we look fat." Another said he had been summoned back to the residence at antisocial hours, sometimes to reheat soup after midnight, other times because he forgot to wish the first lady a good night. Her troubles worsened in May, when the police recommended filing criminal charges over some truly surreal accusations. She might have used state funds to order take-out. She might have stolen patio furniture.

Every journalist in Israel has a notebook full of these "Sara stories", tales of turmoil at home and minor diplomatic incidents abroad. Few publish them, for fear of burning a source—or of a lawsuit. In early 2016 Yigal Sarna, a reporter for *Yediot Aharonot*, wrote on Facebook that Sara had tossed her husband out of their motorcade on the highway between Jerusalem and Tel Aviv. The Netanyahus slapped him with a $70,000 libel case.

More often than not, though, the stories are true. Nearly a decade ago, Channel 10's Drucker introduced the "Bibitours" scandal, accusing Netanyahu (during his time as finance minister) of taking cash from foreign donors to pay for his family's travels. The Netanyahus denied any wrongdoing; three libel cases soon followed. In May 2016, after a long-stalled investigation, the comptroller vindicated Drucker's reporting. In one instance, a British businessman had spent more than $12,000 to host the Netanyahus and their son in a glitzy London hotel. The businessman, identified only as "B", had tourism and real estate dealings in Israel. The donations had not been vetted by the Knesset ethics committee and "created the appearance of a conflict of interest", said the comptroller, who forwarded his findings to the attorney general for a criminal probe.

Corruption is not unique to Israel, nor is it new. Yitzhak Rabin resigned in 1977 over a financial scandal. But attitudes have changed markedly since then. A country romanticized for its socialist *kibbutzim* is now a neoliberal economy, with the attendant inequality; among members of the OECD, it ranks second to only the United States. Much of the Israeli public doubts that the Netanyahus will see the inside of a courtroom. A poll by the Israel Democracy Institute found that 50 per cent of Jews don't trust the authorities to properly investigate the first family.

The men tasked with running the inquiries have not inspired confidence. Comptroller Yosef Shapira has been accused of stalling his investigations and softening their conclusions. The final report on household spending, for example, allegedly deleted an unfavorable comparison to expenses at the White House and Downing Street. Yehuda Weinstein, the attorney general from 2010 until January 2016, was Netanyahu's defense lawyer the first time the prime minister was investigated for corruption. His successor, Avichai Mandelblit, served previously as Netanyahu's cabinet secretary, and is thought to be a personal friend. Netanyahu appointed all three, along with the police chief, Roni Alsheich, who also seems to be shielding his boss. The terse official statement on the Sara Netanyahu probe did not mention that the police backed criminal charges, nor even her name—a break with usual policy. Those details were leaked later by frustrated investigators.

The scandal that felled Rabin was the revelation that his wife Leah had a foreign bank account, which was then illegal; she was later convicted and fined. It was a far less serious offense than anything Netanyahu is accused of, but he stepped down regardless. "We used to be a very homogeneous society, where nobody had a lot of money," said Ifat Zamir, the head of the Israeli branch of Transparency International. "And then in the 1990s, some people earned a lot of money, and the world changed with them. And so did the public's trust in the government."

"It's fun, I enjoy it"

It was, admittedly, a macabre subject: how to handle the bodies of Palestinian attackers. The interviewer was Razi Barkai, a veteran host on Army Radio; though it is run by the military, it often provides tough, balanced journalism. His interviewee, Gilad Erdan (the public security minister in Netanyahu's fourth government), said he did not believe they should be returned to families for burial. Barkai wondered whether their families were any different from the families of the two Israeli soldiers whose bodies have been held by Hamas since the end of the 2014 war in Gaza.

It was an emotionally charged comparison, but nonetheless a valid question about a deeply controversial topic. Moshe Ya'alon, who was then the defense minister, disagreed with Erdan's policy. But the director of Army Radio quickly apologized to listeners, and announced that Barkai's airtime would be cut in half, with the second hour given to Erel Segal, a right-wing commentator who once contemplated running for parliament with the ruling party. "It's no secret that I support Netanyahu and the Likud," he said in 2015. "What was, a few years ago, the opinion of the hard right in Israel has now become the mainstream," said Persico, the media reporter. "And I think journalists are looking around and seeing how the public opinion is moving."

Israel prides itself on having the freest press in the Middle East, and often compares itself to the West in this regard. "As I can personally attest to you, the press in Israel is robust, free, very energetic, and free to say anything that it wants," Netanyahu said in early 2016, during a press conference in Berlin with Angela Merkel, the German chancellor.

The newspaper was the dominant form of media in both the Yishuv, the pre-state Jewish community, and the first few decades after 1948. *Yediot Aharonot*, founded in 1939, is still the country's largest paid newspaper, while the century-old *Ha'aretz* endures as the daily of choice for liberals in Tel Aviv. But there was also a rich tradition of partisan press. Mapai and Herut, the forerunners of today's Labor and Likud, both had their own newspapers. So did the Revisionists, the Religious Zionists, the kibbutz movement, and even the Histadrut, the confederation of Israeli labor unions. As Israel's national library put it, "In general, the Yishuv excelled in political polarization, and the reigning assumption was that each party needed a daily publication of its own."[17]

The Israel Broadcasting Authority started radio transmissions in 1948, but it was the written word that really shaped public opinion. Television came late. The first proper broadcast channel didn't launch until 1968, and it would not have any competition for another two decades. (The "Big Three" networks in the US, for comparison, all started broadcasting in the 1940s; the BBC started daily television newscasts in 1954.) Even today, Hebrew options are limited, particularly for news: the two private stations, plus the state-owned Channel 1. (In late 2016, Channel 20 was granted a news license.)

Non-Israelis often view *Ha'aretz* as the country's newspaper of record, a sort of Israeli *New York Times* (the Grey Bubbe, if you will). But the paper actually has less than a 5 per cent market share. Outside of Tel Aviv, Haifa and other liberal redoubts, it is seen as angry and out-of-touch. Occasional headlines like "Israel is an evil state" do not endear it to the public. Most Israelis get their news from the *Bibiton*, or from *Yediot*. The latter is critical of Netanyahu, but on other issues it takes a nationalist, jingoistic tone that is often indistinguishable from *Israel HaYom*. The same goes for Channel 2, which is hardly known for its crusading investigative journalism. Their military correspondent, Roni Daniel, is sometimes jokingly called the "IDF spokesman" because he hews so closely to the official line. During the 2006 Lebanon war he angrily asked a real army spokesman why they weren't dropping more bombs on Beirut. He also dismissed a video of two Palestinian teenagers shot during a May 2014 protest as a fake, a claim that was swiftly disproved. (A year after the third Gaza war, he made an impassioned call for Israel to "change its policy" and lift the blockade of the strip; a local NGO worker forwarded me the clip, calling it the clearest sign yet that the army was unhappy with Netanyahu's position on Gaza.)

For a foreign journalist, Israel is one of the most accessible countries in the Middle East. It is also the most heavily scrutinized, with pro-Israel groups like CAMERA that pore over every word written about the conflict. The pressure has grown in recent years, partly due to the advent of social media. Michael Oren once suggested that Israel's advocates engage in online "shaming" of journalists—which, I can assure him, they need little encouragement to do.

In February 2016, a Knesset subcommittee called a hearing to discuss unfair media coverage of Israel. It was convened because of a headline published on CBS a week earlier, after three Palestinians armed with guns, knives, and explosives tried to carry out a serious attack in East Jerusalem. Two Israeli policewomen foiled the plot by killing the attackers. Both officers were hurt, and one, Hadar Cohen, died of her wounds that evening. The poorly-worded headline on the CBS website, though, was "Three Palestinians killed as daily violence grinds on". The foreign ministry spokesman immediately sent a screen grab of the headline to journalists, calling it "unprecedented chutzpah". The image rocketed around social media, with Tzipi Livni, a former foreign minister, accusing the network of "choosing sides". Nitzan Chen, the head of the government press office, wrote on Facebook that he would consider revoking press credentials from outlets that published such headlines.

At the hearing, lawmakers asked Chen to provide other examples of media bias. He cited three other headlines from CBS, CNN, and the BBC. That was the extent of his presentation: four faulty headlines, out of thousands filed since October. All four were written by producers in New York, Atlanta, and London. None of them were the fault of Jerusalem-based correspondents. "I fail to see how the media has something to answer for in terms of systemic bias," said Luke Baker, the Reuters bureau chief in Jerusalem, who testified at the hearing.

This kind of petty criticism reflects the growing sense that Israel is losing the battle for public opinion in the West. So does the recent proliferation of English-language outlets that take a broadly pro-Israel line. None of them can exactly claim the mantle of journalistic objectivity. There is *Mosaic*, an online magazine published by the Tikvah Fund, the largest financial backer of the Shalem Center, a neoconservative think tank that has groomed several of Netanyahu's closest associates. *The Tower* is run by The Israel Project, a nonprofit that aims to "communicate proven, effective messages that encourage people to support Israel." *Fathom* is a project of the Britain Israel Communications and Research Center, a *hasbara* shop in London. It mirrors the prime minister's efforts to create his own parallel media, and to use social media to get around the "filter" of the mainstream media. "There's a real sense that Israel is hunkering down," said one longtime wire service reporter. "Attitudes are changing in Europe and in America, and Israelis are blaming us for that."

By the end of 2016, Kan was ready to start broadcasting. The corporation had already hired hundreds of journalists and started building a permanent studio. Weeks before the launch, though, Netanyahu suddenly introduced a bill to close it. Finance Minister Moshe Kahlon opposed the move. They eventually agreed on a four-month delay, amending the broadcasting law to bar Kan from launching before May 2017. The IBA would continue operations in the meantime. "The entire goal of the amendment is to buy time," Netanyahu admitted during a cabinet meeting—time, as everyone knew, that he hoped to use to kill the new broadcaster. The delay will cost Israeli taxpayers 140 million shekels, money that was pulled out of other areas of the budget, like education. Meanwhile, the state finally gave up trying to punish Channel 20, and awarded the right-wing network a license to air news coverage.

In the meanwhile, Netanyahu, emboldened by the rise of Donald Trump, ramped up his hostility to the mainstream press. In November, Channel 2 aired a well-researched documentary on the chaotic and paranoid culture inside the prime minister's office. The program, based on interviews with his associates, reported that his wife sets the agenda for his diplomatic trips and advises him on high-level decisions. One adviser recalled asking Netanyahu how to draft a briefing on the prisoner swap with Hamas that freed Gilad Shalit, the Israeli soldier captured in 2006. "Ask my wife what she thinks," he said. Netanyahu did not respond to the specific allegations. Instead he sent the channel a remarkable three-page tirade, a personal attack that called the presenter, Ilana Dayan, an "extreme leftist" who "hates the prime minister". She read the entire message at the end of the program in a theatrical segment that lasted more than six minutes. "The time has come to unmask Ilana Dayan, who has proved once again that she has not even a drop of professional integrity," the prime minister wrote. "Dayan's show this evening demonstrates perfectly why the media industry needs to undergo reform."

A few weeks later, amidst a swirl of new stories about official corruption, he posted a late-night screed against Raviv Drucker on his Facebook page. "Through daily brainwashing of the public, and character assassination of me and my family, they hope to distract the public's attention from the core issues of political debate in Israel," he wrote.

He was asked about all of this in the winter of 2016, at an annual toast for the foreign press corps: should a head of state offer such sharp criticism of the media? Encouraged, perhaps, by Donald Trump's recent election, he flippantly dismissed the criticism. "It's fun, I enjoy it," he said.

Religion and state

Yisrael Katz was perhaps the only man in Israel wishing he had hit more traffic on the way to work. The transportation minister, a Likud stalwart with nearly two decades in the Knesset, strode into the prime minister's office with an unconvincing grin plastered onto his face. The cabinet was gathering for its weekly meeting, and the rumor swirling around Jerusalem was that it might be Katz's last. He remained overtly buoyant throughout the discussion—at least the part of it open to the press. But the tension in the room was palpable. Katz didn't exchange a single word with the man sitting next to him, his boss, who wasted little time going after his latest enemy. "Ministers are appointed in order to avoid crises and solve problems, not create them," Netanyahu said sternly. He didn't look at Katz. He didn't have to.

Out on the roads, there was indeed a crisis. The highway between Tel Aviv and Haifa, Israel's second- and third-largest cities, was a parking lot in many places. It took three-and-a-half hours for some commuters to reach Tel Aviv from Hadera, a city just thirty miles to the north. One man, trudging off a two-hour bus ride from nearby Netanya, thought back wistfully to his recent family vacation in Greece. "The flight was faster than this," he joked.

The reason for all this was a surreal one, even by local standards. Israel Railways, the state-owned train company, had scheduled a round of maintenance for the previous day, 3 September—a Saturday, the Jewish day of rest. The timing made sense: trains do not run on Saturdays, road traffic is light, and most workers have the day off. Indeed, the company often schedules work for the sabbath. "We've been doing this for years," said Keren Turner, the director-general of Katz's ministry. Just a week earlier, also on Shabbat, the rail company expanded the passenger terminal in central Tel Aviv, which sits in the middle of its main urban freeway, the Ayalon. The project required hoisting two 560-ton, 60-meter-long structures into position, in little over 24 hours—no small feat of engineering, the sort of achievement many governments would brag about. Ultra-Orthodox lawmakers, the self-proclaimed guardians of the sabbath, chose to look the other way.

They are not always so accommodating: there have been mass prayer rallies and protests, occasionally violent ones, against the opening of movie theaters, shopping malls, even a parking lot. This wasn't even Israel's first Shabbat-linked coalition crisis. Yitzhak Rabin barely survived a no-confidence motion in 1976 after Israel received its first shipment of F-15 fighter jets from the United States. The planes landed in the late afternoon, and the welcoming ceremony did not end until well after dark. More than two decades later, in 1999, the electric company needed to move a giant turbine from Tel Aviv to the port city of Ashkelon. It would have snarled weekday traffic across central Israel, because the truck carrying it could only move at a few miles per hour. So the company decided to ship it on a Saturday, which caused United Torah Judaism, one of the two ultra-Orthodox parties, to leave Ehud Barak's coalition.

Netanyahu is secular, like many of his predecessors, but the prime minister's office goes to great lengths to avoid publicly desecrating Shabbat or otherwise violating Jewish law. The ultra-Orthodox press was briefly outraged in 2014 when it learned that he lunched at Fresco by Scotto, an excellent but decidedly un-kosher Italian restaurant in midtown Manhattan; one newspaper called it the "pig restaurant". (He had the veal chops, according to the *New York Post*.) He was forced to explain himself in a television interview the following week, telling Channel 2 that, while he occasionally dines in non-kosher restaurants, "I don't eat non-kosher foods."

But for the railway, a crucial piece of infrastructure in a modern state, the ultra-Orthodox made a quiet exception—until September. The nature of the work made it harder to ignore: the Tel Aviv project wasn't an isolated track repair, after all, but a major logistical operation in the heart of the country. Mostly, though, they spoke up because their constituents did. *Haredi* journalists started to complain about the Shabbat desecration, aiming their criticism not only at Katz and the transport ministry, but also the ultra-Orthodox parties, which they accused of enabling him. The debate started on Twitter, an increasingly popular medium in the ultra-Orthodox world. "Bibi thinks that the *haredim* are stupid," wrote Beni Rabinovich, a writer at *Yated Ne'eman*, a daily ultra-Orthodox newspaper. "I hope the *haredi* parties know how to collect a political price tag from Yisrael Katz," said Arye Erlich, the deputy editor of *Mishpacha*. A third columnist, Ya'akov Rivlin, argued that the ultra-Orthodox parties were desperately trying to avoid a political crisis because they feared leaving the government. "Shabbat is a political pawn," he concluded.

The politicians quickly fell in line. They asked for a meeting with Netanyahu, and warned him that any further construction would force them to leave the coalition. The prime minister, in his usual indecisive fashion, dawdled until the last possible moment—Friday afternoon, 2 September, less than an hour before the start of Shabbat. Then he canceled the maintenance. His decision took the railway by surprise: workers had already started to dismantle sections of track, which meant the trains would be out of service when the day of rest ended. They went home for an unexpected dinner with their families.

So the rail line between Tel Aviv and Haifa was shut during the Sunday rush, with predictable results. Netanyahu's decree inconvenienced a large chunk of the country, and it cost the railway more than $3 million, mostly in the form of lost revenue and compensation paid to the workers who had been scheduled for Saturday. And it didn't even prevent Shabbat desecration: the contractors went home, but the transportation ministry had to call in more than 100 employees to organize shuttle buses and other emergency transit.

The trains, for their part, finally got rolling again on Sunday evening, after a 24-hour delay. The first northbound service made it halfway to Haifa, then screeched to a halt after it hit a wild boar.

Outsmarting God

One of Israel's most unique traditions is the *shmita*, a fallowing of the fields that occurs every seven years. The Torah forbids farmers from plowing or planting; fruits or vegetables that grow naturally are considered public property, and may not be sold. The sabbatical is mandated repeatedly in the Torah, but only within the borders of the ancient lands of Israel. For farmers in the diaspora, from Brod to Baghdad, it was an irrelevant injunction.

It finally became relevant again in the late nineteenth century, as the first large waves of Jewish immigrants settled in Ottoman Palestine. A year-long break would have been devastating for newly-arrived farmers struggling to work the land and feed themselves. But the early Zionist rabbis were keen to honor the Biblical commandment. Their solution was called a *heter mechira*, literally a "permit of sale". Shortly before the start of the seventh year, Jewish farmers would sell their land to non-Jews, albeit temporarily: ownership would automatically revert back one year later. Nonetheless, the sale would remove the obligation to observe the *shmita*, which is only incumbent upon Jewish-owned land. Israel uses a similar sleight of hand before Passover, when the chief rabbis ceremoniously "sell" the country's *chametz* to an Arab citizen, a jovial hotelier from Abu Ghosh, before the holiday. (The contract is voided eight days later, when the buyer inevitably fails to pay the $150 million bill for the national stockpile of bread.)

There is a well-worn joke that goes roughly like this: some years ago, a young Jewish man bought a non-refundable plane ticket to attend his sister's wedding in New York. The ticket, unfortunately, required him to travel on Shabbat. Eager to attend the wedding, however, and unable to afford a different flight, he asked his rabbi if such a thing would ever be permissible. After a moment of thought, the rabbi offered a solution. "Keep your seatbelt fastened," he said. "Then you are not riding the plane, you are wearing it."

Jewish scholars have spent thousands of years inventing ways to dodge the strictures of the religion—to honor them in spirit, if not in practice. First-time visitors to Israel are occasionally confused by the "Shabbat elevators", which run constantly throughout the day. The Torah forbids "building" on the Sabbath, a prohibition extended in modern times to closing an electrical circuit. Pressing the button for your floor would be an act of desecration. So the elevators, a common sight in hotels and tall apartment complexes, stop automatically on each floor, allowing observant passengers to reach their destination (albeit quite slowly).

These compromises, between Jewish tradition and the hum of modern life, are essential to a diverse, industrialized country like Israel. Yet rabbis and politicians who once supported them are now more and more likely to object. Partly this is simple arithmetic: as the ultra-Orthodox population has grown, so has their political clout. And, as the train saga illustrated, journalists and activists have become adept at using modern technology to battle modern life.

Guardians of Shabbat

A Friday evening in August, the sort of languid Shabbat when much of Israel seems to grind to a halt. In Jerusalem, though, thousands of protesters were on the streets, throwing stones at police and shattering the windows of a government building. The reason? A cinema.

Yes Planet, a local chain, had just opened a new sixteen-screen theater in Abu Tor, a mixed Jewish and Palestinian neighborhood south of the Old City. Unusually for Jerusalem, it would stay open on Shabbat. A few months earlier, a second new cinema had tried to do business on the sabbath. The municipality refused because it was built on state-owned land; the case eventually found its way to the supreme court. But the Yes Planet theater was built on private land, and the city couldn't block it. So the ultra-Orthodox community tried to. Flyers quickly went up in their neighborhoods, calling the cinema a "plague" on the city. "Shabbat in Jerusalem is in terrible danger," they warned.

Jewish law forbids almost all forms of work on Shabbat, except activities defined as *pikuach nefesh*—preserving a life. Thus a doctor can perform emergency surgery, but not a cosmetic procedure, and an observant Jew can drive a critically ill patient to the hospital, and the fire brigade can stop a stray Shabbat candle from burning an entire neighborhood.

The state of Israel does not actually have a "Shabbat law". It has a 1951 labor law, which stipulates that members of each faith are entitled to their traditional days of rest: Friday for Muslims, Sunday for Christians, and Shabbat for Jews. The state law also makes a wider class of exceptions for Shabbat than religious law does: it's not just the emergency services that work as normal, but also things like hotels. Critical infrastructure is on the list, too. The electric company will repair downed power lines on a Saturday, and pharmacies set a rotating schedule to ensure the public can buy medicine. The laws on Shabbat observance, in other words, make accommodations for modern life.

A separate law passed in 1990 allows local authorities to impose their own Shabbat regulations. Most of Israel's cities have rules, but when the Knesset surveyed the twenty-five largest cities in 2014, it found that thirteen—more than half—did not rigorously enforce them. Ramat Gan, a suburb of Tel Aviv with a bustling commercial center, handed out 142 fines for Shabbat violations in 2011. The following year it issued two. Either the business community had a sudden crisis of religious conscience, or authorities simply gave up applying the law. "It's not possible for us to map the fines that were handed out by inspectors," said officials in Petah Tikva, a sleepy central city with a largely non-Orthodox population.[18]

Confusing as it is, this arrangement works for cities with a distinct religious character. Secular Tel Aviv winks at the law but largely ignores it, deploying just four inspectors each weekend to patrol a city of 425,000 people; my neighborhood supermarket happily sells bacon on a Saturday morning. Adjacent Bnei Brak has seven qualified inspectors, all of whom stay home on Shabbat. The city is ultra-Orthodox, and nobody would think to desecrate the holy day. The problems arise where Israel's secular and religious tribes rub shoulders.

The ultra-Orthodox don't always win. A *haredi* man named Meir Cohen was briefly famous in 2015 for a series of YouTube videos he made at a shopping center in Ashdod, which does business on Shabbat. He would stand outside the mall and yell *Shabbat HaYom!* ("Today is the Sabbath!") at passersby. Eventually the police got tired of him, and arrested him for harassment. The shopping center is still open. There was also the years-long saga of a humble parking lot in Jerusalem. In a bid to encourage tourism, the municipality decided in 2009 to offer free parking on Shabbat in a garage on Safra Square, near city hall. Thousands of ultra-Orthodox residents came out to protest, some of them throwing stones at police, who hauled out fire hoses to disperse the crowds. A leading rabbi threatened to "burn the city" if the lot was allowed to open. The mayor, Nir Barkat, suspended the plan for two weeks, which prompted a counter-protest by secular Jerusalemites. Seven years later, the lot is open, and the protests have long since stopped. Outside of ultra-Orthodox areas, Shabbat is much more lively today than it was decades ago.

Demographics and economics have helped the secular community. The ultra-Orthodox, with their large families and low incomes, are increasingly priced out of Jerusalem. They move to outlying communities, which dilutes their power. But the same demographics also offer a bad portent for non-Orthodox Israelis.

Jerusalem has a few volunteer "guardians of Shabbat", men who spend the holy day roaming the streets and yelling at motorists. One of them—after he got over his surprise that someone pulled over to chat—offered a confident prediction. "I have sixteen children," he said. "Maybe we're losing for now. But we'll win the demographic war."

"Widespread assimilation"

One day in the summer of 2016, a pickup truck laden with mattresses pulled onto my street, just south of the flea market and the old Jaffa port. The district is a mix of Jews, Christians and Muslims, and a model of coexistence, home to one of Israel's few bilingual Jewish-Arab kindergartens. The park where I walk my dog is called *Gan HaShnaim*, the "Garden of the Two", named for the Jewish woman who was killed in 1992 by a sword-wielding man from Gaza—and the Arab owner of a neighborhood garage, who ran out with a crowbar to defend her and was also cut down. Even at the height of the "stabbing intifada," when tensions were at a boil across the country, the neighborhood was almost entirely peaceful, save for a few teenagers who threw stones at a bus one night. The next morning, most of the local business owners wanted them tossed in prison.

The mattresses were headed for a formerly vacant house a few doors down from my apartment building. The original Arab owners fled in 1948, during Israel's war of independence, and the house was declared "absentee property". It changed hands a few times, until it was bought by a wealthy Argentinean Jew who transferred it to a yeshiva called Shirat Moshe, which is located near the sea, about a kilometer away. The building on my street was to be used as a residence for dozens of students.

Shirat Moshe was founded in 2008, in an effort to establish a "Jewish presence" in Jaffa. Not that one is lacking: about two-thirds of Jaffa's residents are Jewish. But they tend to be secular and liberal. At my neighborhood polling station, center-left Zionist parties and the Joint List won roughly 80 per cent of the vote in 2015. The yeshiva was, in essence, a national-religious settlement inside Israel's 1948 borders. It has posted flyers warning of the widespread "assimilation" in the community. "20 per cent of children are born to mixed marriages", one leaflet claimed. (A gross exaggeration: Jewish-Arab marriages are exceedingly rare, even in Jaffa.) Eliyahu Mali, the yeshiva's reclusive rabbi, once complained to a religious website that Jaffa was "empty of Jewish content".

Mali also described the Arabs in Jaffa as "resident aliens", rather than full citizens. Many of his students seemed to agree. They routinely heckled my neighbors, calling them "inferior", "dirty Arabs", and other derogatory terms. They called the police throughout that first summer, often on spurious grounds—once because a child kicked a ball into their courtyard. Some of my Arab neighbors have been stopped by police and asked for identification on their own street, where their families have lived for decades. The community organized weekly protests, one of which was joined by Knesset members from Meretz and the Joint List. Eitan Shmueli, who lives with his family in the apartment below me, received a letter from the yeshiva's lawyer, warning him to stop "provoking and inciting" against the dormitory.

It was a small, local story, barely covered in the Israeli press, let alone my own newspapers. Yet it was also deeply revealing. For most of Jaffa's residents, the neighborhood's character is a source of pride and optimism, the rare place in greater Israel that suggests Jews and Arabs are not doomed to internecine conflict. Yet for a growing segment of the Israeli population, that *modus vivendi* is a source of anger and disappointment, one they are actively working to undo. The municipality has offered little help, even though it probably could: the building is zoned as a private residence; using it as a dormitory for dozens of students is legally dubious. (After it opened, one of the most common complaints on the street was the lack of parking.)

"Of course the problem isn't that they're Jewish, or that they're religious," another neighbor said. "It's that they're trying to bring the conflict to our street."

Jews have argued for millennia over who is a Jew. The question even has its own Wikipedia page. The establishment of Israel did not resolve that question. On the contrary, it deepened it. In the diaspora, it added a political dimension to Jewishness: some Jews, like President Trump's ambassador to Israel, do not believe that non-Zionists are members of the tribe. And in Israel, the debate—largely irrelevant, of course, to the fifth of the Israeli population that is not Jewish—feels increasingly zero-sum.

Different Israeli Jews have fundamentally incompatible views on how to define Israel as a "Jewish and democratic state". One survey has found that 69 per cent of the ultra-Orthodox, and 46 per cent of the national-religious (a plurality), feel that the state is too democratic. It has also found that 59 per cent of secular Jews think it is too Jewish. A majority of Israeli Jews feel it is inappropriate for Arab lawmakers to sit in the coalition, and majorities of several sub-groups think it is acceptable that the state allocates more money to Jewish communities than to Arab ones.[19]

"We're caught in a crisis of identity. People are worried about globalization, about a sense of losing tradition," said Ofer Zalzberg, a Jerusalem-based analyst for the International Crisis Group. "It's the autonomy of the individual versus Jewish tradition. And nobody knows which side will win."

"I won't forget to die"

It was surely the sort of funeral he would have wanted, with an aerial convoy of world leaders and other bold-faced names flying in to pay their respects. President Obama made the 20-hour round trip from Washington to deliver a 20-minute speech. So did his Democratic predecessor, Bill Clinton, his voice cracking as he remembered his old friend. The Prince of Wales was in the audience, wearing a kippah emblazoned with the royal crest. Dozens of countries, from Canada to Egypt to Australia, sent high-level delegations.

Shimon Peres was the last of Israel's founding fathers, the men who were present at the creation in 1948, when David Ben-Gurion proclaimed a Jewish state in Palestine. His political career went on to span more than half a century. As the master of ceremonies read a list of his roles in public service, it sounded like he was calling the roll of the entire Israeli government, from premier and president to transportation minister and leader of the opposition. Above all, though, he was Israel's elder statesman, a once-controversial politician who achieved something close to universal respect later in life. He stayed active in politics until almost the last of his ninety-three years. In 2007, when an octogenarian Peres ran for Israel's ceremonial presidency, critics wondered if he was too old for the job. "Don't worry," he quipped. "I won't forget to die."

He had a few health scares after his term ended, including a heart attack in January 2016, but at times it seemed he might break his promise. He kept an active schedule, meeting regularly with Israelis and Palestinians, and with world leaders on his frequent trips abroad. On the afternoon of 13 September, however, he suffered a stroke. The prognosis initially looked grim, but surprisingly his condition stabilized overnight, and aides began talking about a recovery. Two weeks later, though, he took another turn for the worse. Doctors said he had suffered organ failure and irreversible brain damage. His family was summoned to Sheba Medical Center in Tel Aviv. Old friends, like Labor leader Isaac Herzog, came to his bedside to say their goodbyes. His children announced his death in the early hours of 28 September. As dawn broke it was, in Prime Minister Netanyahu's words, "the first day that the state of Israel has existed without Shimon Peres."

In Jewish tradition, the dead are buried on the same day. Peres' family made an exception, to allow foreign dignitaries time to arrive. His body was taken to Jerusalem on 29 September, where it lay in state on the stone plaza in front of the Knesset. Tens of thousands of Israelis came to pay their respects, with the twelve-hour viewing period extended until 11 pm to accommodate the crowds. They wept, they lit candles, they took selfies. (A few Israeli journalists complained about the lack of decorum, but Peres, a technophile who had signed up for Snapchat on his 93rd birthday, probably would not have minded.)

The next morning, a Friday, he made his final journey to Mount Herzl, the site of Israel's national cemetery. He was laid to rest between two of his oldest rivals: Yitzhak Rabin, who had fought him for decades over control of their Labor party; and Yitzhak Shamir, the Likud leader who had been forced into a power-sharing agreement with Peres after a tight election in 1984.

Before the final part of the ceremony, though, he was eulogized by Netanyahu, President Rivlin, and Knesset speaker Yuli Edelstein; by Clinton and Obama; and by his children. Only the latter (and Rivlin) really tried to eulogize the man himself. The rest of the speeches were political. Some Israelis thought it tasteless—but again, it was hard to imagine Peres, a lifelong political animal, taking offense. His son Yoni, who works as a veterinarian in Tel Aviv, even alluded to his father's priorities in a melancholy passage of his speech. "He decided to dedicate his life to the country and its people," the younger Peres said. "My sister, my brother and I were raised with great devotion by our beloved mother, Sonia."

In his later years, Peres was dedicated most of all to the peace process. Outside of Israel, he is best known for his work on the Oslo Accords, the treaty that gave the Palestinians a degree of autonomy and launched the formal talks about a two-state solution. He shared a Nobel Peace Prize for his efforts, alongside Rabin and Palestinian leader Yasser Arafat. And he continued to work on the issue for the next two decades—even during his stint as president, when Netanyahu's governments had little interest in peace talks.

In the iconic 1993 photos of the Oslo signing ceremony on the White House lawn, Bill Clinton is flanked by four men from the Holy Land: Rabin, Peres, Arafat, and Mahmoud Abbas. Only Abbas is still alive, and the Palestinian president is a spent force, eighty-two years old and deeply unpopular with his own people. It was hard to escape the symbolism of Peres' funeral—a farewell to the man, but also to his great cause. On the Hebrew calendar, ironically, it fell on 27 Elul, twenty-three years to the day after that optimistic moment in Washington.

"Peace is not only possible, it is essential, because we have nowhere to go from here, and the Palestinians also have nowhere to go from here," said Amos Oz, the celebrated Israeli writer who was a longtime friend of the late president. "Where are the brave leaders who will stand up and make these things a reality? Where are Shimon Peres' successors?"

Hawkish man of peace

Peres was born Szymon Perski in a village in eastern Poland (now part of Belarus). His family emigrated to Palestine in the 1930s, when he was eleven. It was a fateful decision: his relatives who stayed behind were killed during the Holocaust, many of them burned alive in the town synagogue. "The doors were locked from the outside and the wooden structure was torched," he said in 2010 during a speech to the German parliament. "And the only remains of the whole community were embers."

He quickly threw himself into junior politics, rising through the ranks of the Labor movement and attracting the attention of David Ben-Gurion. He joined the Haganah, the main pre-state militia, but never saw combat. Instead he was tasked with procuring weapons. His closeness to Ben-Gurion led to a series of lofty assignments: first head of the Israeli navy, then the director of the defense ministry's mission in New York. In 1952, four years after Israel declared independence—when Peres was just twenty-nine—he was named deputy director-general of the defense ministry.

Despite the mythology of Peres the peacemaker, his work at the defense ministry was his most important legacy. Ben-Gurion tasked him with acquiring a nuclear weapon, a doomsday device that would shield the tiny, vulnerable state. Peres recruited a batch of young physicists to work at two nuclear research centers, at Soreq and Dimona, and funded the project with millions of dollars donated by wealthy Jews who wanted to contribute to Israel's survival.

Then he flew to Paris. The Egyptian president, Gamal Abdel Nasser, had just nationalized the Suez Canal. Britain and France feared that Nasser would restrict access to the waterway, a vital conduit for oil supplies, and started planning an invasion. Israel offered to help. It demanded a few things in return—one of which was France's help in building a research reactor. The Suez crisis was a diplomatic disaster for the European powers, but it paid dividends for Israel. By the end of the decade, hundreds of French engineers were working in the Negev to build what was officially called a "textile plant", the genesis of a nuclear program that has produced an estimated 100–200 warheads. (Israel does not acknowledge its nuclear arsenal under a policy of "strategic ambiguity." But it came close to discarding that policy after Peres died: the reclusive atomic energy commission issued a rare public statement thanking him for his "great contributions to building up the security of the state of Israel.")

From there Peres entered the Knesset as a member of Mapai, the forerunner of the Labor party. He shuttled between various cabinet posts until 1974, when Rabin named him defense minister, a position that allowed Peres to play another fateful role in his country's history.

The settler population grew slowly in the first few years after the 1967 war, because the government was unwilling to approve major construction. Around the time Peres entered the defense ministry, a prominent right-wing activist named Yehuda Etzion decided to create facts on the ground. He secured a contract to build a fence around a military base near Ofra, northeast of Ramallah, and brought a group of would-be settlers (a "work brigade") with him. After eight months on the site, they decided to start sleeping there overnight, the first step toward establishing a community. "They were sent hints that Defense Minister Shimon Peres was looking for a way to approve their settlements in the area," two Israeli writers would later recount. "If they made their move quietly and without publicity, and the settlement was called a 'work camp', with no mention of a permanent 'settlement', there was a chance that they would be allowed to stay."[20]

So they did. One day in April 1975, after their shifts ended, the settlers moved into a group of abandoned buildings, the remnants of a Jordanian military camp. Peres ordered their removal. Then he reversed himself, wondering how he could direct the army "at nine or ten at night to evacuate them by force."[21] Rabin eventually legalized the settlement. Some of the settlers, including Etzion, live there to this day. (He would later join the Jewish Underground, and was jailed in 1984 for plotting to bomb the Dome of the Rock.)

The hawkish Peres saw the settlements as a key part of Israel's security, helping to "fortify Jerusalem... and establish the Jordan River as our security border," he wrote in his 1978 book, *Tomorrow Is Now*. He wasn't worried that a Jewish presence in the West Bank would foreclose the possibility of a Palestinian state. He didn't think one possible. "Maybe this Arab generation cannot live in harmony and peace with Israel," he wrote. "Perhaps this Arab generation can agree only to some interim arrangement, but the arrangement should not involve a withdrawal to the 1967 borders, nor the establishment of a Palestinian state."[22]

Volte-face

The next few years would bring major changes, both for Peres and Israel at large. Likud swept to power in 1977, unseating Labor for the first time in Israel's history. Prime Minister Menachem Begin would soon rapidly expand the settlement enterprise in the West Bank and Gaza—but also sign a peace treaty with Egypt and agree to withdraw from Sinai.

And Peres, the hawk who gave Israel the bomb, would start his journey to the left. Perhaps the pivotal moment came in September 1982, after the Sabra and Shatila massacre in Lebanon, when he spoke at Peace Now's massive anti-war rally in Tel Aviv. "Never have we stood before such a string of wretched decisions that arouse such doubt, sorrow, and mistrust," he said.

Two years later, a close election would force him into a power-sharing agreement with Likud. It was dubbed the *rotatzia*; a cartoonist for the *Jerusalem Post* portrayed it as a horse with a head on each end. The one on the right, Yitzhak Shamir, wanted to build widely in the West Bank. Peres pushed back. They eventually reached a compromise: the government would authorize six of the twenty-seven settlements currently in the planning phase.

Peres never really explained the source of his leftward drift. Cynics would say that he simply read the writing on the wall: surely he had no future as a hawk committed to maintaining a Greater Israel, not with Likud willing to make territorial concessions. Labor had never been in the opposition before. It needed to draw a sharp contrast with the new government, particularly on the crucial issues of war and peace. So politics undoubtedly played a role—but so did experience. In interviews and public appearances, Peres always seemed genuinely convinced that his pivot was necessary and right.

There was a personal component, too. Peres helped Begin sell the Camp David Accords, the peace treaty with Egypt, fighting against both the right and the hawkish members of his own party. He was rewarded for his efforts with threats and scurrilous rumors. In the months before the 1981 general election, Likud activists threw stones at his car, and circulated a "shameful" story: his mother, they said, was really an Arab. "He wanted to be loved, but about half the country got up in arms against him," said his biographer, Michael Bar-Zohar. "He was admired by half of the country, and bitterly criticized by the other half. He got used to that."

As he drifted, he also found ways to offend the left. Arguably the *rotatzia*'s biggest success was the 1985 "economic stabilization plan", a series of emergency measures aimed at curbing hyperinflation (already above 400 per cent). The program cut the budget, devalued the shekel, and imposed a series of wage and price controls. It worked: the inflation rate plunged to less than 20 per cent within two years, though it would take until 1989 for the economy to start growing.

The socialist left still considers the program a betrayal of Peres' Labor roots, because it chipped away at Israel's welfare state and paved the way for privatization and other neoliberal reforms in the 1990s. Yet without those reforms, Israel's modern economy, and particularly its high-tech industry, would not exist. It used to take months, even years, to get a new phone line from Bezeq, the government-owned monopoly. The situation only improved after the market was opened to competition in the 1990s.

The rest of his career is well-known: the Nobel Peace Prize; his role in the peace process; and finally his seven-year period as the country's beloved president, a role that allowed him to bask in the spotlight. He created the President's Conference, a sort of Davos-on-the-Mediterranean that brought together politicians, business leaders and other influential types to discuss everything from politics to art. (The last one was in 2013; to nobody's surprise, Rivlin did not continue the tradition.) He traveled the world, meeting with everyone from heads of state to Mark Zuckerberg, the founder of Facebook. Obama awarded him the Presidential Medal of Freedom, America's highest civilian honor, in 2012.

He was, in other words, the liberal Zionist ideal made flesh, a man who escaped the flames of Europe for a pastoral life on the pre-state kibbutzim, then fought for his newly-established state—not with a rifle, but in his own way, he gave the Jewish homeland physical security. With that accomplished, he turned his attention to its moral security, its long-term destiny. By the end he was a myth, the ninety-three-year-old peacemaker of indomitable spirit who worked harder than his young aides. Admirers and critics would agree on one thing: Peres allowed Israel to show its ideal face to the world. "He was the Israel that everyone wanted it to be, rather than the country that actually is," Chemi Shalev wrote in *Ha'aretz* on the day he died.[23]

"He was what he wanted to be"

The injunction not to speak ill of the dead doesn't really apply to journalists. As Peres lay in the hospital, I found myself musing on what sort of an obituary to write. There was much to criticize, from his role in birthing the settler movement to his political cowardice as president— the substantive failings that were masked by the carefully-crafted image of Peres the indefatigable peacemaker. The bold-faced names at his funeral included some of Israel's wealthiest and most corrupt tycoons, a reminder of one of the seamier sides of his career. Yet there was also something admirable about a politician who reflected deeply on his positions, and genuinely changed them. "The politician you should really suspect is the one who doesn't change his mind over half a century," he once told me. It was the sort of political aphorism for which he was famous. It was also true.

Arguably the most notable guest at his funeral was not Obama or Prince Charles. It was Mahmoud Abbas, the Palestinian president. The leaders of Israel's own Palestinian party, the Joint List, did not attend, a decision for which they were rightly castigated in the local press. But Abbas made the trip from Ramallah, a decision that drew harsh criticism from rivals like Hamas. Even his own Fatah party expressed its displeasure in a Facebook post. At one point during the service, Abbas seemed to tear up; the photo was mockingly circulated on Palestinian social media.

He had a brief photo op with Netanyahu and his wife. The two leaders briefly shook hands and exchanged a few words. "Long time, long time," Abbas said in English, as if they were two old men bumping into each other on the crosstown bus. When it was time to speak, none of the Israeli politicians mentioned his presence, though Netanyahu found time to thank the Grand Duke of Luxembourg. It fell to President Obama to acknowledge him, telling the crowd that his "presence here is a gesture and a reminder of the unfinished business of peace." The prime minister also made no mention of his own party's history of scurrilous attacks on Peres. It was Rivlin, decent as ever, who broached the subject. "We will ask forgiveness", he said. "There were years in which red lines were crossed, between ideological disputes and words and deeds which had no place."

Netanyahu's speech, with a few revisions, could have been delivered on the campaign trail; it was a reminder of his differences with Peres, coated with a layer of schmaltz. "In one of our nearly night-long discussions, we addressed a fundamental question: From Israel's perspective, what is paramount: security or peace?" he recalled. "Shimon enthusiastically replied, 'Bibi, peace is the true security. If there will be peace, there will be security.' And I responded to him, 'Shimon, in the Middle East, security is essential for achieving peace and for maintaining it.'"

Peres, of course, could have taken either side in the peace-versus-security argument; at various points in his career, he did. He arguably contributed more to secure Israel's long-term security than Netanyahu ever has. But then he paid a steep political price for his efforts toward peace—something it is difficult to imagine Netanyahu doing. The prime minister, like many of his contemporaries, is obsessed with short-term tactics, something that would soon come into sharp relief.

It was a funeral for Peres, and the two-state solution—and, for a brief moment in Netanyahu's speech, it also seemed like a funeral for a bygone era in Israeli politics. He reminisced about another late-night meeting with Peres, in which he asked the president to list his Israeli political icons. Peres, to his surprise, named Moshe Dayan, the legendary general and Labor politician, and he explained why: "Moshe never cared what anybody thought about him... Dayan completely ignored political considerations. He was what he wanted to be," Netanyahu recalled him saying.

Netanyahu, more than any of his predecessors, is a politician ruled by political considerations, a short-term tactician who lives in fear of his rivals. It wasn't hard to imagine that Peres meant this as an insult. But Netanyahu utterly missed the point.

Wildfires

For a week at the end of November, a large part of Israel was in flames. The fires started in the north on a Tuesday, in the hilly region between Tel Aviv and Haifa. Others quickly broke out in the south, close to the Gaza border, and in the suburbs of Jerusalem. On Thursday they spread to Haifa itself, which is bordered to the east by wooded mountains. Nearly a dozen neighborhoods were evacuated, forcing more than 60,000 people to flee their homes.

Israel has two seasons: a dry summer and a rainy winter. When the rains are late, the perfect conditions are created for wildfires. This was certainly the case in 2016: Jerusalem had received just 6 millimeters of rain by late November, down from 55 millimeters in a typical year. The northern Galilee was similarly dry, with just 13 millimeters of rainfall, less than a tenth of the normal level. Coupled with high winds—more than 50 kilometers per hour in Haifa, blowing from the arid east—

Israel was a tinderbox. "The conditions are encouraging the development of such fires," said Noah Wolfson, an Israeli meteorologist. "It could start with anything, a glass on the ground, like a magnifying glass, or people who forgot a small fire or barbecue."

The conditions were similar in 2010, the year of Israel's worst-ever wildfires, which started on Mount Carmel (adjacent to Haifa) and quickly spread across more than 12,000 acres. A total of forty-four people were killed, most of them officers in the prison service called in to help evacuate a jail; their bus got stuck on a highway and was consumed by the flames. It was a debacle for the Israeli government, which discovered it was ill-equipped to handle a major natural disaster. The flames were only extinguished with the help of airplanes sent from as far away as the United States.

Netanyahu promised to overhaul the emergency services, especially after a damning comptroller's report issued a few years later. Yet Israel needed help again in 2016, with aircraft dispatched from around the Mediterranean; the Palestinian Authority sent several crews to help, too. But the response was markedly better than during the previous wildfires. While hundreds of people were hurt, there were no fatalities. The crew of a US supertanker spent their Thanksgiving Day flying to Israel. By the time they arrived, the authorities couldn't find many fires for them to douse, and they spent hours doing idle loops over the Mediterranean. One other thing was different, though: the public reaction.

In the winter of 2015, Palestinian news agencies had reported that widespread flooding in Gaza was caused by Israel's decision to open the gates of a nearby dam. It was a transparently false story, as anyone familiar with the region would immediately realize: there are no big rivers near the Gaza border, let alone a dam. But the claim rocketed around the world. Al Jazeera picked it up. So did AFP, one of the largest wire services. Israelis rightly mocked it as an example of shoddy journalism. But then they did the same thing—only with fire, instead of water.

Throughout the week, politicians, journalists, and ordinary citizens described the fires as a wave of terrorism. Naftali Bennett was among the first to suggest they were something sinister. "Only those to whom the land does not belong are capable of burning it," he tweeted. He didn't use the word "Arabs", but the implication was clear. The next day, he said Israel was facing a "major wave of arson", calling it "terrorism in every sense of the word". Shmuel Eliyahu, the chief rabbi of Safed, urged Jewish Israelis to shoot Arabs who were lighting fires, and even gave them special dispensation to do so on Shabbat. *Yediot Aharonot* dubbed it the "intifada of arsons", a name that spread quickly throughout the media. Channel 2 aired an accusatory video of a Palestinian man standing next to a small fire.

The fires were not limited to Jewish areas, or to Israel. Haifa is a mixed city, and the country's best example of Jewish-Arab coexistence. A number of Arab villages in the Galilee were evacuated. Dozens of fires broke out across the West Bank, near Ramallah, Hebron and other cities; the Palestinian fire brigade counted more than thirty on Friday alone. And there were fires in neighboring Lebanon, which has a similar climate and topography.

But the hysteria continued, reaching its peak with the case of Anas Abudaabes, a journalist and photographer from the Bedouin town of Rahat. He spoke out against the incitement in a pair of Facebook posts on Thursday. In the first one, written around noon, Abudaabes decried the "ignorance" of his fellow Arabs. "Our country is burning, and it turns out there are Arabs in countries in the region who are busy praising God for this," he wrote.

A few hours later, he followed up with a second post, outlining some "urgent steps" that Arabs could take to celebrate. The hundreds of thousands of Muslims living near the fires in Haifa and Jerusalem shouldn't worry, he joked, since "what has happened is from God"—just pour the gasoline "in a direction away from your homes," and you'll be fine. He also suggested that "our young thugs" go start fires in "Iqrit, Imwas, Tel al-Khuweilfeh, Asqelon, Bisan, al-Fallujah, al-Tantura and Khabiza." Any Palestinian would have immediately understood his meaning: none of these villages exist anymore. They were destroyed by the Israeli army during the war of independence. Setting fire to Haifa or Jerusalem, he implied, would be no better than what the Israelis did in 1948. He concluded by reminding his readers that a Muslim leader (Abu Bakr, the first caliph) had given instructions to soldiers not to uproot or burn palm trees. In case it still wasn't clear, Abudaabes added a "sarcasm, not serious" hashtag to the bottom of his post.

It was exactly the sort of thing Israeli politicians routinely demand: a prominent figure in the Arab community, speaking out against incitement. So naturally the police arrested him. When he appeared in a Be'er Sheva court on Friday, the state argued that his words could be misunderstood, even if they were meant as satire. The judge, rather than dismiss the case, agreed with the state and extended his detention: he argued that Abudaabes should have considered how his post could be interpreted as "a call and encouragement to hurt the state". It was a surreal scene when he returned a few days later for a bail hearing: the police admitted they'd made a mistake, and pleaded with the judge to release Abudaabes. He did—but ordered him to a brief period of house arrest, and a two-week ban from the internet.

Nearly a month later, only six people had been indicted, all of them for setting minor fires in northern Israel—not the major conflagrations in Haifa or outside Jerusalem. Most of the people arrested were released. Among them was Jawad Qattoush, the Palestinian from Battir whose face was aired on Channel 2 (and other networks). After five days of interrogation, the Shin Bet concluded that he had, in fact, started a fire. He burned some garbage on his own property, a mile away from any Jewish town. And then he extinguished it.

7

CONCLUSION

"The eternal people do not fear a long road."
Yehoshua Weitzman

Around midnight on 23 June 2016, my phone buzzed with a late-night news alert—Nigel Farage was conceding defeat. "It looks like Remain will edge it," said Farage, the leader of the UK Independence Party and an outspoken voice for "Brexit", the euphemism for pulling the United Kingdom out of the European Union. The question had gone to a public referendum, and here was Farage, moments after the polls closed, admitting that early indications weren't good for his camp.

But to borrow an Israeli expression, we went to bed with Remain, and woke up with Leave. The latter pulled out an unexpected victory with almost 52 per cent of the vote, a result that sent shockwaves around the world. Sterling plunged to a thirty-one-year low against the dollar; trillions of dollars were erased from global stock markets in a matter of days; Prime Minister David Cameron announced his resignation, and Britain lapsed into a period of protracted political chaos. "Perhaps you can help by writing a piece about what it's like to live in a small, arrogant, isolated, xenophobic nation when all your neighbors hate you," one of my British editors emailed, only half in jest.

Summer is the silly season for journalists, when the serious news-makers go on holiday and the paper fills up with frivolous stories like

Hamas capturing an alleged spy dolphin off the coast of Gaza. (The more colorful term in Hebrew, borrowed from eastern Europe, is *onat hamelafefonim*, the "season of the cucumbers".) Not so in 2016. The world seemed to be shaking. There was a wave of attacks attributed to the Islamic State: the suicide bombing at Istanbul's main airport; the hit-and-run atrocity that killed eighty-six people on the corniche in Nice; the shooting rampage at a gay nightclub in Orlando; the explosion that killed more than 300 people in a Baghdad market.

The Brexit vote was a victory for right-wing populism, a political current that was making an ominous resurgence across the Western world, with an assist from the jihadis in Raqqa. In a deeply Euroskeptic France, Marine Le Pen, the leader of the xenophobic National Front, was a credible contender for president, though she would eventually be defeated. Yet her poll numbers rose after the deadly truck-ramming attack in Nice. In Austria, a right-wing party founded by former Nazis came within 30,000 votes of winning the presidency. Amidst all of this, the Turkish military tried to stage a coup. It failed, giving the long-serving Islamist president, Recep Tayyip Erdogan, the pretext he needed for a purge that was breathtaking in its scope: tens of thousands of officers, civil servants, academics, even stockbrokers and leaders of the football association caught up in the "cleansing".

Across the Atlantic, meanwhile, Donald Trump continued his unlikely ascent. He was the most ill-qualified presidential candidate in modern American history, a charlatan who based his campaign on racism and hollow nationalism. Yet he easily dispatched a dozen rivals to win the Republican nomination. His 75-minute acceptance speech at the Republican convention in Cleveland that summer was a bleak, despairing portrait of a shattered nation on the brink of collapse.

Israel does not exist in isolation. It likes to see itself as an outpost of the West in the Middle East—the "villa in the jungle," as Ehud Barak infamously put it. By the summer of 2016, with liberalism beating a hasty retreat across Europe and the United States, it was tempting to see Israel as a sort of leading indicator. Indeed, watching the Brexit vote, it was easy to see parallels with Israel's own election, fifteen months earlier. Cameron and his Remain camp cited experts to make an economic argument: leaving the union would sink the pound and roil the markets, they warned. It was a message that proved utterly ineffective. "People in this country have had enough of experts," said Michael Gove, the justice secretary and a Leave supporter, in what became one of the campaign's most memorable lines. The Remain camp never made a positive case for staying in the EU. There was little talk of the centuries of shared history between Britain and the continent, of their common destiny, of the EU's role in ending horrific bloodshed.

Similarly, Israel's center-left parties focused on the economy and social issues, believing they would resonate with voters. They didn't. The center-left bloc actually shrank, from 46 seats to 40, and Netanyahu (who didn't even bother drafting an economic platform) pulled out a surprise victory on a last-minute appeal to security interests and Jewish tribalism.

The morning after Israel's election, I went down to a cafe below my apartment to file some early copy. A man at the next table was tossing back shots at 9 am. The waitress was in tears. "I can't believe it," she said. "I don't know anyone who voted Likud." I heard the same from British friends following the referendum, and from Americans in the aftermath of the presidential election. Across the world, it seemed, liberals were waking up to the realization that large parts of their own countries were foreign territory.

The West

Historians will no doubt spend the next few decades arguing over what caused this lurch toward right-wing populism. Was it a working-class backlash against globalization and neoliberal economics? A response to the fear and uncertainty caused by Islamist militants across the globe? The last gasp of an older, white, Christian majority in an increasingly multicultural West?

This book does not have the answer (though I would lean towards "all of the above"). Viewed from the Middle East, though—where questions of identity are omnipresent—the last point seems to merit particular scrutiny. The countries of Western Europe and North America, to greater or lesser extents, are caught in a painful transition between two models of identity: a narrow one, rooted in shared language or culture or skin color; and a broader one, tied to a loose social contract. Immigration was the animating issue for many Brexit supporters, and for Le Pen's base. Xenophobia was an inseparable part of the Trump campaign.

Israel's identity is simultaneously drawn from both of these models, and from neither. The Jewish population is bound together by Jewish tradition, in a way that America's assimilated and cosmopolitan Jews increasingly are not. Yet an identity based on Judaism excludes one-fifth of the population—so Israel also offers a social contract, granting a degree of autonomy in religious and communal affairs within the broader framework of a liberal (but still explicitly Jewish) society. Ayelet Shaked, the justice minister and a secular Jew, inaugurated a new *shari'a* court in the summer of 2016, a scene that would be unthinkable in, say, republican France.

Still, a shared language and calendar only get you so far. How much do the urban Jewish sophisticates in Tel Aviv have in common with the ideological Jewish settlers living on the hills outside of Nablus, or the ultra-Orthodox Jews in the modern-day *shtetls* of Bnei Brak? Israel feels increasingly like a group of cantons, bound by the most tenuous of threads.

Haviv Rettig Gur, the political analyst for the *Times of Israel*, once offered a third idea for what holds the country together. "Israeli Jews share a profound sense of standing shoulder to shoulder in a pitiless and often bloodthirsty world, a world that has impressed upon them the need to fend for each other, often alone," he wrote in 2015.[1]

This was strong glue in the decades after 1948, when Israel was surrounded by hostile (and much larger) Arab states, and with the memory of the Holocaust still fresh. It weakened after the treaties with Egypt and Jordan. Still, the peace process continued to stitch up Israeli society, albeit into two halves: a "peace camp" which believed that a two-state solution was the only way to safeguard the country's future; and an opposing group which felt otherwise. But there was a sense of shared destiny, that both sides were arguing over a common fate.

By 2016, though, there was no real threat to draw Israelis together in solidarity. The country has peace treaties with two of its four neighbors; a third, Syria, is in ruins; and the fourth, Lebanon, is so weak that Israel routinely uses its airspace to launch strikes in Syria. (Hezbollah poses a serious threat, but hardly an existential one, and it is constrained by both its involvement in Syria and by Israeli deterrence.)

CONCLUSION

Neither the Iranian nuclear program nor the BDS movement currently threatens Israel's survival. And the status quo with the Palestinians, rightly or not, seems sustainable well into the future. Few Israelis give it much thought on a daily basis. So Israeli society cannot be drawn together by the need to stand "shoulder to shoulder" in the face of an existential threat, because one does not exist.

Perhaps there is a fourth option, then: the Israel of 2016 is a society drawn together by nostalgia. This is an odd concept in a state populated mostly by Jews, a people whose history offers little cause for wistfulness. Yet the turmoil of the past few years suggests that a current of nostalgia runs through not only Israel, but societies around the developed world. In the final pages of his 1992 book *The End of History*, the theorist Francis Fukuyama offered a prediction about the future:

> The struggle for recognition, the willingness to risk one's life for a purely abstract goal, the worldwide ideological struggle that called forth daring, courage, imagination, and idealism, will be replaced by economic calculation, the endless solving of technical problems, environmental concerns, and the satisfaction of sophisticated consumer demands.

His words certainly capture the mood in contemporary Western politics. Trump vowed to "make America great again" by building a wall, banning Muslims, and starting a trade war with China. Hillary Clinton promised to tinker with the minimum wage and maternity leave. Brexit campaigners urged the English to "take back control", evoking the days when Old Blighty stood alone against a despotic Europe, while the Remain camp trotted out the much-maligned experts and talked about an "emergency brake" on migrant benefits. Today's center-left is detached from its populist roots, and strongly identified with neoliberalism and globalization, setting the stage for a backlash.

So too in Israel—but across the entire political spectrum. The national-religious movement pines for a Biblical kingdom, an era when Jews had true sovereignty over the entirety of *eretz Israel*. The ultra-Orthodox are nostalgic, in their own way, for a time before modernity: they wall themselves off from the modern society around them and willingly reproduce the stifling *shtetl* that my ancestors fled a century ago. Arab nationalists in Israel, like their counterparts across the region, long for the days of Gamal Abdel Nasser, while Islamists choose a "golden age" that happened a millennium earlier. Even the secular

Zionists, though they share many characteristics with the Western center-left, have developed their own nostalgia, pining for their short-lived kingdom from 1948 to 1977.

And yet even these lofty goals have now become, in Fukuyama's words, "technical problems". The settler movement, Israel's most ideological, has achieved its most basic goals. Half a million Israelis live in territory considered "occupied," and the two-state solution is dead. Today the leaders of the community are often more concerned with zoning laws and water infrastructure than with the overall rightness of their movement. (One of the biggest obstacles to settlement growth today is not ideology, but the simple fact that many settlements are not nice places to live.) The *haredim* cannot roll back the modern world. Instead they make concessions to "kosher smartphones".

Even security and survival, those existential questions that once "called forth daring, courage, imagination, and idealism," are now far more prosaic. The violence of the past few years, from the Gaza war to the "stabbing intifada", was handled in a pragmatic fashion: investments in missile defense and tunnel detection systems; more officers on the streets; and more economic investment in restive communities. There are no more heroic wars, no iconic photographs of paratroopers liberating the Western Wall. Israel approaches its endless conflicts much like the mayor of New York deals with the murder rate.

There is one final divide in Western politics, and it may ultimately be the most decisive: a generational one. Young people overwhelmingly rejected Brexit. Just 25 per cent of those under the age of twenty-four wanted to leave, compared with 80 per cent of pensioners. If only millennials had voted in the US presidential election, Hillary Clinton would have won in a landslide, with 437 electoral votes in her column. For many of us who grew up after the Cold War, who did not experience "history" but rather grew up in technocratic, globalized societies, there seems to be little nostalgia. Views can change, of course, but these demographic trends should be encouraging for anyone who fears a long-term resurgence of right-wing populism.

As we have seen, though, the trend moves in the opposite direction in Israel, where younger voters are more religious and conservative than their parents. Left-wing rallies are a sea of gray hair; right-wing protests are filled with youthful energy. A 2016 poll found that nearly half of Jewish high school students do not believe their Arab compatriots should have the right to vote. This difference cannot simply be attributed to the ongoing conflict with the Palestinians. A recurring theme in this book, after all, is the disconnect between Israel's physical circumstances and its politics. The country has never been more prosperous, more secure, or more accepted in the world than it is today. Yet young Israeli Jews seem far more prone to right-wing views than their American or European counterparts—suggesting that there is another factor at work, a fundamental difference between Israel's identity and the changing identities of Western societies.

A century ago, Zionism had a clear meaning: the desire to establish a homeland for the Jewish people in Palestine. It was not necessarily to be a "Jewish state", however. Many of the early immigrants spoke instead of a "Hebrew state", a new nation that would reject the superstitions and strictures of the *shtetl*, replacing it with an egalitarian society of secular pioneers, hardy men and women who worked the land and fought to defend their borders. Theodor Herzl, the father of Zionism, imagined that the diaspora would eventually disappear, with the entirety of world Jewry concentrated in Israel. "Whoever can, will, and must perish, let him perish. But the distinctive nationality of Jews neither can, will, nor must be destroyed," he wrote in his 1896 pamphlet *Der Judenstaat*. "Whole branches of Judaism may wither and fall, but the trunk will remain."

The pioneers came and settled. But then the country moved on, from socialism to neoliberalism, collective farms to start-ups. The superstitions did not die out but rather endured; the new Hebrews saw their numbers shrink, while the scions of the *shtetl* multiplied. The diaspora did not disappear. World Jewry cleaved in half, one part in Israel, the other largely concentrated in a Western world that became tolerant and open in a way Herzl never dreamt. The vision became obsolete, and nothing took its place. "It is difficult to define Zionism," the World Zionist Organization ironically notes on its website. "But in general, one can say that Zionism is love for the land of Israel, loyalty to the state, and a desire to live in it, despite the difficulties."

It is true that many nations, not just Israel, have only a vague definition of their identity. *The Citizen's Almanac*, an educational booklet for immigrants published by the US government, does not even try to define "Americanism". It only lists the rights and responsibilities of a citizen. But that is exactly the point: American identity is deliberately vague because it is meant to be expansive. When it lives up to its ideals, it can accommodate both the evangelical white farmer in Iowa and the secular daughter of Hindu immigrants in New York.

There are scholars who argue that nationalism is inherently illiberal, because it differentiates between citizens and non-citizens. Maybe so, in a utopian world. But human history suggests that we are not ready to stop dividing ourselves into groups—so the question is what kind of nationalism we practice. And the Western world, in general, has come a long way from nineteenth-century conceptions of nationalism, which were rooted in ethnic identity. This is not to argue that countries like the US are fully "post-racial", as many commentators proclaimed in 2008. Still, the fact that the previous American president was the grandson of a Muslim goat herder from Kenya suggests a certain degree of progress.

Israel, on the other hand, is an explicitly ethno-nationalist state. It cannot be otherwise, or Zionism would lose its final vestiges of meaning.

The rest

In the autumn of 2016, as Netanyahu was plotting to kill the new public broadcaster, one of his cabinet ministers made an unflattering but telling comparison. "We have to put a stop to this Erdoganism," the minister said. "We have to show him he can't have everything he wants."[2]

Despite its cultural affinity for the West, Israel in many ways bears a growing resemblance to two states on the eastern fringes of Europe—Turkey and Russia. Both have a long history, yet their modern incarnations, like Israel's, are recent creations assembled from the ashes of empire by strong leaders: Ataturk, after the fall of the Ottomans; and Vladimir Putin, after the Soviet Union's collapse and the chaos of the Yeltsin years.

For decades, all three countries suppressed elements of their identity. In Russia there was Communism, which tried to supersede both religion and the palette of ethnicities that made up the Soviet Union. Ataturk banned the *hijab* in public institutions, shuttered religious schools and instituted a new system of laws based on European civil codes. "I have no religion, and at times I wish all religions at the bottom of the sea," he once said. "My people are going to learn the principles of democracy, the dictates of truth and the teachings of science." He viewed most of his subjects as uncivilized, not unlike Ben Gurion's assertion that the *mizrahim* lacked any "Jewish and human education." Erdogan's Justice and Development Party (AKP, in Turkish) rose to power for the same reasons as Begin's Likud. It offered a more conservative and traditional majority the chance to end decades of dispossession at the hands of a secular, "European" elite.

The AKP, of course, had to overcome the army, which served as the guardian of Ataturk's order. It carried out three military coups, plus the 1997 "postmodern coup", over the past century. Israel has maintained civilian rule for seventy years (no small wonder, given how few of its citizens can trace their roots back to democratic countries). Yet in its own way, the Israeli army too has emerged as the last guardian of democratic values. Days after Ya'alon was sacked, one of Israel's top security correspondents wrote, "In some conversations I've had recently with high-ranking officers about Mr. Lieberman's appointment as defense minister, the possibility of a military coup has been raised—but only with a smile."[3] It never happened, and no one seriously expects that it will. But the sentiment was telling. Lieberman, a brash right-wing populist with no real military experience, was a sort of spearhead for an attack on the army's inner sanctum.

These are imperfect analogies, of course. The Ottoman Empire and the Soviet Union were both sprawling superpowers humbled by collapse; Ataturk and Putin picked up the pieces. The Jewish people were a weak and scattered diaspora. Connecting all three, though, is a mutual sense of humiliation: Russians by the West; Turks by the army, the nationalist elite, and the Allied powers who carved up the Ottoman Empire after World War I; and Jews by many cultures. All three leaders wrap themselves in the glories of the past, whether a bygone Biblical kingdom, a romanticized empire, or the mighty tsars. And all three promote religion (Russian Orthodoxy, Sunni Islam, and Judaism) as a way to stitch together a diverse and fractious society.

Europeans have a jaundiced view of nationalism because of their history. Long experience suggests that it leads to catastrophic wars and the collapse of the continent, and so a sense of shared identity is seen as a bulwark against disaster. In other places, though, nationalism appears the only way to hold together diverse groups of people. Russia has a number of autonomous regions that do not see themselves as fully Russian, while Turkey has the Kurds, who have fought a decades-long battle against the state. And in greater Israel, of course, a majority of the Jewish state's population is non-Jewish. In contrast to Europe, all three countries share a belief that, without nationalism, their states would literally cease to exist.

None of this is to suggest that the practice of politics in Israel is identical to that in Turkey or Russia. Needless to say, a vast gulf separates Israel from places where opposition voices are jailed or murdered and the security services violently intervene in politics. But one of the lessons of 2016 is that even seemingly solid democracies can be built on shaky foundations. In a number of ways, Netanyahu and his allies have already chipped away at Israel's institutions: through growing control over the media, efforts to sideline the foreign ministry and silence dissent within the army. There has also been open contempt for the Supreme Court, and rhetoric that casts principled critics as unpatriotic traitors.

Yet it does suffer from the same inability to define a modern, inclusive view of citizenship. The never-ending conflict continues to undermine the fragile coexistence with Israel's own Arab minority, even as the latter has become more focused on securing its own rights than liberating the Palestinians across the Green Line. In a state conceived as a home for all Jews, racial and religious divisions have created a strikingly unequal society; the same goes for its supposedly unified capital in Jerusalem. The Likud has controlled politics for much of the past forty years, yet it continues to act like a beleaguered opposition party, lashing out at generals, journalists, artists, activists—the increasingly powerless voices of Israel's real opposition.

Presiding over all of this for nearly a decade is Netanyahu, with his American upbringing and mellifluous Philadelphia accent. In many ways, he has been the perfect prime minister for this inflection point in Israel's history. If he were to leave office tomorrow, it is hard to imagine the headline on his political obituary. Begin signed a lasting peace treaty with Egypt; Rabin did the same with Jordan. Barak ended the decades-long occupation of southern Lebanon. Sharon withdrew from Gaza. Peres oversaw vital economic reforms. Even Ehud Olmert, sitting in his prison cell, can argue that he pursued a serious peace process with both Syria and the Palestinians.

Netanyahu has simply survived. His views on the peace process are flexible, depending on what language he's speaking and whether or not an election is on the calendar. In his third government, he agreed to a plan to draft ultra-Orthodox men into the army; in his fourth, he postponed it. He announced the mixed-gender prayer space at the Western Wall to great fanfare, but never opened it. He spent years describing Iran as the greatest threat to world peace, until he lost the battle to block the nuclear deal, when he promptly stopped talking about it. His promise to lower prices and housing costs has gone unfulfilled. Even his wars have been indecisive. "1973 was the last time when both sides said, okay, let's make a deal," said Oded Eran, a longtime Israeli diplomat. "All of the wars since ended with a UN resolution, which was only partially effective, or the arrangement of 2012. What does it mean that we end it unilaterally? It means that Israel continues to live under the current circumstances. It's not clear what is actually ending."

An army officer once described him as a "character from a Greek tragedy". Netanyahu, after all, is both a gifted politician and an educated man—a keen student of world history and contemporary geopolitics. As a man of the right, the son of a prominent Revisionist historian and a former army commando, he had the stature to be a transformative politician in the mold of Menachem Begin. "But he's full of hubris," the officer said. His lust for power led him to pursue short-term tactics instead of grand strategy, and the fabric of Israeli society unraveled while he did. Of all the many ways I've heard Netanyahu described, it seemed the most apt.

Tofu man

Of course, he will not be in office forever. Yet if he is forced aside, the list of possible replacements is quite thin. Herzog is finished. His inglorious stint as opposition leader has left him struggling to keep control of his own Labor party, now hopelessly adrift. Tzipi Livni is disliked by a large swathe of the Israeli public; so is Barak. Bennett and his party are too narrowly ideological. While the retired generals could challenge Netanyahu on his strongest issues, they would need to find a political home. There is some talk of Netanyahu's eldest son Yair launching a political career, a dynastic succession that would further accelerate Israel's integration into the Middle East, but it seems unlikely. Yair lacks a power base of his own, and his support will likely evaporate when his father's career ends. Israelis desperately want a new leader. But the state of Israeli politics and society makes it difficult to envision one.

The one plausible alternative, at least according to the polls, is Yair Lapid, the chairman of Yesh Atid. He comes from a political family: his Yugoslav-born father Tommy spent nearly a decade in the Knesset as a lawmaker with Shinui ("Change"), a now-defunct secular and libertarian party. Like his dad, Yair started his career as a journalist, with a lengthy stint as a talk show host on Channel 2. He left media for politics ahead of the 2013 election and founded Yesh Atid, a centrist party focused largely on social and economic issues. It was the dark horse of the election, winning 19 seats, enough to make it the second-largest party. In the wake of the 2011 social protests, the party's message resonated with voters. So did his call for the ultra-Orthodox to "share the burden," an ideology he inherited from his father, who was a fierce opponent of the *haredi* parties. (Tommy kept a doll on his desk, a man dressed in a long black coat and top hat. When you pressed a button, the doll tried to punch you. "Just like the ultra-Orthodox," he once told an interviewer).[4]

Two years later, though, Lapid's star had waned. He had achieved little during his stint as finance minister, a job that is often a poisoned chalice. "Israelis never like the man who takes their money," explained one of his colleagues. Moshe Kahlon, the popular ex-communications minister who oversaw the mobile phone reforms, stole Lapid's spotlight when he launched his own centrist socioeconomic party (with better ideas). And some of Lapid's center-left supporters rallied behind Herzog, who seemed to have a shot at unseating Netanyahu. He fell to 11 seats.

Lapid has based his political career on trying to find the exact center of Israeli public opinion. "We're not a center-left party," Yair Zivan, one of his advisers, said over coffee in north Tel Aviv. "This isn't between left and right. It's between left, right, and center, and most Israelis are still in the center." In practical terms, this means Lapid works hard to avoid being tainted with even a whiff of the left. Anshel Pfeffer, my colleague at *The Economist*, called him a "wannabe Netanyahu." Dimi Reider, an Israeli journalist and analyst, memorably dubbed him "tofu man", a television star "who avoided taking any remotely controversial stand on almost any issue."

Though he sits in the opposition, he often refuses to criticize the government: "we're an alternative, not the opposition," in Zivan's words. Sometimes he serves as an unofficial foreign minister, jetting around Europe and North America to meet with senior Western officials. He took credit when the mayor of London removed pro-BDS ads from the Underground in February 2016. "I approached London mayor Boris Johnson, who's a great friend of Israel, and explained that the state of Israel will not accept this," Lapid said afterwards. In August of that year he traveled to Stockholm for a public rally, where he led a small crowd in chants of "we love Israel!"

On the Palestinians, he speaks largely in platitudes, with talk of "regional initiatives" and "involving the Arab states". Like Herzog, he prefers to avoid the issue whenever possible. In a meeting with the foreign press in December, he suggested that a left-wing British newspaper was the real reason for the impasse in peace talks. "The problem is that the Palestinians are encouraged by *The Guardian* and others saying we don't need to do anything in order to work for our future, because the international community will call Israel an apartheid country," he said.

Closer to home, Lapid joined the criticism of Breaking the Silence, accusing them of "undermining the foundations of the state" and supporting a bill to bar them from speaking in Israeli schools. (He spent his own military service working as a journalist for an army magazine.) He endorsed Miri Regev's attempt to cut state funding from the Midan Theater in Haifa, and described the BDS movement as a "puppet" in the hands of Hamas and Islamic Jihad. In late 2016, his party backed a right-wing bill to limit the involvement of NGOs in Israeli election campaigns, an idea cooked up in response to V15, the grassroots organization that tried to unseat Netanyahu the previous year. Perhaps the best example came in November, when he declined to participate in the annual memorial for the slain Prime Minister Yitzhak Rabin. It was a leftist gathering, after all—Lapid would have to share the stage with Labor and Meretz.

The latest polls show Yesh Atid running neck-and-neck with Likud. They have limited utility so far away from the election, as President Jeb Bush can attest. Still, you can discern a few trends. The fragmentation in Israeli politics continues: both parties are polling around 25 seats, barely one-fifth of the Knesset. And crucially, most of Lapid's new-found support is stolen from Labor—trading within the center-left bloc, rather than expanding it. Even if he tried to join with Meretz, Labor, Kulanu and Yisrael Beiteinu, an unwieldy coalition covering the spectrum from the far left to the ultra-nationalist right, he would only have 57 seats, four short of a majority. (His aides also rule out Meretz as a partner, calling it "too ideological".)

So he has spent the past two years trying to woo the ultra-Ortho-dox, the perennial kingmakers of Israeli politics. He sits for long inter-views on *haredi* radio stations. He never misses an opportunity to be photographed in a *kippah* at a religious event. On a visit to Eilat, he even seemed to drop his biggest priority: sharing the burden, he said, "will not be on the table if and when we form the next government." He later tried to "clarify" his statement after a furious reaction from his supporters, but the damage was done.

Lapid's efforts to find the "center" illustrate how Israel does not, in fact, have a coherent center, or even a simple left-right dichotomy. The trend over the past decade has been toward narrow parties, with char-ismatic leaders who focus on a core constituency. This worked for Lapid in 2013, who aimed at middle-class voters in Gush Dan, the coastal plain around Tel Aviv. Kulanu aims a similar message at the "periphery". Fewer than 7 per cent of Israeli voters live in Tel Aviv, but Meretz receives more than 20 per cent of its votes in the city.

As Lapid tries to become a national leader, though, he finds himself mired in contradictions. In an effort to improve relations with the dias-pora, for example, he promises to implement the mixed-gender prayer area at the Western Wall "in his first week" as prime minister. But that would be a hard sell with the ultra-Orthodox, his prospective coalition partners. Bennett, as mentioned earlier, faces the same obstacle with the religious nature of his party.

The political spectrum in Israel is a confusing multi-dimensional con-struct, with different spectra for war and peace, religion and state, the economy, and other issues. The rising star of Israeli politics is a man who tries to stake out the least offensive position on each one—and, in doing so, implicitly promises not to resolve them. "We really need to talk about things like better law enforcement, more traffic police," Zivan said at one point, trying to steer the conversation away from questions of peace and diplomacy. "I realize these aren't the most exciting issues. But if we're elected, we'll enact as many of them as possible."

EPILOGUE

"Um shmum."

David Ben-Gurion

Amona, a cluster of homes perched on a hilltop northeast of Ramallah, never officially existed. To the west was Ofra, one of the oldest settlements in the West Bank; on a hill to the east was Taybeh, a Christian village (and the home of Palestine's only brewery). The residents lived in prefabricated trailers, lofted above the rocky terrain on cinderblocks. They had a few gardens, and a small school at the edge of the hill, and chickens roaming the dirt paths between the caravans. The entire community contained about 300 people, roughly the population of my small street in Jaffa.

Yet for more than a month in late 2016, it was the dominant political issue in Israel. It consumed the government's attention and enraged the Palestinians. There was even overblown talk that this cluster of trailers would bring down Netanyahu's fourth government. It didn't—but it did help to bring about a final diplomatic crisis between Israel and its closest allies, one unprecedented in its fury.

Amona is an "outpost", a settlement built without official permission, and thus considered illegal even under Israeli law. But the government further differentiates between outposts built on privately-owned Palestinian land, and those built on "state land", the large swathe of the West Bank designated as ownerless. The latter are often retroactively legalized. Rechelim, for example, was recognized as a legal settlement in 2012, more than two decades after the first residents pitched tents on a hilltop south of Nablus.

When the land is privately owned, however, the government's hands are tied by a 1979 Supreme Court ruling, which held that the army could not seize Palestinian land to build civilian settlements. It has periodically been forced to demolish those outposts, like it did with Migron, outside of Ramallah, in 2012. (International law, of course, does not recognize any of these distinctions: the Geneva Conventions forbid an occupying power from settling its civilian population in occupied territory, regardless of the circumstances, and thus the United Nations and much of the world view all settlements as illegitimate.)

Amona came under scrutiny in 2014, when a police investigation revealed that the entire outpost was built on privately-owned land. The Supreme Court, unsurprisingly, soon ordered the outpost to be evacuated, and gave the state two years to carry out its ruling. Asher Grunis, then the chief justice, tried to head off any attempt to dodge the order. "Because the structures were built on private lands, it is impossible to authorize them, even retroactively," he wrote in his ruling.

Netanyahu, busy with elections and always loathe to anger the right, dawdled for eighteen months. In the summer of 2016, his government offered to relocate the settlers, following the example of Migron. They would receive new homes nearby, on the outskirts of Ofra, an approved settlement. But they refused. Ayelet Shaked, the justice minister, then drafted a bill to legalize Amona, in exchange for a compensation payment to the Palestinian owners of the land. Her effort was quickly stymied by the attorney general, who advised the cabinet that the bill was probably unconstitutional.

It is worth pausing for a moment to emphasize how exceptional this behavior is. The settlers in Amona (and those in other outposts) were breaking the law—not just international law, but Israeli law. And their own government bent over backwards to retroactively accommodate their illegal behavior. It's an imperfect comparison, but imagine a businessman who built a factory in Yellowstone, then demanded compensation when the government showed up to bulldoze it. And then go a step further: imagine that a powerful faction within Congress drew up a bill to cede that chunk of the park to the factory owner. Avigdor Lieberman, the right-wing defense minister and a settler himself, emerged as one of the few voices of caution. "There is a judgment of the Supreme Court and we shall honor it," he said on 1 September, at an event in an Israeli settlement marking the first day of school. But the prime minister, fearful of losing support to Bennett's party, pressed forward with his search for a "solution". After the High Holidays, like a college student who fell behind on a term paper, he asked the court for a seven-month extension. The settlers ramped up the pressure, holding protest marches, vowing to fight the soldiers who would come to evict them. The court rejected Netanyahu's request.

Netanyahu fashions himself a man of big ideas, an intellectual concerned with the sweep of history. He likes to be photographed in the Knesset with a copy of The Economist, or Henry Kissinger's latest book. By mid-November, though, he was entirely consumed with the plight of forty families living illegally in trailers. "There is no one who is more concerned about settlement than us. Here as well, sagacity and responsibility are needed for the benefit of the settlements," he said at a cabinet meeting on 13 November.

With the deadline approaching, the cabinet drew up a number of "solutions" for Amona, many of them quite broad—aimed at legalizing not just Amona, but dozens of other outposts with thousands of residents. Ministers also discussed labeling the settlers a "protected population" a designation under international law that is applied to the inhabitants of occupied territory. Netanyahu, in a surreal twist, wanted to apply it to the occupiers themselves. On 16 November, a bill to legalize the outposts passed a first reading in the Knesset, by a vote of 58–50. Moshe Kahlon, the finance minister, had threatened to vote against it, but he dropped his opposition after the prime minister swore it would not harm the high court's reputation. Never mind, of course, that the bill was written specifically to undermine a ruling from that same court. The vote drew the requisite condemnations from the international community ("deeply concerned", in the words of John Kirby, the State Department spokesman). But it came at a fortuitous time for the Netanyahu government, days after Trump's election, while the West was preoccupied with the seeming demise of the liberal world order.

Then the attorney general piped up again, warning that any effort to authorize Amona would undermine the Supreme Court and the separation of powers. So in another bizarre twist, the language related to Amona was dropped from the bill. What began as an effort to keep forty families in their homes had metastasized into a law that "legalized" nearly 4,000 illegal residences—but the original forty would still be evicted.

The revised bill passed a first reading in the Knesset on 7 December, by a 60–49 vote. The lone dissenting vote from the coalition came from Benny Begin, the son of Menachem Begin, Israel's first Likud prime minister. It was a telling bit of symbolism. The elder Begin was a right-wing Revisionist, a supporter of settlements and "greater Israel", but also a classical liberal, committed to the rule of law and the separation of powers. In 1979, the Supreme Court ordered him to remove the settlement of Elon Moreh, which was built (like Amona) on privately-owned Palestinian land. "Naturally we shall not make any announcements, which are completely unnecessary, saying that the Supreme Court's decision should be respected," he said at a cabinet meeting shortly after the verdict. "They are unnecessary, because this goes without saying." The settlement was relocated to a nearby hilltop—again, Begin was hardly a leftist—but there was no question about the court's authority.

The younger Begin followed in his father's footsteps, denouncing the outpost bill as a "land grab". After the vote, David Bitan, the coalition chairman, suspended him from his parliamentary committees for breaking coalition discipline. One of those roles, ironically, was on the constitution and law committee.

"It's not the horses"

Thousands of homes in dozens of settlements had been "legalized", but the forty families in Amona—the original reason for this whole sordid affair—still faced eviction in two-and-a-half weeks, with no alternative housing arranged. Naturally, they were upset. By the time I drove out there on a blustery, rainy day in mid-December, they had been joined by hundreds of supporters. Their ranks included Kahanists, "Hilltop Youth" members, and teenagers affiliated with Lehava, the far-right anti-miscegenation group. Many had already spent days camping in the freezing cold. The actual residents of Amona said privately that they planned to resist the demolition order, but peacefully: they would make the police drag them out of their homes, but they wouldn't fight back. Their supporters were less tranquil. They had stockpiled tires, to burn as roadblocks, and also a pile of iron rods.

Amona had been evacuated once before, in 2006, and it was a violent affair. More than 200 people had been wounded, including dozens of police officers. The Likud party had used footage of the melee against Ehud Olmert in the subsequent general election, releasing a video entitled "It's not the horses", which featured clips of mounted cops clad in riot gear. The implication was that Olmert was to blame for the violence. Netanyahu was afraid that a rival—perhaps Bennett— would pull the same stunt against him.

He originally drew up a plan to move the settlers to an adjacent hilltop at state expense. But it was complicated when Yesh Din, an Israeli NGO, filed an appeal, claiming that the new site for Amona was also privately-owned. "The plots that the state is trying to declare as 'abandoned properties' are private lands with recognised owners," said Gilad Grossman, a spokesman for the group. After two years of delay, the government didn't have time to fight the injunction before the Christmas deadline. It hastily drew up another proposal, which moved about a dozen Amona families to a tiny plot of state land on their hill- top, and the rest to the nearby settlement of Ofra. On 15 December, the residents voted overwhelmingly (59–20) to reject it. They called it "Swiss cheese", because it wouldn't accommodate all of the outpost's families, and it didn't guarantee permanent homes on their new land.

Two days later, after Shabbat, Netanyahu convened a late-night meeting to discuss another compromise. The meeting ran until the small hours of the morning. Again, stop to consider the imagery: the Israeli prime minister sitting at 3 am with the emissaries of a group of scofflaws whose supporters were threatening violence against the state. While the cabinet was talking, a group of soldiers from the Givati Brigade ordered to secure the roads around Amona briefly abandoned their posts. They told their commanders that they would not take part in the evacuation, and only returned to duty after they were assured they would have no direct role. "The IDF condemns any kind of refusal to obey orders and will show zero tolerance towards it," the army spokesman said in a brief statement—but the soldiers were not pun- ished for their protest.

Finally, with less than a week before the deadline, the residents accepted the offer. The final agreement, which also included a state commitment to build a new settlement in the northern West Bank, allowed two-thirds of the families to stay on a plot of land near Amona (the rest would go to Ofra). It would cost 130 million shekels.

The "regularization bill", as it is known in Hebrew, will almost certainly be overturned by the courts: even before it passed, the attorney general said he would struggle to defend it. The seemingly inevitable verdict will cement the high court's reputation as a leftist body. (Miriam Naor, the chief justice, had her security detail increased at the height of the Amona debate.) Many of the young supporters who flocked to Amona opposed the community's deal with the state. "We have to convince the youth to accept it," a resident said. On 15 December, days before the evacuation deadline, police arrested a 22-year-old man for threatening to kill Bennett. He allegedly sent a message to a Whatsapp group that included a photo of the Israeli flag next to an Uzi. "Someone ought to take out Naftali Bennett," he wrote. The Shin Bet had already increased Bennett's security detail, too.

Yet Shmuel Rosner, a peripatetic Israeli journalist, wrote an op-ed for the *New York Times* arguing that all of this was actually a positive sign. "The government—even if reluctantly—abides by the law and will follow the court's ruling," he wrote. "It's now a cliché that the settler movement has an undue influence over the Israeli government. But the Amona evacuation is evidence, once again, that this common knowledge is wrong."[1]

To borrow a phrase from George W. Bush, this was the soft bigotry of low expectations: arguing that a few hundred settlers didn't have "undue influence" because the government was unwilling to totally subvert the rule of law to support them. Ignore how the prime minister spent literally weeks trying to placate forty families who violated Israeli law, and how the Knesset spent hours debating their fate instead of, say, the 21 per cent of Israelis who live in poverty, or the hundreds of thousands of students lagging behind their Western peers in math and science. Disregard the fact that lawmakers ultimately voted to authorize thousands of other illegal homes across the West Bank, creating a supreme moral hazard. The caravans in Amona would be bulldozed. Israeli democracy was healthy.

The backstabber

The rest of the world wasn't convinced. On 21 December, Egypt circulated a resolution at the Security Council that declared Israeli settlements to "have no legal validity". Such measures pop up every few years; they are usually swatted down by the United States, which wields a veto. But there was a sense in Jerusalem that President Obama, after eight years of clashes with Netanyahu, had finally reached the end of his tether, and would allow it to pass.

Hours before the vote, though, Egypt unexpectedly pulled the measure. The reason, according to diplomats, was Donald Trump. The Israeli ambassador in Washington, Ron Dermer, called him on the afternoon of 22 December and asked him to intervene. He did so first in a surprisingly sober statement that urged a US veto. "This puts Israel in a very poor negotiating position and is extremely unfair to all Israelis," he said. Then he went a step further and called the Egyptian president. Relations between the US and Egypt soured after the 2013 coup, but Abdel Fattah al-Sisi had high hopes for the new administration. The two men met in New York in September, on the sidelines of the General Assembly, and Sisi was the first world leader to call with congratulations after the election. He didn't want to start the new relationship on a sour note.

So he postponed the measure, only to have four other states— Malaysia, New Zealand, Senegal and Venezuela—pick it up. They brought it to a vote the next evening. It passed by a 14–0 vote, with an abstention from the United States. "It is sad because our most important ally has abandoned a policy which has existed since 1967," said Michael Oren. This was untrue. The measure was hardly unprecedented: its language was nearly identical to a 1979 resolution that the US also declined to veto. Since then, the settler population has grown thirty-fold, and no blue-helmeted peacekeepers have descended on Ariel and Efrat. It was purely symbolic. "The United States has been sending the message that the settlements must stop—privately and publicly—for nearly five decades," said Samantha Power, the US ambassador at the UN. "So our vote today is fully in line with the bipartisan history of how American presidents have approached both the issue."

Israel, needless to say, took a different view. The reaction was unprecedented in its fury. "The Obama administration carried out a shameful anti-Israel ploy at the UN," Netanyahu said the following night in his first public comments on the matter. "The entire Middle East is going up in flames and the Obama administration and the Security Council choose to gang up on the only democracy in the

Middle East." On Christmas Day, the foreign ministry summoned the ambassador from each country that voted "yes" for an individual démarche. Dan Shapiro, the outgoing US ambassador, got a higher-level reprimand, in the form of a forty-minute meeting with Netanyahu, who also canceled meetings with Theresa May and the Ukrainian prime minister, halted Israel's contributions to various UN bodies, and suspended economic aid to countries like Senegal and Angola that voted yes.

The worst vitriol was reserved for President Obama. Politicians and journalists called him a coward, a traitor—even Antiochus, the villain of the Hanukkah story. Oren Hazan, a freshman lawmaker from Likud (and, reportedly, a former pimp), said the vote "brought out the Hussein in Obama." An illustration that made the rounds on social media showed the president, clad in a *keffiyeh*, stabbing an Israeli soldier in the back. (One of the first people to share it, not surprisingly, was The Shadow.) Netanyahu would later accuse Obama of secretly conspiring with the Palestinians to draft the resolution, though the only evidence he offered was a story from an Egyptian tabloid.

The center-left, as usual, was merely a faint echo of the right. Herzog was invisible: many journalists didn't even bother to seek out his opinion. When he did speak, it was unremarkable. "This is a difficult night for Israel... it seriously harms our capital Jerusalem, the settlement blocs and Israel's status and diplomatic achievements accumulated over the years." Lapid blamed Netanyahu for the diplomatic failure, but he too condemned the resolution. "The nations of the world should know there is no coalition or opposition within Israel," he said. "We won't be forced to act against our national security interests." There was no substantive debate about whether settlements were, in fact, an impediment to Israel's peace and security. Foreign diplomats drew a connection between the American vote and the Amona farce—but Israeli politicians ignored it.

The following Wednesday, 28 December, John Kerry delivered what was billed as a major address on the Israeli-Palestinian conflict. Again, on substance, it was nothing new. He outlined his vision of a two-state solution, a list of parameters that everyone in Israel and Palestine has known for decades. "Ultimately I think the parameters he lays out are well-known to all of us. There are no major surprises," said Michael Herzog, a former Israeli peace negotiator.

But in style, it was a scathing criticism of Israel. Kerry laid some blame on the Palestinians, for inciting violence and for their internal political dysfunction. But he spent nearly an hour castigating the Netanyahu government, particularly its settlement policy. Israel was drifting toward a binational state, he warned, in which the Palestinians would be "separate but unequal"—an ode to the civil rights movement, of course, and thus a powerful phrase for an American diplomat to use. "The settler agenda is defining the future in Israel," Kerry said. "And their stated purpose is clear. They believe in one state: greater Israel."

Three times during his speech, Kerry quoted Naftali Bennett, though he never mentioned him by name. Bennett nonetheless picked up on the reference, and he tweeted approvingly about it. "Kerry quoted me three times, anonymously, to show that we are opposed to a Palestinian state," he wrote. "Correct."

This was once a fringe position in Israel. No longer. In November, weeks before Kerry's speech, the Israel Democracy Institute found that 44 per cent of Israelis supported annexing the entire West Bank, while just 38 per cent opposed it. A similar share, 42 per cent, felt that the Palestinians should not be granted equal rights under such an arrangement. "That is, a small but significant minority of the Jewish public supports a situation that the international community regards as apartheid," the pollsters noted.[2]

The Jewish Sparta

Foreign diplomats often argue that the settlements are the core problem in the Israeli-Palestinian conflict. I personally disagree: the issues on both sides run much deeper. Yet this story of contemporary Israel began and ended in settlements—and tiny, ideological ones to boot.

Their establishment, half a century ago, helped to create a sort of feedback loop in Israeli politics and society. For one thing, it undermined the rationale for a two-state solution, decades before peace talks even started. If the government allowed Jews to settle in one corner of the territories, it had no moral argument for keeping them out of others. Indeed, it's possible to sympathize with the settlers forced out of Gaza in 2005. There was a pragmatic argument for removing them— they required a huge amount of manpower and resources to protect—

but a similar argument applies to, say, the residents of Hebron. The same goes for the residents of Amona: Why is their settlement illegal when Yitzhar, an ideological, violent community deep in the West Bank, is not?

The settlers wield power that is vastly disproportional to both their numbers and their contribution to the Israeli economy. They make up perhaps 5 per cent of the population, but ten members of the current Knesset live in settlements. Add to that the deeply pro-settler politicians who live inside of Israel proper—Naftali Bennett, Ayelet Shaked, Tzipi Hotovely, and others—and their level of representation is more than double their size. Their political views, meanwhile, have moved further and faster to the right than those of Israelis inside the Green Line. In Ma'ale Adumim, a relatively non-ideological settlement (effectively a suburb of Jerusalem), the Likud party received 48 per cent of the vote in 2015, double its nationwide tally. As a whole, the right-wing bloc won 73 per cent there, up from 46 per cent in elections a decade earlier. The Zionist Camp received just 5 per cent—less than a third of its national average.

The extremist Yachad didn't clear the threshold to enter the Knesset. In a few small settlements, though, where even Bennett is now seen as too liberal, it won a majority. It turns out, in other words, that living illegally on occupied land, while ideologues insist on your religious claim to that land, is an incubator for extreme views.

Here the narrative comes full circle. Over the past few years, a growing number of liberal Jews in the diaspora have called for a settlement boycott. Except on the far left, though, they are quick to stress that they do not wish to boycott Israel as a whole. "A settlement boycott is not enough. It must be paired with an equally vigorous embrace of democratic Israel," Peter Beinart wrote in the *New York Times* in 2012.[3]

But as the Amona fiasco demonstrated, it is impossible to separate "democratic Israel" from the settlements, because the former supports the latter. The residents of Amona moved there illegally, without the state's permission, yet it was the state that ponied up nearly $1 million per family to relocate them. The number is striking, but it is a tiny fraction of the overall budget allocation for settlers. A 2010 analysis by an Israeli think tank found that the settler roads and highways alone were worth $1.7 billion (a number which has only grown since the study was conducted). The schools, synagogues and other public institutions cost another $500 million. The think tank, the Macro Center for Political Economics, reported in 2015 that settlers received about 1,013 shekels per capita for development; the residents of impoverished southern Israel received less than 400.[4] All of this money comes from "democratic Israel". Indeed, days after the Amona plan was agreed, Netanyahu announced hundreds of millions of shekels in budget cuts for education, health care, and grants to local authorities.

In one sense, then, Rosner is right. The settlers do not have "undue influence" over the Israeli government. Every Israeli government for the past fifty years, from center-left to far-right, has aided and abetted them. Nor does the ultra-Orthodox minority: prime ministers as far back as Ben-Gurion allowed them to maintain a grip on the religious identity of the state.

Seventy years ago, as the Zionist leaders were preparing to declare independence, Hannah Arendt mused about the sort of country they would create. Arendt was born in Germany, but left in the 1930s, as the Nazis were first consolidating power. She is remembered today for her writings on fascism and for "Eichmann in Jerusalem", her coverage of the Nazi leader's 1961 trial, which coined the phrase "the banality of evil". But she also wrote about Israel and Zionism, often critically. On 1 May 1948, just two weeks before Israel declared independence, she published a scathing essay in *Commentary*, then the most prominent journal of the Jewish intellectual left. (Today it takes a belligerent right-wing line on Israel; it marked the fiftieth anniversary of Eichmann in Jerusalem with a piece entitled "The Lies of Hannah Arendt".)

Arendt predicted that a small Jewish state, surrounded by hostile Arab neighbors, would inevitably become warlike, "absorbed with physical self-defense"—unrecognizable to her American Jewish readers: "Under such circumstances… the Palestinian Jews would degenerate into one of those small warrior tribes about whose possibilities and importance history has amply informed us since the days of Sparta. Their relations with world Jewry would become problematical, since their defense interests might clash at any moment with those of other countries where large numbers of Jews lived. Palestine Jewry would eventually separate itself from the larger body of world Jewry and in its isolation develop into an entirely new people. Thus it becomes plain that at this moment and under present circumstances a Jewish state can only be erected at the price of the Jewish homeland."[5]

The title of this book is a question: How long will Israel survive? I have no definitive answer. Nobody does. But the status quo is unsustainable. In a few decades, one-third of Israelis will be *haredim*, a group that mostly lives in poverty and contributes little to the national economy. More than half the country will not serve in the army, that longtime melting pot. Similarly, if trends continue, a solid majority of Israeli Jews will view Judaism as more important than democracy. Racism and nationalism are increasing, despite the tremendous improvement in Israel's physical security. And the long-serving prime minister, instead of trying to address these long-term concerns, is busy trying to quash the few remaining bastions of dissent.

This, most of all, is the tragedy of the Netanyahu era. While the West is having similar arguments about identity and democracy, the choices are clear. Obama was a cosmopolitan liberal; Trump is a nationalist with authoritarian tendencies. Voters in Germany have a stark choice between Angela Merkel and the populist, Euroskeptic AfD. But the man who rules Israel, and the man who wants to replace him, look almost identical. They encourage the anti-democratic tendencies of the right for short-term political reasons, but they don't go far enough to appease the right. They ignore the left—justifiably so, because it has utterly failed to articulate a vision for how Israelis can overcome their differences and forge a new identity. And so they create a space for the ideologues, the sectarians and the extremists, who are eagerly working to undo the delicate social contract that has held the country together since its creation.

NOTES

PREFACE

1. Lazaroff, Tovah, "One in Every Five Jewish Israelis Knows a Terror Victim, Survey Finds", *The Jerusalem Post*, 12 May 2015.
2. "Chief Rabbi Urges Israeli Soldiers to Kill Palestinian Assailants, Not Worry About Court or Chief of Staff", *Ha'aretz*, 13 March 2016.
3. "PM Netanyahu Speaks with Father of Soldier Involved in Hebron Incident",Government Press Office, 31 March 2016.
4. Arens, Moshe, "Defense Minister Ya'alon's Ouster Is a Turning Point in Israeli Political History", *Ha'aretz*, 23 May 2016.

1. THE BATTLE FOR ISRAEL'S SOUL

1. Freedland, Jonathan, "The Liberal Zionists", *New York Review of Books*, 14 August 2014.
2. Lerman, Antony, "The End of Liberal Zionism", *The New York Times*, 24 August 2014.
3. Cohen, Roger, "What Will Israel Become?", *The New York Times*, 21 December 2014.
4. Beinart, Peter, "Letter to the Israeli Voter: If You Reelect Netanyahu, You Risk Losing the US", *Ha'aretz*, 11 March 2015.
5. A Portrait of Jewish Americans, Pew Research Center, 1 October 2013.
6. 2014 National-Religious Sector Survey, Israel Democracy Institute, 27 January 2015, http://en.idi.org.il/about-idi/news-and-updates/2014-national-religious-sector-survey/
7. Saban Forum 2014, "Israel's Future: A Conversation with Naftali Bennett", Brookings Institution, 17 December 2014.
8. Obama, Barack, "Remarks by the President on Jewish American Heritage Month", Washington, DC, 22 May 2015.

9. Lipka, Michael, "A closer look at Jewish identity in Israel and the US Publication", Pew Research Center, 2016.

2. CONFLICT

1. "The Monthly Humanitarian Monitor | January 2012", Jerusalem: United Nations Office for the Coordination of Humanitarian Affairs, 16 February 2012.
2. Zertal, Idith, and Akiva Eldar, *Lords of the Land: The War over Israel's Settlements in the Occupied Territories, 1967–2007*, New York: Nation, 2007.
3. Novik, Akiva, "Arrest of a Girl from Yitzhar who Justified the Murder of a Soldier", *Yediot Aharonot*, 5 July 2014.
4. Beilin, Yossi, "The Transformation of Shimon Peres", *Foreign Policy*, 24 July 2014.
5. "SPIEGEL Interview with Israeli President Shimon Peres: 'We Have to Open Negotiations Right Away'", *Der Spiegel*, 12 October 2012.
6. "Peres Says Israel Could Face an Eternal War", Associated Press, 11 February 2015.
7. The phrase he used, *avodah zarah*, literally means "foreign worship". It referred in antiquity to pagan idol worshippers, but in recent times it has been applied to other "false" religions, including Christianity, Islam, and even some strains of Judaism.
8. Kershner, Isabel, "Israel Parliament Elects Ex-Speaker as President to Succeed Peres", *The New York Times*, 6 October 2014.
9. Rivlin, Reuven, "The Parliamentary Fists of the Majority", *Ha'aretz*. N.p., 15 July 2011.
10. Lis, Jonathan, "Rivlin Hints Sara Netanyahu Had Hand in His Dismissal as Knesset Speaker", *Ha'aretz*. N.p., 28 March 2013.
11. The latter part, *yimakh shemo ve'zikhro*, is the sort of curse Jews typically reserve for figures like Haman and Hitler.
12. Tibon, Amir, "The Secret Back Channel That Doomed the Israel-Palestine Negotiations", *The New Republic*, 26 November 2014.
13. Yehoshua, Yossi, "A night in the city of terror", *Yediot Aharonot*, 20 June 2014.
14. Shaer, Gilad, Telephone call to police, 2014; http://news.walla.co.il/?w=/2689/2760392
15. Harel, Amos, "Missing Teens: Time Is Not on Their Side", *Ha'aretz*, 13 June 2014, http://www.haaretz.com/news/diplomacy-defense/1.598633
16. Shragai, Nadav, "The murderers: A strange and dangerous fire", *Israel HaYom*, 7 July 2014.

17. Shein, Chaim, "A knife in the heart of the nation", *Arutz Sheva*, 8 July 2014, http://www.inn.co.il/Articles/Article.aspx/12533

18. Brown, John, "Ayelet Shaked Incites, and Invents the Burning of a Jewish Cemetery", *Local Call*, 12 July 2014.

19. Shaked, Ayelet, "Exposing Militant Leftist Propaganda", *Jerusalem Post*, 16 July 2014.

20. Melman, Yossi, "Comment: Nightmare Scenario", *Jerusalem Post*, 7 July 2014.

21. Mandel, Ralph, "Israel in 1982: The War in Lebanon", American Jewish Year Book 84 (1984)

22. Nir, Amiram, "Sheket—Yorim [Quiet—We're Shooting]" *Yediot Aharonot*, 6 June 1982.

23. "100,000 Demonstrate in Tel Aviv Against War in Lebanon", Jewish Telegraphic Agency, 5 July 1982.

24. "July 2014 Peace Index—The Israel Democracy Institute", Accessed 9 August 2014; http://en.idi.org.il/about-idi/news-and-updates/july-2014-peaceindex/

25. Goldberg, J. J., "How Politics and Lies Triggered an Unintended War in Gaza", *The Forward*, 7 October 2014.

26. Levy, Gideon, "Hara'im L'tayyis [The Worst to the Air Force]", *Ha'aretz*, 14 July 2014.

27. Levy, Gideon, "Tayyasinu Lo Shavu B'shalom [Our Pilots Did Not Return in Peace]", *Ha'aretz*, 31 December 2008

28. "News" Israel: Channel 2, 14 July 2014.

29. "Interview with Yariv Levin", Israel: Channel 2, 3 August 2014, http://www.mako.co.il/news-israel/local/Article-2c7078b86ca9741004.htm

30. Levi, Yonit, and Segal, Udi, "Why the Gaza War Looked Different on Israeli TV Than It Did on CNN", *Tablet Magazine*, 10 July 2014.

31. Schneider, Tal, "Bibi's Public Diplomacy Chief, Herzog", *HaPlog*, August 2014

32. Shikaki, Khalil, Special Gaza War Poll, Ramallah: Palestine Center for Policy and Survey Research, 2 September 2014, http://www.pcpsr.org/en/special-gaza-war-poll.

3. INEQUALITY

1. Wasserstein, Bernard, *Divided Jerusalem: The Struggle for the Holy City*, New Haven, CT: Yale University Press, 2001.

2. Lubell, Maayan, "Breaking Taboo, Jerusalem Palestinians Seek Israeli Citizenship", Reuters, 3 August 2015.

3. "The Palestinian Economy in East Jerusalem: Enduring Annexation,

Isolation and Disintegration", United Nations Conference on Trade and Development, April 2013.

4. Punitive house demolitions. Rep. Jerusalem: HaMoked, 2015.
5. Khatib, Hashim, "The Arabs in Israel—Three Years after the Or Commission Report", Tel Aviv University, Tel Aviv, 11 September 2006. Lecture.
6. Maltz, Judy, "Russian Immigrants Leaving Israel, Discouraged by Conversion Woes", *Ha'aretz*. 2 November 2014.
7. Hendely, Igal, Saul Lachz, and Yossi Spiegel, "Consumers' Activism: The Cottage Cheese Boycott", 2016. MS. Tel Aviv University, Tel Aviv.
8. "63% Favor Civil Marriage", *Hiddush*, 28 July 2011, http://hiddush. org/article-2244–0–63_favor_civil_marriage.aspx
9. Mansour, Bahij, "Israel's Druze Ambassador Can't Defend the Nation-state Law", *Ha'aretz*. 6 December 2014.
10. Diskin, Yuval, "Apropos the 'National Law'", Facebook, 24 November 2014,   https://www.facebook.com/yuval.diskin.9/ posts/1741270999430915.
11. Peres, Shimon and David Landau, *Ben-Gurion: A Political Life*, New York: Nextbook/Schocken, 2011.
12. Dattel, Lior, "Israel's Funding for High Schools Favors State Religious Stream Over Arabs, Haredim", *Ha'aretz*. 19 July 2013.
13. Yadid, Judd, and Carlo Strenger, "How Cantonization Can Save Israel", *Ha'aretz*. 7 October 2014.

4. THE ELECTION

1. Plesner, Yohanan, and Gideon Rahat, "Reforming Israel's Political System: A Plan for the Knesset", Rep. Israel Democracy Institute, 2015.

5. THE DIVIDE

1. Klein, Tzvika, "The Secret Messages of Israel: 'How You Respond to BDS Activists'", *NRG*, 22 February 2016.
2. Gross, Terry, "Frank Luntz Explains 'Words That Work'", *Fresh Air*, NPR, 9 January 2007.
3. "How to Sell Americans on Israeli Settlements", *Newsweek*, 10 July 2009.
4. Horovitz, David, "Israel Losing Democrats, 'Can't Claim Bipartisan US Support,' Top Pollster Warns", *Times of Israel*, 5 July 2015.
5. Vorspan, Albert, "Soul-Searching", *New York Times Magazine*, 8 May 1988.
6. "A Portrait of Jewish Americans", Pew Research Center, 1 October 2013.
7. Lis, Jonathan, "Israeli Ultra-Orthodox Lawmaker Compares Reform Jews to Mentally Ill", *Ha'aretz*, 23 February 2016.

8. Shapiro, Daniel, "Ambassador Daniel B Shapiro's Remarks at the Institute for National Security Studies 9th International Conference", Tel Aviv, 18 January 2016.
9. Kirby, John, "Daily Press Briefing", Washington, DC, 19 January 2016.

6. DEMOCRACY

1. Fendel, Hillel, "'Settler' Pays Troubling Condolence Visit to Arab Village", *Arutz Sheva*, 3 Augus 2015.
2. Bar-Stav, Liat, "Inside radical right-wing group Lehava", *Yediot Aharonot*, 3 Jan, 2015.
3. "Fatalities after Operation Cast Lead", B'Tselem, 24 Oct, 2016.
4. Ben-Gurion, David. "*The Eternity of Israel*", Tel Aviv: Ayanot, 1964.
5. Indyk, Martin S, "The Peace General", Brookings Institution 7 December 2016.
6. Schmemann, Serge, "10 More Die in Mideast Riots as Violence Enters 3rd Day; Mosque Is Scene of a Clash", *New York Times*, 28 September 1996.
7. Lipkin-Shahak, Amnon, "Speech at Memorial for Yitzhak Rabin" *Ha'aretz* B2, 31 October 1996.
8. Wilkinson, Tracy, "Barak Is Elected Israeli Leader by a Landslide", *Los Angeles Times* N.p., 18 May 1999.
9. Alon, Gideon, "Knesset Okays 3-year Cooling-off Period for Security Officials", *Ha'aretz*, 12 Mar 2007.
10. Bergman, Ronen, "Dagan Before His Death: 'Bibi is the Worst Manager I Know'", *Yediot Aharonot*, 7 April 2016.
11. Ravid, Barak, "Mossad Chief: Palestinian Conflict Top Threat to Israel's Security, Not Iran", *Ha'aretz*. 5 July 2014.
12. Lanski, Naama. "'You Don't Dictate What Is Right and Wrong'" *Israel HaYom* [Jerusalem], 11 Sept 2015.
13. Coutinho, Paulo, "Sheldon Adelson: 'My Gaming License is a Privilege, It's Not a Right'", *Macau Daily Times*. 24 December 2015.
14. Baz, Itamar, "Cheap Propaganda". The Seventh Eye, 11 July 2014.
15. Tucker, Nati, "Netanyahu Admits He Opposes Establishment of New Public Broadcast Corporation", *Ha'aretz*, 9 August 2016.
16. Eichner, Itamar and Yuval Karni, "'If There's No Control, Why Give Money'", *Yediot Aharonot* [Jerusalem], 1 August 2016.
17. "The Yishuv and State of Israel Press Section", National Library of Israel, Accessed 22 February 2016.
18. "Akifat Hahoraot B'dvar Petikhat Esekim U'sgiratem B'yimi Hamnokhah Al-Ydei Harshuyot Hamekomiyot [Enforcement of the Provisions Regarding Opening and Closing of Businesses on Days of Rest by

Local Authorities]", Jerusalem: Knesset, 6 February 2014, http://www.knesset.gov.il/mmm/data/pdf/m03360.pdf

19. Hermann, Tamar, "The Israel Democracy Index: 2016", Rep. Israel Democracy Institute, 19 December 2016.
20. Zertal, Idith and Akiva Eldar, *Lords of the Land: The War over Israel's Settlements in the Occupied Territories*, 1967–2007, New York: Nation, 2007.
21. Ibid.
22. Peres, Shimon, *Ka'et Mahar [Tomorrow Is Now]*, Crown, 1978.
23. Shalev, Chemi, "The Countless Contradictions of the Late and Great Shimon Peres", *Ha'aretz*, 28 September 2016.

7. CONCLUSION

1. Rettig Gur, Haviv, "Another Kind of Unity", *Mosaic Magazine*, 24 June 2015.
2. Verter, Yossi, "Despite Growing Pushback, Netanyahu Is Obsessed With Killing the Public Broadcaster", *Ha'aretz*, 29 October 2016.
3. Bergman, Ronen, "Israel's Army Goes to War With Its Politicians", *New York Times*, 21 May 2016.
4. Gradstein, Linda, "Profile: Campaign of Shinui Party Leader Tommy Lapid", NPR, 9 January 2003.

EPILOGUE

1. Rosner, Shmuel, "No, Settlers Don't Control Israeli Politics", *New York Times*, 15 December 2016.
2. "The Peace Index: November 2016", Rep. Jerusalem: Israel Democracy Institute, 2016.
3. Beinart, Peter, "To Save Israel, Boycott the Settlements", *New York Times*, 18 March 2012.
4. A comprehensive analysis of economic and other costs which the state of Israel bears for settlements in the West Bank, Rep. Tel Aviv: Macro Center for Political Economics, 2015.
5. Arendt, Hannah, "To Save the Jewish Homeland", *Commentary*, 1 May 1948.

INDEX

INDEX

INDEX

245

INDEX

INDEX

INDEX

Persian Empire: xi
Persico, Oren: 177, 185
Pew Research Center: 6, 10–11,
133; polling efforts of, 146
Pfeffer, Anshel: 177, 221
Piron, Shai: Israeli Education
Minister, 91
Plesner, Yohanan: President of IDI,
125
Poland: 9–10; Katowice
(Kattowitz), 92
Porat, Hanan: 15
Power, Samantha: US Ambassador
to UN, 231
'price tag' attacks: 17, 20, 148;
concept of, 14
Putin, Vladimir: 181, 216–17

Al-Qaeda: 107; Jabhat Fatah al-
Sham, 25
Qatar: Doha, 48, 59
Qattoush, Jawad: 208

Rabin, Yitzhak: 1, 44, 158–9, 198,
218; administration of, 200;
assassination of (1995), xiv, 18,
35, 38, 159–60, 221; Israeli
Defense Minister, 152; no-
confidence vote against (1976),
190; resignation of (1977),
184; role in ethnic cleansing of
Lydda/Lod, 167; signing of Oslo
Accords (1993), 117
Rabinovich, Beni: 190–1
al-Rai, Bishara: 22–3
Ravid, Barak: 110
Regev, Mark: 70
Regev, Miri: 170, 180; background
of, 171–2; Israeli Culture
Minister, 171, 176; restriction
of funding for Israeli cultural
institutions unwilling to perform

in underdeveloped regions, 172,
221
Reider, Dimi: 221
Remley, Rennick: 100
Republican Party (USA): 6, 210;
ideology of, 125; support for
sanctions, 142; supporters of,
140–1
Reshet: 179
Revisionism: 9
Rivlin, Reuven: xv, 27, 29–31,
38–9, 78–9, 87, 98, 125–7, 146,
181, 204; election to Knesset
(1988), 28; family of, 28–9;
opposition to 'Boycott Law'
(2011), 29
Rivlin, Ya'akov: 191
Rivlin, Yosef: family of, 28–9
Romney, Mitt: 141; Israeli public
support for, 141
Rosenblum, Herzl: 44
Rosner, Shmuel: 230
Russian Federation: 216; Kremlin,
181; Moscow, 181–2

Sa'ad, Omar: 88
Sa'ar, Gideon: 32–3
Sabbah, Michel: 24
Saban Forum: 9
Sabra/Shatila Massacres (1982):
83, 132; political impact of,
201–2
Salafism: 18
Samri, Luba: 73
Sarid, Yossi: 173
Sarna, Yigal: 183
Saudi Arabia: 135
Sayeret Matkal: background of, 117
Schneider, Tal: 57, 114
Sea of Galilee: 148
Second Intifada (2000–5): 14, 33,
70, 151; casualties of, 152–3;

INDEX